BEARING WITNESS

BEARING WITNESS

Gay Men's Health Crisis and the Politics of AIDS

PHILIP M. KAYAL

Westview Press
Boulder • San Francisco • Oxford

Copyright © 1993 by Westview Press, Inc.

We gratefully acknowledge permission to reprint portions of this work from JAI Press, *Humanity and Society, The Nonprofit and Voluntary Sector Quarterly, The Journal of Religion and Health,* and *Journal of Gay and Lesbian Social Service.*

Published in 1993 in the United States of America by Westview Press, Inc., 5500 Central Avenue, Boulder, Colorado 80301-2877, and in the United Kingdom by Westview Press, 36 Lonsdale Road, Summertown, Oxford OX2 7EW

Library of Congress Cataloging-in-Publication Data
Kayal, Philip M., 1943–
  Bearing witness : Gay Men's Health Crisis and the politics of AIDS
/ Philip M. Kayal.
    p. cm.
  Includes bibliographical references and index.
  ISBN 0-8133-1728-2. — ISBN 0-8133-1729-0 (pbk.)
  1. Gay Men's Health Crisis, Inc.   2. Gay men—New York (N.Y.)—
Social conditions.   3. Gay men—New York (N.Y.)—Attitudes.
4. Volunteer workers in community health services—New York (N.Y.)
5. Gay men—United States—Public opinion.   6. Public opinion—
United States.   7. Homophobia—United States.   8. AIDS phobia—
United States.   9. AIDS (Disease)—Political aspects—United
States.   I. Title.
HQ76.2.U5K39   1993
305.38'9664—dc20   92-40293
                                                                                      CIP

Printed and bound in the United States of America

The paper used in this publication meets the requirements
of the American National Standard for Permanence of Paper
for Printed Library Materials Z39.48-1984.

10   9   8   7   6   5   4   3   2   1

Contents

Dedication

THIS BOOK IS DEDICATED to past friends who have died of acquired immune deficiency syndrome (AIDS) and to present and future friends who struggle daily with gross illness in both their personal lives and community. To Diego Lopez, the creator and initiator of client services at Gay Men's Health Crisis (GMHC); to Michael Doyle, a dedicated sociologist and volunteer who was just beginning his career as a psychoanalyst when he fell ill with pneumocystis; to Horatio Benegas and Victor Bender, who lived and died proudly as gay people by taking care of each other and who intimately and directly introduced me to the process of dying; to Howard Goodkin, a dear friend who was diagnosed with AIDS just as he was beginning to edit this manuscript; to theologian Kevin Gordon, whose brilliant use of systematic theology to undermine Catholic arguments about homosexual legitimacy was cut short by AIDS; to Jerry Norman, a wonderful opera singer who died not long after his final moving recital at Cooper Union; to his lover, my beloved friend Leonard Barton, who introduced me to high art and culture, and in whose loving arms Jerry died; to Dan Bailey, first "official" hotline director at GMHC and my longtime friend and confidant; and to Dr. Paul Jerro, a friend and cousin, who chose to burden no one with his illness, keeping it to himself until the very end. Like all the others, he was a good, generous, honest, and kind person.

They were all in their late thirties and early forties and had led honorable lives when their AIDS diagnoses were made, often only weeks or months apart. As friends, our loyalty never wavered. Over time, we pulled even closer together. Though the heavens fell on us, we made ourselves available to one another and to dozens more.

Then there were Terry and Chris, lovers who came out to each other and stayed together for life. They were among my closest friends, parts of myself. They taught me a lot, offering a different perspective because they were not trained, official AIDS volunteers, preferring to informally help their sick friends by themselves. And help they did, perhaps a dozen or so friends.

They had built a cabin in a gay campground near Scranton, Pennsylvania, and took it upon themselves to provide safer-sex education for their camping buddies who lacked access to gay or AIDS news. They were both diagnosed in November 1989 after the three of us took the "AIDS test." Having been with me on this project from the very beginning, Terry died the day this book was finished, entrusting Chris to us, his friends. Less than a year before, Chris's only brother had died of AIDS.

Like most people living with AIDS, those I have known who have died from its ravages led rewarding lives, always giving of themselves as generously as they could. Each had his own personality and died as he lived, in ways that were unique and special. For no particular reason, some died quickly and quietly while others struggled and lived on for years. Most died true to themselves and with a public acknowledgment of who they were, how they had lived, and why they died.

For the most part, my friends left in peace, free of shame and guilt, and with their business on earth completed. Unexpectedly, their lives and deaths became signs of hope and symbols of love and service. Their deaths have taught us—their many carepartners and friends—how to live joyfully and mourn unabashedly. Though often ill and grieving themselves, they helped us come together as a family. Our dying friends gave us, the living, the opportunity to "do good," to discover our fears and limitations and our capacity to absorb suffering.

Perhaps they are the lucky ones because they do not have to face AIDS and the world alone. Today, we survivors have little to be joyful about. In a friendless world, what's the point of being the last of a generation to live, perhaps even to die?

Generally, the people that I mourned were all surrounded by love. As friends and families, we shared their enormous suffering and pain, their endless loneliness and fear. For many of us, those living with AIDS appear heroic and their anguish seems profound.

AIDS shatters everyone's hopes and dreams; its unpredictability and its inconsistencies are monumental. Not knowing how, or who, or when, or why him or her and not me or them is a harrowing experience. Looking for an answer or *the* answer becomes a journey inward to the depths of the soul. For this reason, AIDS remains a primary mystery in the human journey toward self-discovery.

Because AIDS affects so many people in one way or another, it simultaneously produces both anger and the need to forgive—to be reconciled to ourselves as individuals and as part of a community. It makes one want to run away—to be detached from the world.

Nothing really matters during or after AIDS. Yet, for all the deaths to be remembered and understood, the meaning of AIDS in human terms needs to be made known, if not highlighted.

It is for this reason that this book is also dedicated to all those who witness the suffering of AIDS, in particular to the families, friends, and carepartner volunteers at Gay Men's Health Crisis, who are forced as much by circumstances as by choice to daily take up the cross of caring in ways that bring peace and respite instead of despair.

AIDS forces us to mourn reflectively and creatively, and to have hope. We now know how to rely on our own mourning rituals to transcend the tedium of everyday life. Relevant ceremony, especially when mourning, gives us back our identity and unites us together as innocent, worthy, and honorable people.

When my cousin Paul died in his prime, nearly everyone knew his pneumonia was AIDS related. His brother and sisters who nursed him (as did his mother, nieces, nephews, and cousins) were more than supportive and generous of their time and energy. I am proud to be related to them and to know his friends and lover. By accepting, loving, and supporting Paul as a person, they brought us all through with pride and dignity.

Not everyone at the wake and funeral could articulate his or her grief so honestly because not everyone knew of Paul's life as a proud and happy gay man. An older generation of relatives and family friends believed he was single, not realizing that Jack, his "special friend," was more than an ordinary buddy. Jack was always with him at family affairs and during his illness was at his bedside.

It was with these others—the silent ones—the neighbors, friends, and business associates who came to mourn, that it was difficult for us to share our sorrow. It is not that they were or would have been hostile or indifferent to Paul for having AIDS or being gay. It was just that they were uninformed or misinformed about what it all meant. We did not know how to share our experiences and memories of him, since so many of us were strangers.

Not being able to mourn aloud and honestly fuels the fear and loneliness of being gay and/or of having AIDS. Not being able to bring everyone in the life of a Person with AIDS (PWA) together in one place at one time to do one thing—grieve together in an authentic way—devastates the psyche.

What I keep learning at the wakes of so many friends and neighbors is that for outcasts, mourning takes on a special meaning and function. For gay people, lamenting a friend or lover becomes a time of affirmation, an opportunity for healing. When done only by a family, it is too often done in silence and in hiding, leaving the gay friends alone and removed. It also distorts and debases the personality and life of the PWA. While a wake and a funeral are normally moments of personal sharing, with an AIDS death they become something else altogether. In a gay context, a wake or funeral becomes a political statement about support systems, community, personal identity, and loyalties.

They are opportunities to experience the misery and pain of AIDS directly. With an AIDS death, the human face of gay people comes alive.

Yet I find myself asking over and over how any one ritual, ceremony, or eulogy could be expected to meaningfully unite friends, family, believers, skeptics, the angry, and the reconciled. There were so many people at Paul's wake, from so many disparate walks of life and so many distinct parts of his own life, that it was impossible to find a common way to symbolize our shared loss. Who has first claim on the life of a gay person or PWA? Family, friends, lovers, the community? Who should arrange the burial? After all, he was loved alike by everyone.

Were we, his mourners, ashamed of Paul? Did we blame him? Were we angry at him for dying? Did he disappoint us? Did we think deep down that something about his life and death should be hidden from the neighbors, from ourselves? Would Paul want us to bury him secretly? He lived his life openly and with pride. Why don't we accept why he, like all the others, really had to die? We need to accept that homophobia, like AIDS, also kills.

I suppose that if Paul had died an ordinary death in ordinary times, it would not be as important to raise these questions. But he didn't, and his death remains as much a personal loss as a political issue. Do we add to the dilemma, to the conspiracy of silence, by not acknowledging aloud how and why someone has died? Should the death of a Person with AIDS be forcibly acknowledged as such? Should a wake become an educational opportunity, so that everyone understands that a Person with AIDS died of an illness and not a curse from God? Should mourners be reminded that their loved one was but one of many who died unexpectedly and unnecessarily this year? How many funerals must be held before we all cry out loud about our grief and demand that this horror, this conspiracy of silence, stop?

Why doesn't everyone already understand that Paul and the others had to deal with hate, fear, and ignorance every day and that this environment was daily sapping their spirits and slowly killing them anyway? Why don't we yet know that all of this ignorance, terror, and homophobia is unnecessary, that it is all preventable, that there is nothing to hide, nothing to be ashamed of when you are gay or have AIDS?

People with AIDS can be anyone and are everywhere. Gays and PWAs are family, neighbors, friends, doctors, priests, workers, and teachers. We will not go away. We will not be silent because we are not sorry about who we are and how we live, and, now, how we might die. Nor will we cooperate with silence or live with shame. We have no apologies and no regrets. We only ask that *we* be allowed to tell who we are on our terms, how we really live and love, why we are really dying, what has happened to us because of AIDS, and what we are now doing for one another in the midst of tragedy.

The only sin in AIDS is that we are not allowed to share our lives and our wisdom more deeply with those who claim they love us.

I want anyone and everyone who reads this book to understand that we will survive this scourge and that we are proud of the way we have responded to it. I hope this book will help explain our crisis and that you, the reader, will come to know and love us as we are: a hopeful people, a compassionate people, a holy people.

No more hidden obituaries, no more shallow ceremonies, no more empty rituals, no more meaningless gestures. Our lives are eternal and will be forever celebrated.

Philip M. Kayal
Seton Hall University

Preface

BEARING WITNESS IS A STORY ABOUT HOPE, a statement of faith in the human spirit. By dint of circumstance, it is two stories rolled into one. On the one hand, it is the tale of how volunteerism became the most necessary and reliable response to the political problems caused by AIDS and, on the other, it is a chronicle of how the gay community mobilized itself in the service of transformation to contain and resolve the social, psychological, and spiritual issues that the disease raised.

Transformation is about how volunteers ended gay self-estrangement through their bearing witness to People with AIDS and how the formalization of this effort at Gay Men's Health Crisis in New York encapsulated community interests in a way that empowered and forever changed the relationships and fortunes of gay people everywhere.

When I began my research, I had not realized that volunteerism in AIDS represented yet another chapter in the long American tradition of problem solving at the local level. Nor had I known that those most at risk themselves would be expected, albeit forced, to take on the burden of responding to AIDS with any magnitude virtually alone. While the voluntary response to AIDS was spontaneous and altruistic, it became increasingly evident that it was as much a heroic reaction to fear and hatred as it was practical.

By first titling this book *Angels at War*, I wanted to acknowledge those who responded in a way that gave their work a deeper meaning. AIDS is such a shattering human event that it is only possible to capture its horror in a direct face-to-face encounter—by living in a relationship with a PWA. Looking at the meaning of AIDS in the life and work of gay/AIDS volunteers is the prime opportunity for both intimately knowing AIDS and understanding its political dimensions.

The carepartnering of PWAs takes us beyond our everyday assumptions about what illness means, what voluntary work should consist of, and what being political entails. It forcibly brings to light why AIDS has greater sociological significance than its medical and biological dimensions alone suggest.

The many distinguishing characteristics of AIDS volunteerism can be recognized only when looked at from the vantage point of gay men—those who are simultaneously most collectively at risk of infection and those most absorbed as a community in its suffering. This book intends to give testimony to these untiring carepartners because they too are being ignored in many of the same ways that AIDS still is.

What is needed is an explanation of why there is still no mention of what the loss of so many lives to AIDS will cost American society in human and economic terms as there is, for example, of African AIDS. From a sociological perspective, it is the lack of power over the course of events in AIDS that permits such a profound silence to last.

For gays with AIDS, isolation and powerlessness are sustained by the stigma of sinfulness. And if society can legitimate its abhorrence of homosexual activity this way, as Catholic theologian Kevin Gordon (1986:42) maintains, this hatred will become even more virulent because a deadly illness can now be attributed to a morally suspect sexuality: "Gays had AIDS; gays harbor 'the AIDS virus.' Gays, therefore, should die."

Fortunately, it is this same linking of gays with illness and moral corruption that also gives us reason to bear witness to one another. If the prevailing social (moral) meaning of AIDS is not continually challenged, death rates, especially among the stigmatized poor, will increase even more dramatically than they have. Power over AIDS comes with autonomy and authority over life events. And it is on this process of empowerment through volunteerism that this book is based.

AIDS volunteers are people who in the midst of a massacre somehow keep on going. It is a story about the significance of gay efforts that is being recounted here and now, while the memories and people who bear them remain alive. Otherwise, the painful details will be criminally forgotten. Neither the commitment that the gay community has made to helping PWAs nor its efforts to contain AIDS have been publicly celebrated. And this needs to be done so that everyone will know and no one will ever forget.

In her book *AIDS: The Ultimate Challenge*, Elisabeth Kübler-Ross notes that of the thousands of patients she has seen worldwide, none have had as much mutual support and solidarity as AIDS patients and their carepartners.

> If there is ever a vaccine for AIDS, it will not in the least be the result of their strength and their efforts. For more than half a decade they have been isolated by most communities, have allowed doctors to experiment with them, suffered incredible side effects from experimental drugs, ruined the lives of their families, and participated in anything that promised a cure. (1987:155)

In a deadly war of attrition, it is important to document the story of these "unheralded angels," these good people doing what sociologists call "dirty work." Gay/AIDS volunteerism is a significant event because it is a human story of resurrection over despair and triumph over impotence and loss. What distinguishes virtually all community-based initiatives responding to AIDS is not that they come almost entirely from one at-risk population "even before AIDS had a name" (Levine 1989:13) but that all those participating had to confront prejudice and fear and overcome denial and guilt before the help could be given effectively.

"The initial shock at this dawning social disaster," writes Michael Denneny (1990:16), "was compounded by the peculiar relations of the gay community to the surrounding society, that has always favored resounding silence as the most effective means of gay repression."

Internationally recognized parasitologist Kevin Cahill was the first to note that whereas toxic shock syndrome and Legionnaire's disease received enthusiastic and concerned responses from the medical community, no major research programs were announced when homosexuals and Haitians became ill until it became clear that the disease could spread to the general population through blood transfusions. "Organized medicine," he writes, "seemed part of the curious conspiracy of silence" (Cahill 1983:2). Without doubt, this silence, more than anything else, forced the voluntary community response to AIDS by gays. If the silence continued, genocide would occur.

Gay/AIDS volunteerism is a response to a lack of response, to being ignored and unserved. It is a reaction to exclusion and marginalization, to being defined and treated as "an other." It is for this reason that this story has to be written from experience and with conviction. If not, the event becomes antiseptic, something merely academic. Gay/AIDS volunteerism is more than a naturally occurring and expected community mobilization responding to a demand for services or certainty, as Susan Chambre (1991) suggests. It is an upheaval in relationships and identities.

If the unarticulated issue in AIDS is hatred and rejection of "the other," then the emphasis in studies of AIDS volunteerism has to be on the linkages that the disease generates within the community, among and between gays, PWAs, and the broader society. The focus is thus on empowerment and how and why AIDS needs first to be resolved politically so that its suffering can be alleviated and a cure can be found. It is in the volunteers' connection with PWAs that the political economy of AIDS volunteerism is revealed.

While aptly mirroring the way AIDS volunteers are generally perceived by PWAs, my early identification of volunteers as "angels at war" failed to address not only this drama of self-discovery in connections with others but how the exigencies of AIDS were shaping the direction and content of both the larger, societal reaction (disinterest) as well as the local community response (mobilization). Moreover, "angels" failed to capture the tremendous impact of the epidemic on institutional patterns. This early approach missed the effects of

AIDS on the ordinary and interactive ways that gay people live daily. The political meaning and social connection of AIDS to gay life are ignored in most studies. To grasp this dimension, AIDS needs to be approached from the perspective and experience of volunteers as carepartners. There is no other way for empathy to develop and the human face of AIDS to be known.

Gay/AIDS volunteerism is an experience in self-recognition and as such is a fundamental political act, connecting the question of why PWAs are being disregarded by society to the rejection and hatred of gays by conservative, "stateside" religions.[1] It thus epitomizes a rebirth of the spirit, of the will to survive. In response, and in kind, volunteerism becomes the process through which gay people are restored to the community as a sacred, hence empowering, source undermining social arrangements.

It is this link to similar others that empowers, and it is for this reason that this text is written with political intent, identifying issues and recommending both goals and strategies to achieve them. Looking at AIDS through the perspective of volunteerism draws a more complete picture of what AIDS symbolizes and implies for the gay community within the political economy of traditional American expectations as they pertain to problem solving.

The title, *Bearing Witness: Gay Men's Health Crisis and the Politics of AIDS*, reflects this shift in emphasis by acknowledging not only the quality and nature of the collective gay response but also its political context and meaning, and thus its deeper importance as a process that empowers. Through carepartnering, gay/AIDS volunteerism becomes an opportunity for the community to ingather by identifying with and taking in its most beleaguered members. This integration of interests essentially summarizes what the volunteer effort in AIDS consists of and what it entails politically. By accepting the humanity of each Person with AIDS, volunteerism, likewise, takes on a radical and fundamental religious quality.

The theological concept "bearing witness" is quite appropriate to an analysis of gay/AIDS volunteerism. In its basic form, bearing witness means taking on the cross or the suffering of others as if it were one's own. "To witness," notes Sarah Petit (1989:43), "is not simply to make note, not simply to record, although there is a power in that. It is to go out and see what is going on." Bearing witness is what volunteers actually do and accomplish for themselves and for others. It captures the quality of their relationship with PWAs and identifies healing as the task at hand. Volunteering personalizes AIDS by drawing carepartners out of themselves and placing them in the situation of another person as hated for his gayness as they are.

Through this activity and its call for justice, the gay community becomes the biblical *anawin*—the poor of God or the prophetic community that calls people out of isolation and into commitment to one another in a way that challenges the structural sources of indifference to AIDS and of gay oppression. This way, of course, is the way of self-acceptance, which means acknowledging the community that one is identified with as an extension and reinforcement of the personal self, even when stigma, fear, and, now, the specter of death make it painful to do so.

P.M.K.

Acknowledgments

OF THE MANY PEOPLE who lent me a gracious hand, there are an especial few to whom I am particularly grateful. In the very beginning, Barbara Bari of the College of St. Elizabeth's (Convent Station, New Jersey) graciously read the early drafts. She not only enthusiastically supported me but also pointed me to the historical role of women in nonprofit work. Her input made me realize how much of a minority phenomenon the gay response to AIDS actually was.

Then, there was my colleague and friend David Abalos, whose imprint on this book should not be mistaken or ignored. David both guided and advised. He helped me to understand the model of transformation he used so caringly to illustrate the Mexican-American experience and to apply it to the ordeal of gays during AIDS. He went over every word, taking the opportunity at each meeting to encourage me to bring the book into the first person and to develop its cathectic elements. He was right: Moral outrage cannot be dispassionately stated or addressed.

My special friend and fervent editor Howard Goodkin came through up to the end. He read and reread the text, even while ill himself with AIDS in the hospital. His patience and support are unsurpassed. His editorial objectivity is beyond question. We were very different, yet he discussed fairly what I wrote, querying and testing me constantly. He too wanted to know what AIDS meant, and in finding answers for him I sharpened my own thoughts and feelings. He tested me by not letting me assume anything.

There were tenfold others—from librarians to GMHC staff and personnel. There were volunteers and People with AIDS, doctors and hospital workers, family, parents, and colleagues. There were all the people who gave me leads and direction, support and advice. The Seton Hall University Summer Research Council made it possible for me to take two summers off to finish the manuscript. The university's computer center staff worked with me for over a year to create, file, and later retrieve the data. My own college and department gave me release time to facilitate finding a publisher.

I can't even begin to acknowledge all the friends who opened doors for me and offered help. They inspired me by their own commitment. Everyone I needed to talk to made themselves available, as many times as I asked them. This was equally true of the editors at Westview Press—Ellen Williams, Nancy Carlston, Amy Eisenberg, Cindy Hirschfeld, and Sarah Tomasek—whose enthusiasm and support never wavered. This book is truly a team effort. Thank you.

P.M.K.

Introduction

 $\mathbf{G}$ AY VOLUNTEERISM IN acquired immune deficiency syndrome (AIDS) is a unique phenomenon shaped completely by its own exigencies and social contours. AIDS is still a disease of minorities, the disinherited, and the stigmatized. Therefore traditional models of either social movement development (which is what AIDS volunteerism essentially began as) or formal organizational growth (which is what successful voluntary community efforts typically develop into) cannot fully capture the significance of how homophobia (the inordinate fear of homosexuality and gay people) shapes the evolution of volunteerism as a response to abandonment.

It was in New York City that the first mobilization against AIDS developed. It took the name Gay Men's Health Crisis, Inc. (GMHC), and the perspective and information of this report are derived from my volunteer experience there between 1983 and 1986 and my informal affiliation with the agency up until now. Among other things, volunteering offered a unique opportunity to simultaneously study the evolution of AIDS as a political event and the evolution of GMHC as a minority-identified, community-based initiative that was specifically founded to define AIDS and contain its effects.

AIDS was first brought to broad public consciousness in the summer of 1981. On July 3, the *New York Times* reported that forty-one American homosexuals were dying from a rare cancer and infectious complications stemming from an unexplainable depression of the immune system. That same summer, an influential group of gay men met in the Greenwich Village apartment of playwright Larry Kramer and evaluated the situation. Having lost friends and lovers, they were to become the core of a volunteer organization popularly known as GMHC.

As an outspoken community representative, Kramer had been advised by New York University Medical Center doctors to spread the word about this new disease that the media described as a "gay cancer" and to raise money for research. In August, after a larger meeting of eighty men, journalist Nathan

1

Fain remarked that "each man swallowed his panic and found himself shocked into action." These volunteers were responsible for organizing the country's first major support programs for People with AIDS and AIDS-related complex (ARC) and their lovers, families, friends, and carepartners.

When not using their own money to assist needy sufferers, these early "volunteers" and their friends stood outside discos and gay bars soliciting donations for research. In just three months they donated $11,000 to the Kaposi Sarcoma Fund established at New York University Medical Center. By mid-1982, they were able to give nearly $50,000 more to individual doctors, social workers, and hospital research centers. By summer 1982, GMHC received its corporate charter and remained for some time the only organized response to AIDS on the entire East Coast. It was then housed in a decrepit Chelsea brownstone donated by a concerned community member.

Now, with a yearly budget approaching $20 million and an active volunteer corps of over 2,000 (and a volunteer registry in the thousands), GMHC is the largest and most recognized AIDS-specific agency and gay organization in the world. Located in its own community-owned building, it is still able to offer direct personal support to about 35 percent of all New Yorkers with AIDS, servicing a wide range of needs free of charge without regard to race, gender, or sexual orientation. It has outreach services in every borough and in New Jersey. While GMHC now only minimally funds AIDS research, it still enthusiastically develops and staffs new educational and prevention programs. By the close of 1992, GMHC had directly helped nearly 14,000 People with AIDS (PWAs).

Although GMHC lobbies for entitlements and reviews and instigates hospital treatment protocols, its main emphasis has been on palliative services. These differ from traditional medical or social services because they do not identify, label, or cure illness but rather assist and support the sick, much the same way that a family, community, or group of friends would. Until the founding of the AIDS Coalition to Unleash Power (ACT-UP) in fall 1987, GMHC was the most outspoken advocate for PWA entitlements, delivering a wide range of social services to well over 3,000 PWAs a year.

In 1992 alone, GMHC's AIDS Hotline received over 80,000 calls. Its own publication, *The Volunteer,* estimates that in any given month anywhere from 100 to 200 new clients arrive. They are served by an energetic corps of trained volunteers who each donate about seven hours a week to hands-on supportive care for a PWA. By 1992 1,300 new volunteers were yearly recruited and assigned tasks.

Nationally, GMHC remains central to the way AIDS is engaged as a social issue. "It now appears to be de riguer," notes Kobasa (1990:286), "for all levels of government to include a representative of GMHC in any major AIDS-related group that they establish." However, when first begun,

GMHC's immediate intention was not policy formation or care delivery, but to monitor the spread of the illness, fund and conduct research, and increase public awareness of AIDS as a growing and lethal public health emergency.

Understanding the political dimensions of AIDS and their implications for gay people, GMHC also hoped to generate political pressure to ensure a more rapid resolution to the crisis. Its founders simply assumed that everyone would rally around its call for justice, compassion, and a more enlivened response from the medical profession. Unfortunately, popular concern for what was presented as a gay plague did not begin to materialize until after 1985 when the public was led to believe by *Life* magazine (July 8, 1985) that now "no one was safe."

So rapid was the spread of AIDS and the desperation of People with AIDS that GMHC was eventually catapulted into "being on everyone's list." Knowingly, GMHC responded directly to the moralization about gays that AIDS inevitably caused and thus became, in the words of former board member Dan Bailey, "the only game in town." Since the social worth of gays and drug-users would intersect with heath care delivery and the search for a cause and cure, GMHC always had to combat AIDS hysteria—the fear of homosexuality and the denial of the humanity of a Person with AIDS.

Shaping GMHC's Agenda

Until 1988, AIDS, GMHC, and the gay community had been conterminous with each other. They evolved together. Both GMHC and the gay community became more sophisticated in the workings of government and the non-profit sector just as the social implications of AIDS became more apparent. GMHC's founders were neophytes (like everyone else) in the politics of AIDS. A major concern was defining and directing the burgeoning social movement that they had unwittingly inspired.

Community concern was high because in the vacuum of information enough people were motivated to become aware and keep guard. Between 1982 and 1986, the gay community sought out GMHC because there was no other way to represent and articulate the collective interest. There was no other vehicle to bring gays, PWAs, and the community together in an interaction that would politicize.

In the beginning, GMHC's "street-level bureaucracy" was pliable and its volunteers had easy access to one another, to staff, and to PWAs because they were tied together through trusted, interconnecting social networks. For a time, it seemed that to be identifiably gay in New York meant to be affiliated with GMHC. Together, everyone was learning what AIDS meant and what needed to be done. Comprehensive education, prevention, advocacy programs, and organized service delivery would come soon thereafter.

In 1982, Mel Rosen, a social worker with administrative experience, became GMHC's first director. Through goodwill and personal contacts, he kept GMHC accessible and responsive. By 1983, the agency needed a full-time paid administrator and appointed Rodger McFarlane as executive director. Before his arrival, he kept getting phone calls from friends in Houston, Los Angeles, and San Francisco who were horrified about AIDS. "No one knew what the hell was going on. No one was doing anything," he is quoted as saying (Howard 1984:274–275).

Picking up on Rosen's lead, McFarlane opened a hotline in his home, a twenty-four hour service, taking names and numbers of people who called from around the country with questions about AIDS. "I'd call every one of them back personally, explain everything. I started screams for help from every social agency I could think of. I was most unhappy with medical information about AIDS"—a growing gay concern. With board determination and support, he moved GMHC into larger and more useful office space, hired more staff and fund-raisers, and coordinated program delivery.

While McFarlane was director, GMHC psychologists and social workers laid the groundwork for both an inventive crisis intervention protocol and a supportive "buddy system" for PWAs. Help for lovers, friends, and family would come a short time thereafter. These programs gave GMHC its fame and character. McFarlane was very successful in networking with the media; in 1984 he was identified as "the warrior" in *Esquire* magazine's special issue entitled "The Best of the New Generation." Throughout his tenure, and well into that of his successor, Richard Dunne (1985–1989), it would be impossible (if not unnecessary) to easily distinguish between what volunteers and GMHC or the gay community did. They were one and the same, speaking in one voice and with one mind as a functioning community. However, when the full horror and extent of AIDS became known, and the complexity of service delivery revealed, an unsophisticated bureaucracy would no longer do.

Richard Dunne quietly established the reputation of GMHC as the premier gay organization and AIDS-specific service delivery agency. He had a master's degree in public administration. GMHC grew coherent under his tenure. He was determined to maintain GMHC's sensitivity during its bureaucratic transition into an AIDS agency, a goal he desired. His short-term successor in 1990, Jeffrey Braff, though from out of state, likewise had good administrative credentials earned in the communications industry. GMHC was holding its own at the time of his sudden resignation.

The next and current director, Timothy Sweeney, is a longtime gay activist and GMHC insider (former director of policy). He has the responsibility of maintaining GMHC's reputation and vigor. Sweeney is a highly respected and efficient coordinator, visionary, and community spokesperson. He is director at a time when an AIDS industry is emerging and the demographics of AIDS are changing; he is thus presiding over GMHC's potential transition from a gay initiative into an AIDS community organization. In any case, GMHC's "informality" will be put totally to rest during his administration.

Despite its accessibility, personalized care delivery, and the ideological intent of its staff and volunteers, GMHC's formal organization has become very complex. It is now both possible and necessary to separate what volunteers do as carepartners from what the agency as an organization does. We can now speak of the volunteer role, even the volunteers themselves, independently of GMHC's organizational structure and community affiliation.

As a result, the agency remains in a constant and significant dialectic over how to define and integrate its organizational expectations with its social service commitments and the affective demands and needs of both volunteers and PWAs.

This book is written in the spirit of GMHC's early years and explains why more attention is paid to the process of community empowerment through the primary role of witnessing than to how and why GMHC organizationally developed the way it did. This emphasis on GMHC as a gay community initiative (not as a formal organization) is important because GMHC is a product and reflection of the community it serves and gives it life. GMHC is the product of social relationships and these linkages give the agency its character.

GMHC and AIDS-Homophobia

Up until the end of 1982, I was certain that the broader public would react to AIDS with compassion and concern. It was quite a shock to discover firsthand that this was not to be the case. There even were gays who were not convinced there was a problem, never mind an epidemic (Levine 1982). No one was sure exactly what the issues were, would be, or what to do about them when they did materialize. Instead of offering assistance, social institutions disavowed minority entitlements and virtually ignored AIDS.

GMHC was shaped by two undeniable social facts: homophobic disinterest and the rebirth of American volunteer ideology under President Ronald Reagan. Disease always solicits specific responses "at historically defined moments," writes Brandt (1988:418) "and AIDS is no exception." Gay/AIDS volunteerism was created and given its political character by AIDS-homophobia, wherein gay people and their lives are further denounced because of AIDS and the disease is disavowed because it is thought of as gay.

In an interview with Charles Ortleb, editor of the once influential gay-owned and -operated weekly the *New York Native*, Ann Guidici Fettner, coauthor of *The Truth About AIDS*, says:

> Before I got involved with AIDS, I never realized the depth of prejudice against gays, Haitians and junkies. ... The lack of conscience on the part of this govern-

ment has bothered me worse than anything, but it's just a crystallization of the lack of concern for the health of the population outside the politically and financially advantaged. (Fettner and Check 1984:27–28)

For Dr. Allan L. Goldstein, a leading Washington-based thymosin researcher, the political component of AIDS is a tragedy. "There are individuals in the health-political arena," he writes, "that couldn't care less about what happens to people in the gay community." In other words, as "perverts" and "sinners," "they're getting what they deserve" (D'Eramo 1984: 19).

The consequences of characterizing a medical problem in a moral language of this type colors and distorts AIDS as a human tragedy (see Chapter 2). It also affects perceptions and acceptance of People with AIDS. More important, blaming victims and calling gays names (perverts, sinners) discounts the significant efforts of the gay community to stave off its own disintegration by owning AIDS so unashamedly.

Because of stigma, AIDS is ignored or disavowed as a significant illness despite its biological virulence. The "sin" of homosexuality, the social science treatment of gays as deviants, the fact that AIDS is sexually transmitted (especially through anal intercourse), and the social status of gays explain why AIDS-homophobia exists and why People with AIDS are feared and hated so much.

It is the inordinate loathing of homosexuals and homosexuality by individuals, institutions, and moral entrepreneurs that turns gay people into "others." As a political tool, homophobia is used to deny gay civil entitlements. It sustains morality and society, and creates both fear and disconcern about PWAs. AIDS-homophobia splits the gay psyche and separates gays from community; this is why gay oppression is so accepted and unchallenged and why despair often exists among those confronting AIDS. Guilt and fear explain why gay volunteerism is an act of healing.

Because homophobes blame gays for AIDS, volunteerism is affected in two general ways: internally, when homosexuals refuse to identify with AIDS, preferring private solutions over political movements for common benefit, and externally (or socially), when GMHC volunteers try to negotiate adequate responses from the health care and social service industry, when they deal with anguished parents grieving as much over their son's impending death as his homosexuality, when they can't "heal the guilt" so prevalent in many sufferers with AIDS, when they attempt to educate people about safer sex, and when they try to get the medical establishment to be more supportive and compassionate.

Being an active GMHC volunteer at a time when the agency had not yet fully developed its complex organizational structure, I had numerous informal conversations with PWAs, fellow hotline workers, staff, and a random assortment of callers about the loneliness that AIDS-homophobia causes and sustains. In listening to the stories of the dying for over a year there (and privately, for years thereafter), I experienced the tremendous guilt and denial that AIDS almost universally causes, even among the most self-accepting.

In contrast to this doubt is simply being in GMHC's zone of comfort. It renders an appreciation of what "coming home" means, how nonjudgmental acceptance heals and integrates the individual with the community and with himself. Volunteerism, I now know, is really about self-acceptance because the PWA suffers more than anyone from hate, isolation, and self-doubt.

Homophobia is *the* most important social dimension of AIDS. It needs to be contested because it colors AIDS analysis and clouds the issues involved. It also impedes self-discovery and acceptance. When internalized, homophobia makes gays and PWAs depoliticized nonpersons by fragmenting their identities and feelings, separating their inner selves from themselves as "a sacred source." It leads to self-estrangement and powerlessness by destroying the potential for personal linkages with the community as a life-giving source. Homophobia, thus, makes volunteerism in AIDS unlikely, if not impossible. Institutionalized and "morally" justified, it encourages violence toward gays, legitimating our total abandonment with moral certitude.

In its organized form, homophobia is systematic and is expressed in the disregard of gay people by public institutions. In this way, the theologies of Roman Catholicism and fundamentalist Christian sects (as legitimating institutions) become especially central to AIDS fulmination. Because of the indifference that they generate toward PWAs and their negation of the morality of nonprocreative sexual activity and the use of safer-sex protocols as an AIDS preventive, the spread of disease through alienated sexual behavior remains unchecked.

Paying attention to AIDS through the lens of homophobia and volunteerism is appropriate because mixing morals and medicine has implications for the collective well-being and security of gay people. It is *the* defining issue in AIDS. Health care rights have always been tied to the social, legal, and "moral" status of the sick, and this is especially the case in AIDS, where religious stigma intersects with gay community needs to create and recreate the content and character of AIDS volunteerism at GMHC.

Volunteerism, GMHC, and AIDS

Because of the timing of AIDS (the 1980s, the presidencies of Reagan and Bush), GMHC creates, as its name suggests, a sense of community ownership in AIDS and gay responsibility for PWA care. As such, it represents three basic themes in American civic culture: *volunteerism as ideology* (a set of beliefs about American society and our "sacredness" as a people and nation), *volunteerism as activity* (the way individuals and communities apply themselves to problem solving by assuming responsibility), and *volunteerism as voluntary association* (the organization of the voluntary response). As the title of this book suggests, I introduce a fourth possibility: *volunteerism as bearing witness politically.*

The first eschews state intervention, preferring to emphasize philanthropy and communal self-help in the solution of social problems. Voluntary activity can be understood as the mobilization and assignment of volunteers to a host of activities designed to benefit either the sponsoring agency or its "clients" or members. Volunteerism as voluntary association, which is quite different, replaces virtually all government social services programs with private, not-for-profit, voluntary ones. Volunteerism, then, is both a set of values and a collection of formal structures. By bearing witness in AIDS, volunteerism empowers the gay community by joining the individual and collective interest.

AIDS brings all gays and PWAs together as one, and GMHC, in its organized form, represents and demonstrates this union. With AIDS being labeled a "gay plague," gay people and homosexuality were irrevocably implicated in AIDS. This automatically makes GMHC the "alternative" community-based initiative favored as the seat of responsible problem solving in our national ideology.

AIDS was originally called GRID (gay-related immune deficiency). Equally specific, the name Gay Men's Health Crisis clearly identifies the nature and character of the issues involved as they pertain to the community's survival and integrity. The name describes and locates the problem in social arrangements by pointing to its urgent medical and political dimensions. Given that GMHC had to first force the definition of AIDS as a medical, not "moral," problem, its willful identification of AIDS as a "gay man's crisis" is both significant and wise.

By accepting the disease as a gay-specific crisis, GMHC recognized AIDS as a threat of potentially cosmic proportions. "When death is a social event," writes Denneny (1990:16), "both the individual *and the community* are threatened with irreparable loss." One of GMHC's overtly stated goals was to prevent this from happening. In some ways, however, the gay identification with AIDS further isolated both the disease and the gay community. The response to AIDS, therefore, mirrors social arrangements and the system of intergroup relations between gays and established institutions.

Because of gay concerns about the civil issues surrounding AIDS and the medicalization of deviance and/or gay life, GMHC has identified and capitalized on the political implications of relating germs and illness to sexual behavior. Through the instigation of protests and the placing of pressure on gay insiders in influential places (especially at the *New York Times*) to write about AIDS to bring it to public attention, GMHC skillfully turned AIDS into a broader international and humanitarian issue.

GMHC demanded its share of citizen entitlements because it assumed the humanity of gays and PWAs. It could mobilize the community because virtually all gay people are numbered among the "worried well." With growing numbers of PWAs, the community could not wait for either government or mainstream agency responses, should they ever be made available. In the beginning, there simply were no services offered to people with an assumedly infectious, yet thought to be contagious, illness. GMHC had to appoint ombudsmen and make liaisons with city hospitals and health care institutions to push for improved care and service delivery. There was no precedent in New York for such a singularly large and concerted health-related effort by stigmatized minorities. But because PWAs were being left to die unfed and uncared for, the community had to respond and create a specific, often militant, gay/AIDS agenda. At first, however, GMHC did not appear threatening to city officials because of its informality and minority origins.

While the urgency of dealing with AIDS was the same in San Francisco, gays there had achieved a modicum of political power. Hence AIDS has been less a political crisis and more a health and service issue in that city. In New York, gay political impotence, relatively indifferent mayors, and the power of the Catholic archbishop there clearly make AIDS a continuous political crisis.

To effectively protect gay rights against such an entrenched establishment, GMHC developed a complex administrative structure. By 1985, it could easily articulate the community's concerns, keep track of the business at hand, and interact professionally with other city and state agencies and institutions.

More significant, however, gay/AIDS volunteers become part of the suffering of gay humanity at critical historical and biographical moments. In more ways than one, the PWA and the volunteer are one and the same. This significant feature of AIDS volunteerism, where volunteers become clients and the clients become volunteers, is astutely noted by volunteer specialist Susan Chambre. She writes:

> While this is not unique to AIDS volunteering, it has significant implications for the creation and maintenance of organizations because the leadership and the volunteers are terminally ill. Their deaths have an overwhelming impact on the viability of organizations and the continued reliance on volunteers. This is the only epidemic in history in which relatively large numbers of people have actively assisted the dying over a prolonged period of time. It is even more distinctive because it represents an epidemic where the dying themselves also provided help to others and where helping others was viewed as a way to prolong their own lives. (Chambre 1989:8)

This situation, I believe, keeps the gay commitment to AIDS dramatic and peculiarly responsive. As at the People with AIDS Coalition, where three executive directors have died within four years and in a normal week anywhere from 25 to 40 percent of staff time is lost to illness, GMHC is also caught up in the drama of staff loss. At the coalition, fifteen board members have died and another six have had to leave it in the span of two years. At GMHC, virtually all but two of its founding board, staff, and department coordinators are either infected with HIV or have already died of AIDS. Yet both organizations remain committed to keeping PWAs working, thinking, and retaining control over medical procedures and living conditions.

In this context, AIDS volunteerism becomes an opportunity to express connections and love to gay men and ideally, if not problematically, to all People with AIDS.

PART ONE

AIDS: The Issues

1

Getting Involved

BEING A PRODUCT OF the gay rights movement, I considered myself part of the energy that produced and shaped GMHC even though my direct involvement in its earliest formulation and activities was minimal. In the fall of 1981, just about when GMHC was being established, I had developed many of the symptoms of AIDS at a time when not much was known about the disease. My symptoms made me suspicious and reflective, if not sympathetic.

I was extraordinarily fatigued, had mood changes and bizarre temperature fluctuations, lost considerable weight, and was simply out of it, as if with dementia. My interest in AIDS and GMHC, therefore, was more than academic or even altruistic. Given my AIDS symptoms, staying abreast of developments and news was central to my own survival, even though I believed, for no apparent reason, that I did not have AIDS. Unawares, I was living the life of a PWA, literally "taking the role of the other."

Given my own health, there was very little I could offer in the way of support or consolation to other PWAs. I simply went along, trying to survive each day on my own. I felt cheated out of the opportunity to help my brothers and sisters "do something about AIDS." As a gesture of sympathy and support, I kept myself busy worrying about my friends. After three years of illness, I began to accept my diagnoses of AIDS-related complex (ARC), chronic flu/fatigue, irritable bowel syndrome, and depression. While AIDS ravaged my peers, I, nevertheless, went through the routine of living, concentrating on my own affairs and the need to get better. I was learning how to survive, make do, and get on with life, much like the chronically ill have always done and People with AIDS were now daily learning to do.

I talked about AIDS a lot and speculated about its nature and meaning with friends and colleagues, but I was still not fully or directly involved with carepartnering a PWA. Quite the contrary, I tended to myself. Being a firm believer in medicine and science, I was pursuing every hypothesis offering explanations for my own illness. I received gladly as many diagnoses and treatments

13

as the doctors and specialists offered as long as it was not AIDS. And there were a lot of them, including psychological ones.

My real wish, however, was to directly help PWAs. I was surrounded by death and dying. AIDS volunteerism was becoming central to the physical and social survival of the community and I needed to do something responsible and find an outlet for my rage. People were being abandoned, friends were dying, and their pain (our tremendous losses) was being discounted. Little did I know that volunteering and being with People with AIDS would give me a chance to do something rewarding, useful, and politically significant, all at the same time.

Bearing Witness

George Whitmore (1988:14) describes involvement in the "AIDS struggle" as the "need to bear witness." For me, bearing witness is the willingness to take on the suffering of others as if it were one's own, but in a way that brings the carepartners into deep conversation with themselves about their own value or sacredness as human beings.

At first, it was impossible for me to fully appreciate AIDS's social implications, political dimensions, or impact on individual lives, let alone its emotional cost. I had not yet fully understood the suffering and loneliness that PWAs were experiencing, their desperation to make us understand what it was like to have AIDS, and what human needs it creates. Volunteering soon changed all this.

It was with some fear and doubt, then, that in fall 1983 I entered GMHC's tiny but new "office" on West 22nd Street in Manhattan. A community benefactor, one among many, had a short time before donated space in an old brownstone for GMHC's temporary use. The office quickly became a haven, a place to go to. In the early days, volunteers and staff, though generally unknown to one another, worked as equals out of private homes, apartments, and workplaces.

Having a central office permitted the volunteer enterprise to begin in earnest. Volunteers were made to feel welcome and useful by executive director Rodger McFarlane and his staff (Barry Davidson, Diego Lopez, Christopher Clark, and Paul Carro). The staff also endured my academic and sociological inquiries. Together with an activist and accessible board, their level of commitment and concern made GMHC a successful community organization and set the tone for volunteers. I soon became aware that nothing I could do, short of quitting my teaching job, would equal their dedication and output. It seemed to me that virtually all volunteers were, likewise, putting in extra time and always making themselves available.

While my introduction into GMHC was gentle and done under the most auspicious of circumstances, I soon felt overwhelmed by the magnitude and significance of the drama unfolding. As early as 1982, it looked like an entire generation of gay men, my generation in particular, was going to be wiped out, but no one seemed capable or concerned about preventing it—except two or three informed gay activists and doctors in New York and San Francisco.

The only viable option available was to do something that empowered us as a community. For all practical purposes, this meant becoming part of GMHC in New York or some other local AIDS service organization like the People with AIDS Coalition or the AIDS Resource Center.[1]

According to Des Pres (1976), this need or "will to bear witness," to stand by those in need and in unfortunate circumstances, characterizes many survivors of "gross tragedy," especially those who had lived or are living in "death camps"—the exact environment that AIDS creates. Playwright Scott McPherson puts it this way in the *Playbill* for *Marvin's Room*.

> Now I am 31 and my lover has AIDS. Our friends have AIDS. And we all take care of each other, the less sick caring for the more sick. At times, an unbelievably harsh fate is transcended by a simple act of love, by caring for another. By most, we are thought of as "dying." But as dying becomes a way of life, the meaning of the word blurs.

For many of us, this is precisely the reality that AIDS conjures up. Holleran (1987:6) says that being gay today "is living in terror," made worse by the collective and compounded loneliness it generates for the gay community. In the face of absolute horror, the need to do something becomes an overwhelming emotion, if not activity, and GMHC was, for a time, the only vehicle for channeling this need and absolving the terror.

AIDS gives new meaning to the phrase "suffering alone in silence." Unlike most diseases, AIDS reverses the natural order: young children watch their mothers and fathers die; as in warfare, friends and lovers lose each other in their prime; aging parents have to nurse their children all over again. The disease destroys trust and friendship, the basis of community. AIDS impoverishes society, depriving it of talent and creativity. Carriers may go on for years unaware of their infection and risk to others. AIDS affects the most powerful of human emotions and the most personal human activities. With the lack of cure or vaccine, it is almost always debilitating, if not fatal, over time. "Collectively," writes Heise (1988:27), "these factors give AIDS a psychological charge that is unmatched by any other disease."

As an early GMHC volunteer notes, "We started out just to find out who was supposed to be dealing with the problems [of AIDS sufferers]. Then we realized no one was: it would have to be us" (Byron 1983:19). Like many others, I just couldn't give in to the emptiness or helplessness now surrounding gay life. I felt, or kept on believing, that good should triumph over evil, returning life to normal. After all, the 1960s and 1970s were the best times ever for gay people and I yearned for that creativity, celebration, and accomplishment that so defined that period. I had no idea that those days seemingly would be gone forever or that AIDS transforms everything.

It was inconceivable to me that the disease could claim so many lives, destroy so many families and relationships, test so many friendships, or bring so many assumptions and expectations into question without immediately generating scholarly interest. The research on AIDS that did exist examined its sociological context, nature, and character, but in a way that failed to create empathy.[2] Isolation and loneliness are the most devastating results of the disease for both PWAs and all gays. This situation needs to be grasped by society in order for the life of the PWA and the work of the volunteer to be understood.

When compared to the suffering of those with AIDS, however, my own health problem paled. Horror story after horror story came with the epidemic and I began to feel fortunate relative to those I came to view as "really sick." In her book on the problems and rewards of "living with chronic illness," Cheri Register (1987) notes that chronic illness makes one appreciate better days. It makes one accept life on its own terms. She demonstrates that living fully the experience of illness frees a person from the curse of "perfectionism" or the belief that happiness is dependent upon having everything just right or in place. Through suffering, I soon learned to be tolerant and compassionate. This in turn protected me from apathy.

For a "sympathetic person," however, I became strangely insensitive to lives that were free of pain. Chronically ill people often come to believe that things work out eventually for the better precisely when and if they fully examine their lives, which is what I was always doing. I soon learned that one need not be sick to identify with PWAs; one simply had to be gay or be involved with the life and spirit of the community or just have gay friends to understand the tragedy that was unfolding. I marveled that PWAs, who were facing much greater deterioration than I was, often came to see the world the same way. If psychological terror were not enough for them, intense physical pain remained a constant and defining reality.

It was at this point that I gathered the strength to give more time to GMHC and understanding AIDS, and devote energy to volunteering. While that commitment in that environment generated my interest in the social psychology of medicine and health, more important, it forced me to enter into a deep conversation with my own inner voice, my own sacred source. I soon discovered a world of meaning and strength that had been unknown to me. Rediscovering my own spirit and accepting my own personhood and integrating them with my heart, mind, and body freed me to move on despite the destruction of AIDS around me. I could do this because I was no longer alone, having discovered the place and meaning of community. Such is the case and story of so many PWAs and volunteers.

Up until then, the very grounding of my existence was shattered, since any notion of a just society or loving god became unreasonable. Theologian Kevin Gordon (1988) summarized the dilemma succinctly with the question, Can there be faith and theology after AIDS? Fortunately, my despair ended when I discovered that AIDS forever transformed anyone willing to personally connect with a PWA. This experience and awareness also helped me understand the essence of faith and hope and the relationship of religion, god,* and "the sacred" to AIDS and gay self-acceptance and empowerment.

AIDS is a crime happening to good people, but very few care to understand its magnitude—to see its meaning for American society or its place in gay history or even world history. Yet it is virtually impossible to live as a gay man in New York City and not be aware of the surrounding specter of death. The city is simply dying. Even when in the best of health, legions of men are simply waiting to be diagnosed. The most common ailments unleash the most neurotic reactions and fears. When one is faced with AIDS, one feels little hope or joy. The gay/AIDS service sector is at least able to create a sense of safety, if not comfort.

Being ill motivated me even further to make some sense out of and find some purpose in the drama of AIDS. I became even more determined to do something to make the horror disappear and the anxiety stop. Reasonable people, when in the middle of a catastrophe characterized by regular visits to hospitals, funeral parlors, and cemeteries, *will* act. My life became a ritual of both mourning aloud and constantly grieving in private. This simple solution—of getting involved, participating in communal works of mercy—was also chosen by many others.

Fortunately for me, my own health improved dramatically at about the same time I got more deeply involved in GMHC and AIDS work. I underwent a routine test for strongyloidiasis, which indicated a nematode infection amenable to a three-day treatment of Vermox, an anti-worm drug. Not having AIDS, I was now "reborn," a person instead of a victim and free to attend to the needs of my friends and the community that sustained and nurtured me in turn for over three years. Unfortunately, hope and a change of venue are never possible for PWAs.

After stumbling around the agency for days on end, doing what I could when possible and attempting the impossible when not, I realized that the

---

*Here "god" refers to the new spirituality, while "God" refers to the historical patriarchal God of organizations.

best contribution I could make was to use my own sociological imagination to help explicate AIDS, if not for the community, then at least for myself and my profession. I was fascinated by the personality of GMHC and the stamina, character, and politics of the people it attracted. GMHC had a unique relationship to the beleaguered gay community, both transforming it and being transformed by it as it went along. While I wanted to understand GMHC's complex and intriguing evolution, I was also moved by the experiences and struggles of the volunteers.

I could now repay a debt—"collect on a deal" by working for and within an agency that had given me a sense of purpose and worthiness that I had not even realized I had needed. After all, I was a member of the "Stonewall generation," the generation that learned to publicly celebrate gay life and sexuality, and thought I was sufficiently healed because I was politically correct. But AIDS and GMHC changed all that. AIDS has a way of putting things into perspective.

Unknown to me at the time, GMHC volunteers were daily living out the experience of crucifixion, despair, and death. Were the volunteers, I wondered, similar to me in their experience of AIDS and in their motivations to volunteer? For PWAs and volunteers, any resurrection was always followed by more illness and more dying. Hopes ran high, but dreams were continuously shattered, then, remarkably, often suddenly, remade. How would GMHC and the volunteers survive this emotional roller coaster?

For me, volunteering at GMHC became the logical vehicle for understanding and experiencing AIDS. The volunteers were the activists, the link between the Person with AIDS, the gay community, the public at large, and the medical and health professions. I wanted to experience what went on between the volunteers and the PWAs and to know how this would politically affect what happened to the larger gay community.

Researching Volunteerism at GMHC

To successfully study "outsider" or subcultural "deviant" groups like gay/AIDS volunteers, Adler and Adler (1987) note than an ethnographer must be an "insider." As a GMHC member, I was able to secure the trust of the volunteers and agency staff, unwittingly becoming myself an object of study. I would now be able to look at both AIDS and volunteerism as it touched on both individual PWAs and the gay community. The problem of determining the best way to proceed, nevertheless, remained. My instincts as a sociologist favored the *verstehen* (experientially intuitive) approach, but my desire for objectivity and accuracy led me to a more traditional methodology (survey research).

Quantitative research methods, however, were not my forte or even my main interest. Nevertheless, a lengthy fourteen-page questionnaire testing everything from homophobia to religious imagery, nurturing skills, and gay pride was distributed to a random sample of 300 volunteers.[3] I inquired about motives, perceptions of AIDS and volunteerism, images of self-worth, capacity to nurture, and so on. To my surprise, I received a 65 percent return, a fact that further enlivened my interest. It soon became obvious, however, that the survey would be useful only in combination with my intuitive sense of what was happening. Putting the data together and interpreting them in the context of volunteerism would be challenging, to say the least.

While based on this tabulated survey data, my main arguments are drawn mainly from years of ethnographic research. This "etic" approach (popularized in anthropology) is a derivative analytical construction that builds and elaborates upon interviews with informants as well as participant observation. It influences the type of information collected and the way it is gathered. My analysis and conclusions, therefore, were not necessarily expressed as such by my respondents and informants. "Interpretive sociology," writes Torpey (1989:393), "typically has less to do with statistics and uses the cultural meaning and subjective focus of investigation" to interpret social reality. Its "truth" comes from insider experience as understood and validated by the community. It is collective wisdom, articulated by individuals but representative of the many.

In any case, writing about AIDS and volunteerism would not be easy. Volunteer studies simply ignore sexual orientation as an explanatory variable, concentrating for the most part on the organizational volunteerism done by and for mainstream Americans. Of the studies of homophile community organizations that exist, none are construed or assessed in the context of volunteerism as an ideology. While gay studies are generally handicapped by the presence of stigma, stereotypes, ethical considerations, and the criminal law, I had not realized that my own *verstehen* approach was not only central to AIDS research but was also one of the main methodological and political questions surrounding AIDS in general. Both Lessor (1987) and Murray (1987) attest that the contingencies of AIDS render typical survey research less informative or accurate than one would expect or hope.

Whether it is the outsider or the insider who can know, understand, appreciate, and even resolve the problems of AIDS better remains a primary research issue. The "truth about AIDS" is claimed to be known by the gay community, People with AIDS, so-called impartial scientists, policymakers, moralists, ethicists, and bureaucrats. I similarly had to wonder whether my own experiences at GMHC were generally representative of all AIDS agency volunteers. All I can say is that I have lived within the shadow of AIDS, GMHC's development, and the volunteer experience of serving PWAs from virtually the beginning of the epidemic. It is my generation, my friends and my community who are at risk and who bore witness the most desperately and devotedly.

In researching the phenomenon of gay/AIDS volunteerism and the development of a unique volunteer role in AIDS, I became involved with earnest people living with and under extraordinary stress that went beyond simply working with the sick. Suzanne C. Ouellette Kobasa writes: "To conclude . . . that AIDS is a stressful illness is to risk absurd understatement." She identifies several sources of volunteer stress that are unique to volunteerism in AIDS:

> Their tasks are numerous and varied and often highly stressful. Responding to pressing and often overwhelming emotional and material needs of clients with hands-on assistance, facilitating groups for recently bereaved lovers and other family members, coming up against an unresponsive legal system, convincing the media to report on AIDS in an informed way by avoiding techniques that foster panic and hysteria are only some of the strenuous tasks that volunteers meet on a regular basis. (Kobasa 1987:15)

Volunteers, like so many others, also have a fear of contagion. They frequently overidentify with their clients and have feelings of helplessness and hopelessness. They may lack support from family or friends and their volunteering may actually isolate them from their normal social contacts and activities. I also experienced these conflicts while volunteering.

On any given day, emotions range from exhilaration to profound despair, from feeling connected to feeling abject loneliness. No sooner is one problem resolved than other, even more painful and complex, problems are born. The only satisfaction for volunteers is knowing that they make a difference in the lives of the people and community that they love. The horror of an AIDS death remains with them forever, its terror somewhat contained by the memory of a few cherished "thank yous".

Most early AIDS volunteers carepartnered for two to three years. Today, volunteers do so for about a year. When their first burnout occurs, these volunteers generally feel satisfied that they have done what they can to help. If they return to carepartnering, they do so informally and with a more realistic attitude. There is no way of escaping: The needs of PWAs and the need to help them are great. Though few informal and even fewer formal rewards are available, volunteerism in AIDS persists and remains a viable way of coping with disregard, abandonment, and loss. There are now approximately 300 AIDS-specific voluntary community organizations in the United States and dozens in New York.

As a GMHC volunteer, I found it virtually impossible to separate the sociological from the personal and professional. Fellow volunteers and PWAs become friends and confidants, and there was no limit to the variety of experiences and emergency situations in which volunteers and staff found themselves. What being at GMHC primarily taught me, however, was that being with PWAs for any length of time dramatically brings the reality of homophobia home to roost. It is ubiquitous in society, cannot be avoided institutionally, and is daily experienced as real. Its intensity is made worse by AIDS. It is this realization that continually shaped the contours of this study.

There are dramatic effects on intra- and interpersonal relations for those who choose to identify with a stigmatized population and disease. I wanted to know what they were and why so many gay men chose volunteering at GMHC as a way of addressing the problems that both AIDS and homophobia created. To identify with AIDS, I reasoned, volunteers would have to be less homophobic themselves (by being more community identified) and be more willing and able to nurture, that is, bring individuals to a sense of their own valuableness—a necessary objective in AIDS care.

In addition to identifying the salience of homophobia to any AIDS research, I studied volunteers, the gay community, and GMHC, which required subtle yet accurate measurements of realities not necessarily or even consciously known to either the volunteers or to the GMHC staff. As a researcher, my task included interpreting volunteer behavior and motivations. Since the community was obviously being empowered, it was clear that volunteerism was its genesis. The problem was not whether empirical evidence confirmed this but rather how to access and operationalize concepts such as political behavior, community, homophobia, healing, and empowerment.

My first step was to develop a set of questions concerning topics that I thought needed to be covered. These questions reflected the conceptual assumption of the project that homophobia was not only at the root of AIDS as both a social and medical problem but that it would also generate and shape the community response that, I reasoned, would occur among those who were free of homophobic guilt. Because the research questions matched my personal understanding of how GMHC and gay volunteerism evolved together, it became obvious that the study would have to be mainly descriptive and exploratory and that this would be the best way to proceed in any case.

Quite honestly, my choice of roles, from detached observer to insider member and participant observer, does affect the perspective of this book, the type of information sought, the way the data were collected, how and why this ethnography is written, and how the volunteer experience in AIDS is being interpreted. My being a sociologist simply informs my own volunteer experience, which I obviously believe to be typical of GMHC volunteers. This "problem" of objectivity is unique to AIDS precisely because of its "collective" and emotionally charged nature.

Most certainly, a psychologist doing the same study would concentrate on different variables (Omoto and Snyder 1990) and would draw a different picture of what GMHC, volunteerism, and AIDS are all about. All I want to do is record the need for what Griggs (1989) calls "simple acts of kindness," or what I believe to be acts of collective altruism in AIDS. I hope to do this by using both qualitative and quantitative sociological methods. I trust that the readers of the manuscript during its preparation corrected for any generalizations that might be too subjective, inaccurate, or unrepresentative.

2

The Sin Stigma and Gay/AIDS Volunteerism

I
T WAS MY OWN CHRONIC ILLNESS and fear, not social responsibility or altruism, that generated my immersion in both AIDS research and GMHC. My interest was also fueled by my dissatisfaction with the way moral entrepreneurs, supported by many religious leaders, were encouraging "AIDS hysteria."

The celebrated gay culture of the late 1960s and 1970s is gone, eclipsed by a so-called moral majority that determinedly acts on its agenda to have gays, who are already oppressed, punished further. In some bizarre way, AIDS is a victory of Anglo culture over multiculturalism, at least as far as gays are concerned. For once, we were living—dancing, as it were—and we were happy. Now, we are dying, in part because of this carefree abandonment. It is this shock and hostility that makes our world, which was taken for granted, suddenly suspect and leads to questioning anew the nature of god and organized religion, and their relationship to both the state and society.

As a disease, AIDS continuously raises questions about the meaning of sexuality, equality, and morality. It deeply affects our collective images of the church and the sacred. In writing about "the faith challenge" that AIDS poses for the gay and lesbian community, Kevin Gordon quotes Tolstoy:

> If the thought comes to you that everything that you have thought about God is mistaken and that there is no God, do not be dismayed. It happens to many people. But do not think that the source of your unbelief is that there is no God. If you no longer believe in the God in whom you believed before, this comes from the fact that there is something wrong with your belief and you must strive to grasp better that which you call God. When a savage ceases to believe in his wooden God, this does not mean there is no God, but only that the true God is not made of wood.

When one searches for the "message" in AIDS, the question of god's relationship to illness, people, and society and the question of being gay or having

23

AIDS, or both, are inevitably raised. When religious organizations are identified as the true or only source of divine knowledge, and when religious ideologies are imposed on the state and society, the free interchange of ideas becomes a proscribed activity. The corrupt union of church and state creates a bankrupt "corporate theology" relative to AIDS and gay people.

Religion, AIDS, and Homosexuality

The power that religion had in defining the parameters of AIDS when it first appeared is significant for two reasons. First, by successfully mixing morals with medicine, those in established religion have made their perspectives and concerns central to any discussions of the problem of AIDS. For the "moral majority," AIDS is proof of a patriarchal God's condemnation of homosexuality. For them, the solution to AIDS is either death or celibacy; homosexuals should spend their lives "in the closet."

Second, AIDS pushes questions of sexuality and holiness into remarkably new and diverse directions, forcing us to establish the sacredness (humanity) of gay people outside the confines of religion and in a way that joins sexuality with identity and community life. Bearing witness does this for us by celebrating the self and the community as mutual life-giving realities. The ground of religious orthodoxy and the relevance of stateside religion are undermined by this shift in sacredness from organizational approval to self-acceptance and shared consciousness.

Within "incorporated" forms of religion, the gay or lesbian individual as a unique, special, and sacred gift is lost forever. Equality and validity in simply being oneself is passed over in favor of patriarchal notions of order, law, hierarchy, obedience and their corollaries of deviance, sin, and punishment. The common good is defined as what is normative for the political majority or religious establishment rather than what is just for both the individual and society. "Whatever is not male, preferably white, hierarchical and patriarchal, is other than and less than—that is, women, women not wanting men, and men perceived as acting otherwise than within the prerogatives of their privileged gender" (Gordon 1989:183).

The "assimilationist" ideology of the political majority justifies denying outsiders their rights. By definition, gays and lesbians are neither centrists nor compatible in life-style with a patriarchal social world. To identify with mainstream culture, a condition for acceptance, means to live in the closet. The out-group has to accommodate and imitate the in-group to be considered a neighbor, never mind a neighbor in need—an unnecessary, hypocritical, and impossible demand to be made of gays, to say nothing of PWAs.

Raising and resolving the justice issues generated by AIDS cannot be done by moralizing entrepreneurs who have a vested interest in the prevailing power arrangements anchored in the control of sexual activity. Moral, philosophical, and theological thinking becomes sabotaged whenever inquiry or thought is tied to a particular distribution of social power. As Ranke-Heinemann (1991) demonstrates, this makes objectivity impossible.

It is a corrupt and distorted theology, not a redemptive one, that produces and legitimates homophobia (see Chapter 11). Such theology sustains heterosexist power at the expense of women and gays. The denial in so many Western religions of the validity of female and gay experiences precludes thinking of them (us) as knowing people, as part of god's plan (society), and as instruments of revelation. Patriarchy not only interferes with our appreciation of the work of gay volunteers in AIDS but also undermines and distorts the relationship of men and women to themselves and to one another as sacred sources.

The questions of "women's church" as believing and faith-filled community and of "gay church" as legitimate revelation need to be addressed, since AIDS calls the religious establishment to task on all accounts, the way the Nazi holocaust still does. "Some may think that this disease provides a natural occasion for the churches to judge AIDS," notes Gordon (1989:171), but "ironically, and in the long run, it will be AIDS that judges the churches."

Traditional religious ideologies have serious implications for the life journey of all minorities, especially PWAs. By being segregated out, their human value is diminished. For AIDS sufferers, these ideologies result in their being misidentified, having mismanaged health needs, and having to endure misjudgments about which treatments they should undergo, often becoming guinea pigs for pharmaceutical companies. Creating and employing a "punishing God" in the war on AIDS weighs heavily on the psyche and spirit, frequently inducing fear, guilt, shame, and silence.

Organizational theology, then, can find neither answers nor a perspective on the question of gay rights and the suffering of PWAs. It can't because it won't acknowledge either the notion of sexual orientation as a valid ontological category or the legitimacy of nonprocreative sexual behavior as a fact of a free, human life. Because of their implications for social structure and church-state relations, the authenticity of homosexuality and gay holiness cannot even be raised for discussion. Therefore, a new "theology of liberation" (gay liberation) and a theology of AIDS are emerging now precisely because the exigencies of AIDS demand that such a theology be written—and that it be written by those who are suffering from and responding to AIDS on a daily basis. To be useful, it would have to be a theology rooted in the sociological experience of being outsiders.

To be sure, moral entrepreneurs understand the centrality of gay legitimacy and women's equality to the continuation of masculinist or patriarchal privilege in general. This is why they moralize about AIDS the way that they do and obsess about the propriety of anal intercourse. Organized moral enterprises require a corporate theology that ensures that sexism never be dismantled or that gays be accepted. Roman Catholicism, for example, recognizes very acutely the centrality of AIDS to the reordering of both social structure and cultural values relative to male privilege and, subsequently, its own power in society.

When gays survive AIDS and thus legitimate nonprocreative sex, then the very basis for Roman Catholic moral theology is undermined. Its emphasis, dependency on, and support of hierarchical, organizational, and patriarchal family systems become less credible, if not unnecessary, in a nurturing society of equality and respect for all human life. "It is the same age-old tradition of male control, domination, and oppression of women which underlies the oppression of the homosexual," writes silenced gay Jesuit priest John McNeill (1976:189).

Gay civil rights would legitimate diverse and personalized sexualities expressed in nonprocreative ways outside of marriage. Normalizing homosexual relations dismisses the social control of sexuality by stateside religions and the parallel social institutions they influence and legitimate. Both gays and AIDS pose challenges to the church-state connection and the social and institutional status quo built on the repression of women and the denial of sexual expression for pleasure in a relationship.

The continuous confrontation with the Catholic church by the AIDS Coalition to Unleash Power (ACT-UP) on the steps of St. Patrick's Cathedral throughout 1989 and 1990 is not, therefore, an insignificant, random event. AIDS has revealed for gays who the mortal enemy is. To survive, the community goes for the jugular vein of homophobia when it attacks the power of religion over personal and sexual identity and behavior. ACT-UP responds in kind to the violence that religion causes to the gay psyche.

"Incorporated religion" is a legitimating social institution with considerable power to define social morality. Moral stigma excludes people from human community, and from the very beginning AIDS was cast in moralistic terms to inhibit a more rational and humanistic reaction. So responding would give legitimacy to gays living through a crisis redefined as not of our own making. It is in the context of this marginality and exclusion that the transformation of gay identity and relations takes place at GMHC. Gordon refers to this phenomenon as "fraternal friendship." "The response of gay men to one another, especially in creating organizations like the Gay Men's Health Crisis in New York City, and similar institutions across the country, makes it clear that something new, exciting, and moving has come alive within the gay community and its friends across the country" (1989:204).

For many, AIDS has become an opportunity to affirm the self, renew the community, remain distinctive, and lay claim to wholeness (or holiness) once and for all. For gay volunteers, bearing witness to PWAs becomes a celebration of hope and self-acceptance, bringing the community back to itself on its own terms. AIDS volunteerism allows gays, at least those with some degree of pride, to avoid collective despair and impotence. It ends withdrawal and inertia, forcing a decisive pro-life stand by the community.

Promulgated and legitimated corporate theology retards our survival and gives religious organizations advantages by allowing them to make gays scapegoats for national ills. The bizarre notion of "justified suffering" as an explanation for AIDS, for example, while horrifying for many, has seemingly became tenable for the political majority, who continue to use the idea to sustain their social and political hegemony.

Ironically, given the American need to find a scapegoat for AIDS, the resurgence of religious fundamentalism, and the popularity of the self-styled "moral majority," a "revengeful God" almost seems believable. By itself, this one vindictive idea fueled and sustained the prevailing political morality and, because AIDS was sexually transmitted, brought the general public back onto religion's side in the homophobic "healthy society" and "natural law" debate. It generated what Poirier (1988) identifies as "the war on homosexuality," which is considered the moral cause of AIDS.

Equally as important as the indifference and hostility to gays and PWAs generated by the "gay-AIDS-sin" stigma is religion's role in the production and maintenance of violent homophobia. Note especially the argument and logic of the October 1986 "Letter to the Bishops of the Catholic Church on the Pastoral Care of Homosexual Persons." Not only does it intentionally join together AIDS and homosexuality, but it also legitimates violence toward both gays and PWAs. "Even when the practice of homosexuality may seriously threaten their lives and well-being of a large number of people, its advocates remain undeterred and refuse to consider the magnitude of the risks involved." This view of gays as unrepentant and self-destructive actually encourages violence because this stateside theology creates the image of gays as sinners, hence dispensable, others. Moreover, it is patently untrue. Also in the letter: "When civil legislation is introduced to protect behavior to which no one has any conceivable right, neither the Church nor society at large should be surprised when other distorted notions and practices gain ground, and irrational and violent reactions increase."

Despite modern psychology, this deceptive document defines homosexual "inclinations" as "ordered towards an intrinsic moral evil," making the homosexual condition itself "an objective disorder." Homosexuality is not, for the Roman Catholic church, an orientation or state of being. In so ignoring the naturalness of homosexuality, corporatized Catholic theology shifts the grounds of the longtime discussion with psychology to medieval philosophy.

"This strategic move," writes Gordon (1989:177), "renders an already unconscionable and violent document literally incredible."

The idea of an all-loving, embracing, and inclusive god rendering grotesque punishment on people who behave on their natural instincts was bad, but useful, theology. Because it sustained the discriminatory status quo, publicly calling gays "sinners" was unacceptable as much to me as it was for most reasonable theologians. In the context of a "liberated theology" in AIDS, it is a sign of bankruptcy that any religious person or institution remains committed to the "AIDS as sin and divine retribution" argument *and* to the violence that such a stand engenders.

Morals and Medicine

By dint of historical circumstances, patriarchal religious ideas have prevailed throughout the spread of AIDS and have made gays seem morally culpable, hence ignorable. Parroting President Reagan's speech writer Patrick Buchanan (who blames AIDS on the unceasing insistence of gays to have unnatural, suicidal sex), Archbishop John Kroll announced that AIDS "is an act of vengeance against the sin of homosexuality." And so it seems to many.

People not in need of partisan theological reasoning or a patriarchal God produced by corporate insiders, however, would be less likely to see AIDS and gays the way entrenched "moralists" and religionists do. Nonconformists would reject beliefs that were based neither on real knowledge of "the other" nor the direct experience of their own and others' inner sacredness. Nor would they react to People with AIDS and women the way that Roman Catholicism so consistently does. Their religious imagery would be of an equitable god.

AIDS is haunting, indeed threatening, sexually phobic religions because AIDS brings sexuality and the sacred together in powerful new ways. Corporate theological beliefs create a crisis in justice and forgiveness for those who either know gays, know god's love, or have faith and want to believe in a just god. I believe that the intent of any god, and the purpose of the sacred, is to be reconciled to people in the fullness of their humanity. This is best done by incorporation, by ending marginality and fear, rather than by casting judgments and making threatening condemnations.

Gays are feared because AIDS challenges the power and plausibility of the old patriarchal God of rules, power, and punishment. As a disease, it threatens the social order by making society examine the truth about gay men and women, sexuality, *and* god. AIDS forces all believers to determine whether the god they believe in is a god of love or a God of vengeance. Our god is the former. AIDS, then, is the issue around which the urgent questions of sexuality, sexual ethics, gay rights, and even women's equality all hinge. Because it stigmatizes, it identifies anew who does and does not belong to "the community," the people of god, and the society.

These questions of sexuality, gay rights, women's autonomy, individual freedom, and sexual expression for pleasure are all interconnected and are at the core of all things dear to social engineers or moral entrepreneurs—from the organization of their religions to their stateside, theological definitions of sin and morality. These questions are the central issues because, when openly and honestly addressed, they undermine the social and political control of individual sexuality by orthodox social and religious institutions.

AIDS and the response of gays fundamentally challenge the location and uses of authority, the domain of the sacred, and the meaning of society and community. By reordering personal relationships, AIDS volunteerism redefines the source and nature of the sacred. It threatens the religious establishment by reappropriating the sacred. It is in moving from an androcentric and heterosexist characterization into a wider human application that gay life becomes comprehensible, thus, threatening.

AIDS tells us a lot about the nature of both homophobia and morality, and religion's manipulative, legitimating functions in society. The political majority now uses AIDS to sustain homophobia in new and dramatic ways. It gives homophobia a medical basis in addition to a religious one. Together with conservative images of god, members of the political majority maintain the status quo, excluding and marginalizing those who threaten the social order. And one way of reinstating authority over gays is to ignore AIDS by defining it morally. This leaves gays vulnerable and medical practitioners free of moral and professional obligations.

Transformation: A Model for Understanding AIDS Volunteerism

Because it is an issue in civic culture (rights and entitlements), gays' publicly owning AIDS challenges institutionalized homophobia. The drama of this oft-made psychosocial identification with the human face of AIDS cannot be easily captured from the outside or from the sidelines. Gordon (1989:193) calls this activity "the sacrament of coming-out," which, in an epidemic, is heroic work. For Gordon, coming out "is the organic unfolding of our deepest being."

> [It means] giving public witness the incarnational witness of a human face of God, shattering the quiet and dark closet, unmasking anonymity and hypocrisy. Here public would mean "out in the light," the realm in which human life is sustained and fully exercised, as contrasted with "in the shadow," the realm of necessity, restriction, and isolation, "privation." What is hidden and concealed is revealed and made manifest. It discloses itself.

Coming out, changing, and facing death are a central part of the process of becoming fully human. It is implicit in our humanity that our past selves die and that we grow and change, have hope, and seek to overcome—to have, as it were, a resurrection. For gays, confronting the horror and depth of AIDS initiates this process and journey. The willingness to volunteer springs from deep within the human heart, making volunteering a way of affirming the human need for hope, meaning, and purpose.

If AIDS volunteerism brings one out and establishes, in Gordon's understanding, "the truth of being," then a new approach combining sociology, political science, and theology is needed to recognize the true sources of sacredness and the mystery of self-adjudication through communal acceptance that he refers to. By themselves, traditional social science paradigms cannot explain this "truth renewal and commitment" and why it happens except in a static, functional way. Classical sociology relies too heavily on models of society and behavior that are pervaded by homophobia (Phillips 1991). Likewise, human qualities such as altruism, selflessness, hope, belief, and forgiveness are all unintelligible in traditional scientific paradigms.

If sociology, however, acknowledges the sacred squarely in human experience, making it concomitant with the variety of human existence, then it can be used together with theology to explain gay/AIDS volunteerism as both political and sacred activity. Since it is an individual's sense of his or her own personhood that renews and gives meaning, hope, direction, and purpose to life, political activity is the result of this consciousness and self-acceptance.

In gay AIDS, it is the acceptance of our own humanity that radicalizes us and sets us in opposition to the status quo. AIDS volunteers are, by definition, in an authenticating experience as growing, connected persons. As such, gays become political actors. This empowerment through connectedness makes it possible to say *no* to misanthropic oppression and rejection and *yes* to survival as gay people.

Because AIDS, established religious prejudices, and homophobia are so intimately and oppressively linked, I use an unorthodox sociotheological language (e.g., healing, transformation, self-actualization, communalization, linkages, sacred sources, and so on) to analyze and interpret the significance and meaning of gay/AIDS volunteerism. This approach and vocabulary will allow us to go beyond the ordinary limits of sociology.

Liberated sociology creates shared insights (grounded in experience) that force us to adopt a public philosophy ideally committed to political action as a way of ending AIDS-homophobia. Any approach to solving problems like AIDS and homophobia is justifiable only if it serves the liberation struggle. As such, writes Kruijer (1987:3), it "must make a contribution to it, to a process that involves a leap forward in consciousness, organization, and activity, and that leads to a society based on liberty, fraternity, and equality."

It is the absence of these conditions, the disinheritedness or desanctification of gays, and the fallacy of social science objectivity about gays and AIDS that explains the reason this book is written with fervor and conviction and a certain degree of iconoclasm and irreverence toward establishment truth.

An emotive language is used in this analysis because it reflects pain, struggle, loss, and the perpetual and universal hope of overcoming compounded grief and despair. It is not intended to be an irritant, but to go beyond both sociology and traditional theology, which are too staid to interpret the gay community as a valid sacred source in its own right. If a static language were applied to AIDS, we would miss the dynamics of how homophobia oppresses and how it needs to be dismantled for the destructiveness of AIDS to the soul and spirit to be known.

In response to this AIDS-inspired incoherence is the phenomenon of volunteerism. It is an affirmation precisely because it witnesses to the pain of similar yet even more disadvantaged, faceless, and dehumanized others. So severe was the marginalization of PWAs in the early 1980s that an appropriate AIDS language actually had to be created by AIDS sufferers themselves to protect their integrity and identity as persons (Navarre 1988). They did this by insisting on being called People with AIDS rather than "AIDS victims." By using this new language, GMHC makes the PWA an extension of the community, the group with which an individual gay person's fate is tied. This link becomes the nexus and praxis of gay empowerment. GMHC's development discredits the claim that voluntary action is an apolitical, secular activity.

An informed "sociotheological imagination" is necessary to make sense of this connection between AIDS volunteerism, self-acceptance, the location of sacredness, and the politicization process. This perspective, emphasizing the links between social arrangements, images of god, and personal troubles, is implied in the "theory of transformation" first developed by Manfred Halpern (1987, 1969). As deftly utilized by David Abalos (1986) in his analysis of the social experiences and politicization of Latinos in the United States, this approach to political change is based on strategies of personal and communal transformation through the establishment of binding and affirming links between individuals.

Like Halpern, Abalos sees politicization as a derivative of connectedness between individuals and the communities that define them. For him, these linkages are sacred and political because they bring people to their own fullness. Abalos's insights are particularly applicable to AIDS because they help us recognize that being political means establishing ties within and between a segmented and fractured gay community so as to withstand its own dissolution.

> Political activity is a fundamental human right that has always belonged to us but was taken away from all of us, both minority and majority groups. To be political

is to participate, to struggle with others on a plan of equality so as to be able to create, nourish, and destroy inadequate institutions and to build new ones. (Abalos 1986:140)

If it is anything at all, gay/AIDS volunteerism is about the breaking and re-establishment of connections to the self, to the community, and to the surrounding society. Since AIDS is a shared experience that turns individual death into a notable social occurrence, it has infected and diseased all relationships. In AIDS, not only individuals but the gay community in its entirety are implicated and at risk of annihilation. The interconnectedness of gays, AIDS, and volunteerism highlights the effects of other, more oppressive, institutional linkages on the relations of homosexual individuals to themselves, to one another, to the gay community, and of both homosexual individuals and the gay community to the larger, surrounding society.

Using Halpern's model raises consciousness about how the personal is political and allows us to identify volunteerism as an ingredient in the empowerment of both the individual and the community. It permits us to integrate both accurate historical data and subjective experiences of oppression and rejection with psychosocial facts such as homophobic discrimination and rejection. Concentrating on the volunteer role in AIDS will help us grasp these connections and, hopefully, to take sides.

Because the starting point of the model of transformation is the position and condition of those who have traditionally been most powerless in society, for gays, connections to the community and to the "others" are established by claiming the self as an authentic source. It is an act of liberation for all gay people when the rejected PWA becomes the symbol or emblem of the community. In Halpern's model, gay/AIDS volunteerism can be recognized as political activity because it renews and restores individuals to one another and to the community as a sacred source, challenging psychic, social, and spiritual fragmentation, if not physical death, in the process.

Volunteerism as Prophetic Witnessing

To be sure, GMHC, an avowedly secular community service, does not define its work as either sacred or political, never mind as "prophetic," although this is very much what it is. Actually, the organization is often attacked for appearing too *apolitical* (as opposed to untypically political) because it operates within an organizational political economy. GMHC sees its service ethic to the "other" as its defining attribute, not its volunteers' healing of homophobia or empowerment of the community. Since its response is secular, it prefers to see itself in humanistic and culturally ethical terms.

GMHC's overt secularization is understandable, even commendable. It allows for objectivity and freedom to create a reasonable and useful response to AIDS-homophobia. This is why the model of transformation is useful: It offers a vocabulary of analysis to understand GMHC and the work of the volunteers. Interpreting its mission and task in either traditional secular or religious languages would actually be inaccurate, harmful, and counterproductive. Anyway, the old images of holiness or wholeness can not capture the human or faith journey of volunteers, gays, and People with AIDS and it would be irresponsible to interpret GMHC's ethos, commitments, and effects in terms of the patriarchal God of organized religion.

In the theory of transformation, however, the work of volunteers produces a "sacred humanism" by integrating people with themselves through the act of bearing witness. Volunteering takes the experience of gays beyond ordinary religious concerns or capabilities. To paraphrase Peter Berger (1967:117), there are many people today who joyfully look upon the world and their own lives without the benefit of traditional religious interpretations.[1]

Stateside religions are the bane of gay existence and there is no solace to be found in them since much of their "compassionate" concern in AIDS is to dying homosexuals, not gay people as such. Kateb (1988:456) suggests that while PWAs know that some people in society want to help them, "others, in their religious or nonreligious puritanical or prurient hostility, want to use the procedures needed to study AIDS and to help those sick from it as devices of humiliation and punishment."[2] For him, "the sick and those who may one day become sick are driven to cooperate with those who want to help them, and driven also to resist them. The sick are in a dilemma and so are those who want to help them."

There are now numerous "pastoral ministry" programs for AIDS patients; the hypocrisy of them is overwhelming. Oppressed and ignored when alive, denounced as sinners from the pulpits and often denied civil rights because of religious hostility, gays as AIDS patients are prayed for and ministered to as *victims*.[3] These "pastoral counselors" are normally members of hostile religious organizations and therefore cannot fully address their own homophobia or that of their own congregations. This would undermine their own institutional commitments and loyalties and increase their own cognitive dissonance. Their energy is misdirected since they do not generally call their own church organizations into service to gay people, just to AIDS "victims." They do not even try to bring their church organizations to the same level of commitment as themselves.[4] Except for the Episcopalians, they have not asked their superiors to address the issue of homophobia.

GMHC's volunteers, in contrast, are able to do so much more. They can address the humanity of PWAs, their needs, personally and directly, without benefit of sanction and support by the religious establishment. Their corporal works of mercy occur concomitantly with the restoration of pride, dignity, meaning, and purpose to the lives of PWAs. That GMHC does not see this restoration as empowering and politically unsettling is simply a function of the conservative way it and so many gay activists understand the sacred, see religion, and practice politics. The volunteers, however, in the simple act of witnessing, perform fundamentally religious (political) activities with radical political (spiritual) consequences.

In this sense, the silence of the churches is useful to GMHC because it allows for a greater radicalization and community mobilization. Now gay people can do sacred work for one another unencumbered by traditional religious imagery and organizational constraints. GMHC volunteers step outside of the state-church union to create an alternative system in which gays and PWAs can relate to themselves and to one another. Bearing witness is a fundamental religious service yet is not entangled with organized religion and does not make PWAs think that being holy or worthy has something to do with going to church or belonging to a religion.[5] This is why the state religions must crush gay religiosity: It stands, by definition, in opposition to the established patriarchal order in all its duplicity and pseudolegitimacy.

Of necessity, AIDS forces us to ask ultimate questions about social justice and the nature of relationships. The answers can be found only *outside* the parameters of church-related religion and theology. This way, the truth that the gay community is really a life-giving sacred source can emerge. Although not self-defined in theological terms as such, the volunteer experience is liberation theology at its best because it offers hope and access to self-discovery, especially to the poor. In very profound ways, GMHC is different from other community organizations because it reflects an alternative way of being in the world. Its "humanism" is sacred and therefore fundamentally religious. It is more than merely secular because it generates radically new relationships that take AIDS volunteerism beyond the ordinary and mundane.

While my primary emphasis is sociological, this foray into this relationship of religion to both the tragedy of AIDS and the gay community mobilization has to be noted, but in a way that brings into question philosophy, theology, sociology, psychology, political science, and history all at once. The discussion that follows, therefore, will perhaps meet with resistance because of its implications about our everyday understanding and experience of ourselves as a people and society. It will also challenge the prevailing wisdom about god, the relationship of the sacred to being gay and political, and the significance of the suffering of PWAs. The argument of this book, therefore, will be construed as subversive to prevailing social knowledge and the societal arrangements it is based on.

3

"Morality" and AIDS Issues

THROUGHOUT THE 1980s, young men were dying in their prime without explanation, and few scientists and public officials viewed these deaths as critical because the victims were primarily homosexual men. Not until the dramatic spread of AIDS (doubling every six months from 1982 through 1986) and the destigmatization of the disease (through its heterosexualization) permitted objective research were scientists earnestly willing to look for a cause and cure. Yet even today, interest in AIDS fluctuates in terms of what groups are considered at risk. Sensationalist AIDS stories grab headlines and are particular media favorites.

Compounding and reflecting this heedlessness is the social destitution of PWAs. In the context of being addressed as an illness of "disposable others," at least for gays, AIDS-homophobia becomes an isolating political strategy. It encourages a "morally justified" anti-gay backlash based on fear and ignorance.

Early scientific inquiry was jeopardized by moral judgments and the convenient disinformation generally accepted as true about gays (Treichler 1987). Because of this attitude toward gays and the social disdain for minority drug-users, little biomedical inquiry was conducted between 1981 and 1983.

In 1982, when the distinction between T-4 and T-8 cells and their relationship to immune function became clearer, gay activist Dr. Joseph Sonnabend called researcher Stuart Schlossman, the Harvard immunologist who did the original research with monoclonal antibodies. "I suppose you've been deluged with phone calls about people wanting to work on this new disease, which involves T-cell subsets," asked Sonnabend. "No, you're the first one who's called" (Harrington 1990:28).

It is a sociological truism that if a white, heterosexual male is not directly and generally affected by a particular disease, committed social and medical responses to this disease are unlikely. And when, as in AIDS or HIV infection, a response does occur, it is likely to happen for economic rather than humanistic reasons. This fact is central to the whole evolution of AIDS ontology and, together with homophobia, are the fundamental reasons behind the urgency of the gay mobilization. Thousands of lives had been lost to AIDS by 1990, when the U.S. Senate finally realized that no less than $3 billion needed to be spent on AIDS relief for hospitals and clinics. Experts claimed it would be too expensive in the long run to spend any less.

AIDS, however, was as much a profound social and political crisis as an expensive medical problem. This is why GMHC's concern was centered on how AIDS was being conceptualized as an issue. The question for gays was how its cause or causes would be determined and the categories of analysis established. Gay politicos intuitively knew the social consequences of identifying an infectious illness in arbitrary social terms like "life-style" or "sexual orientation." "The gay and lesbian response to AIDS is an ordinary effort drawn from centuries of community wisdom—'Do for yourselves, before you are done for,'" writes Gordon (1989:202).

It is only now being acknowledged that the social status of HIV sufferers, more than anything else, inhibits supportive public policy. Until 1987, AIDS had been dismissed as an irritant, something that happens to people who live outside the parameter of normative moral constraints. Most politicians, journalists, and bureaucrats simply wanted and still would like to wish it away.

Ignoring such "allowable" horror and suffering is explained by the presence of a "political morality" that posits nonprocreative sexual activity as sinful, the diseases that result from it as justifiable, and Third World people as dispensable.[1] Government is disinterested in the health problems of gay men, prostitutes, drug-users, Latinos, and African-Americans—groups that are politically impotent. Urban gays, often wealthy, articulate, and seasoned civil rights veterans, had to respond swiftly to political inertia and inadequate health care service delivery. Almost by design (necessity), if not default, gays took control of the field.

Stigma and GMHC

The reasons why people choose to help PWAs at GMHC are directly related to who these people actually are. Individuals' social characteristics determine whether they are willing to daily clean up vomit, wipe away splattered diarrhea, or stand vigil at the closing hours of life. What is extraordinary, however, is GMHC's ability to continually harness the energy of "tarnished outsiders" to help severely "tarnished others," accepting them as part of the community. For all practical purposes, GMHC is an effort of a stigmatized minority undertaken on behalf of other alien minority groups. Even if AIDS is not gay, GMHC most certainly is. GMHC is the prototype of community on both the political and affective level.

Given the pervasiveness of homophobia, GMHC's success is astonishing. Gays have triumphed over stigma and rejection to get involved in PWA care. Despite the effectiveness of the gay civil rights movement of the previous decade, gays still had to take charge of the AIDS situation. No one else would, and no one else could, own up to AIDS so magnanimously and uniquely. This is reflected in GMHC's name. Also, Americans believe that problems should be solved on the local level; this means that no one else should care for PWAs.

For gays, AIDS is a crisis in relationship, a threat to community. It calls everything into question, from social institutions to personal emotions, sexual behavior, and religious beliefs. AIDS undermines identities by destroying trust in simply being oneself and living with others. Because it attacks whole classes of people, AIDS has structural origins and collective implications. It is for this reason that the resolution of AIDS can be found as much in the political process as in medical science. Now the political is truly personal and the personal clearly political.

To be sure, all gay people did not respond immediately or enthusiastically to GMHC's concerns about AIDS. Early gay indifference came from fear, ignorance, and disbelief as well as deeply entrenched and internalized homophobia, often manifested as fear of exposure.[2] Yet since the disease alarmingly intertwined the personal and collective interest almost immediately, the gay response would have to be as great and prompt. Not to mobilize in this instance and circumstance would be collectively suicidal.

Unlike the broader society, which felt fearful and apathetic toward AIDS, social or medical scientists were not interested in relevant AIDS research and accurate information on gay life-styles not only because of stigma, hatred, or ignorance but also because of unethical political considerations, the need to protect reputations, and moral self-righteousness.

Fortunately, Larry Kramer and Dr. Larry Mass, two singularly insightful individuals within the gay community, began conceptualizing the disease politically, even though their major and immediate concern was finding its natural cause. Through informal gay social networks, the awareness that the social dimensions of AIDS and its civil implications were as significant as its fatal, biological effects became widespread. This knowledge was facilitated by the coverage given AIDS by Ann Guidici Fettner and epidemiologist James D'Eramo, staff writers at the *New York Native*. Kramer was further encouraged and drew support from several concerned doctors at New York University Medical Center.

AIDS and gay civil rights issues were inherently intertwined and GMHC understood that it required political power to protect the community's interest in the context of morally justified social abandonment. Public health is simply not a national priority; that it is not a priority even with the presence of AIDS is because minority illnesses guarantee an apathetic response.

By stressing this link between personal welfare and political arrangements, GMHC began garnering wide community support. By paying particular attention to the medical entitlements of PWAs and relating their needs to the civil rights of the larger gay community, GMHC guaranteed its own continuity, never mind the humane services it was delivering. Somehow, GMHC was going to be both a gay community initiative and a private agency serving the needs of all People with AIDS regardless of their personal identities, life-styles, or social affiliations. This was a unique yet inevitable dilemma for the agency and community to be in.

Unaware that being unabashedly identified as a gay agency would be its greatest accomplishment, GMHC took on AIDS by producing position papers on virtually every aspect of the disease, including scientific issues. It was able to draw support from educated and activist gays who hounded homophobic researchers, politicians, and moralists. Fortuitously, it succeeded in winning its case over delayed AIDS entitlements, research snags, and inadequate service delivery. In the beginning, just trying to define the illness and keep count of infections occupied much of its time. Were it not for GMHC's public posturing, AIDS would have remained unnoticed even longer and more lives would have needlessly been lost.

Labeling AIDS a "gay plague" had contradictory, though positive, consequences. Unfortunately, the social identification of AIDS with gay life first resulted in bad science and a delayed appreciation of AIDS's pervasiveness and complexity. Moralizing this connection with gay life resulted in a lack of response to AIDS as a global and life-threatening disease of significant human import. GMHC's identity also contextualized the illness and gave it social meaning. But the gay community was empowered in response to these perceptions because GMHC represented the feelings that gays had about the value and beauty of being gay.

Communalizing AIDS through bearing witness (which is what GMHC essentially did) proved to be the best antidote to internalized guilt and potential depoliticization. But were it not for the fortitude and know-how of gay politicos in this country, pushing GMHC to make institutions pay attention, AIDS would have ultimately wreaked even greater havoc on many other populations. If AIDS was limited, for example, to an underclass in Africa, it might never have emerged as a world crisis.

> Without doubt, credit for a good deal of what has been accomplished in terms of raising public and government awareness of AIDS, developing and adopting safer sex procedures, creating community models for caring for PWAs, organizing political pressure for increased government spending on research and care, opening access to experimental treatments, collaborating with all manner of AIDS research, and combating AIDS hysteria belongs to gay and lesbian activists. (Singer et al. 1990:197)

Even though it hit hard on American gays, no one could have predicted that the gay response, at least in New York, would be so swift and decisive, which it might not have been had there not been the Stonewall riot of 1969. The Stonewall, a popular gay bar in New York, is considered the birthplace of both a new collective gay consciousness and the contemporary gay liberation movement. In late June of that year, gays directly confronted police corruption, harassment, and brutality on the streets of Greenwich Village after they raided the Stonewall (Adam 1987:75). In attenuated form, GMHC is the child of Stonewall, likewise moving the community in a new political direction.

People with AIDS in New York

Since 1981, over 50,000 cases of AIDS have been reported in New York State, but the cumulative total may actually exceed 100,000 if blood cell counts and HIV infection itself (without opportunistic infection) are included. The vast majority are in New York City, yet "despite rising caseloads, New York's non-profit AIDS agencies say they may be forced to reduce services because the government support they depend on is being curtailed by the budget problems of the city and state" (Lambert 1990a:38). In October 1990, GMHC announced that it would have to curtail its caseload growth because it was swamped by a surge in AIDS cases.

According to AIDS specialist Bruce Lambert (1988e), in July 1988 New York City had to lower its estimate of the number of expected AIDS cases in order to accommodate its already poorly financed health care budget. GMHC cares for about 35 percent of all AIDS cases in the city. In 1991 its caseload jumped from around 3,000 a year to 4,000, where it remains today.

San Francisco, with one-third the number of cases, which are concentrated predominately among homosexually active men rather than among drug-users, has consistently spent millions more than New York in AIDS prevention and care. That San Francisco was willing to mount a massive and publicly funded response to AIDS rather than rely so desperately on community-based initiatives proves that organized gay interest groups can influence the American political process to their advantage. San Francisco had a gay rights ordinance in effect years before New York did.

New York City's response improved somewhat after 1986 when the city passed its "gay rights bill." Really effective gay political power relative to AIDS, however, has yet to be fully realized. In 1992, a hostile councilman from Brooklyn was left in charge of AIDS disbursements by Mayor David Dinkins over strong gay objections. A report that New York's commissioner of health admits that New York City is "two years behind where we should be" has yet to be addressed (Gross 1988:38). In 1990 the gay community was also unable to halt the appointment of a city health commissioner who once indicated support for quarantine and contact tracing for HIV-positive individuals, themes anathema to gay interests.

In 1989, AIDS reporter Bruce Lambert (1989:A1) wrote that "unless things change in New York, AIDS organizations say people will be suffering and dying in the streets." He also notes that "most experts agree that New York—with 200,000 or more infected people, many impoverished, and with housing in short supply—faces singular challenges."

What is remarkable about this estimate and projection is its redundancy. Putting the politics and usefulness of inflated numbers aside for the moment, for all practical purposes GMHC has consistently warned the city of the impending crisis, yet the city continues to simply augment GMHC's social services, doing little directly on its own for PWAs. With the distribution of condoms in New York City schools, the city's record on AIDS prevention has somewhat improved, though the city seems unable or unwilling to engage AIDS prevention education forthrightly, arguing over an emphasis on abstinence.

City by city, people from high-risk groups face and present unique and different crises. In New York, for example, emergency room facilities are being grossly overtaxed because of the growing number of minority drug-related AIDS cases.

If drug-addicted AIDS sufferers are normally located in large urban centers, gay AIDS is more dispersed both occupationally and residentially, making the problems for gays diverse and more complex. The discrimination and the social and psychological losses are different for gay AIDS sufferers than for drug-addicted AIDS sufferers because with diagnosis and illness, identity and family relations as well as employment and health benefits are often called into question.

In effect, because of its collective and communal nature, AIDS now defines gay life. For all practical purposes, gay life is now lived as in an inferno. For Larry Kramer (1989), this newest gay genocide is the result of direct and purposeful intent, manifested as conscious indifference and silent neglect.

For the second time in recent history—the first being World War II, with the concentration camps—thousands upon thousands of gay men are again being systematically allowed to die and most people, including the potentially "prophetic" voices of many religious leaders, are not only silent but in many instances add coal to the fire. The issue is not whether conservative, stateside religions are theologically homophobic or pornographic. Rather it is their desire and ability to make such prejudice state policy that is the concern here.

The Social Categorization of AIDS

When the origin of an illness is framed in a "religious language," and that illness affects morally suspect minorities, those stricken ill will be blamed for its causality. I fear the political, social, and personal implications of fusing or confusing social categories like homosexual and drug-abuser with morals and medicine. I cannot imagine other illnesses being defined by sexual orientation and I think it dangerous that AIDS has been conceptualized as such. There are no heterosexual diseases, I reason, so how can there be homosexual ones? I dread the consequences of such a conceptual alignment.

It is increasingly obvious that, in its American setting, stigma and social identity define the boundaries of both the politics and science of AIDS. Now that gay people have fallen on hard times, it is easier for everyone to justify AIDS as "their problem." Social abandonment is commonplace, even among the fair-weather, liberal friends of gays. With hostility and indifference confirming the community's worst fears, it is evident that gays are being threatened by yet another epidemic of the basest homophobia imaginable. Unlike AIDS, however, homophobia is endemic to *every* American institution and is not only related to AIDS causality and fulmination, but also to its control and "management."

Within a year of its recognition as a disease (1981–1982), gays were being depicted as dangerous sociopaths, making AIDS the latest metaphor for being a feared "outsider" and threat to public safety (Sontag 1988). Medical experts were using life-style issues rather than scientific evidence to explain disease. The appeal to ignorant, moral arguments was facilitated by the lack of accurate scientific information (Kateb 1988:455).

Insensitivity to and intolerance of AIDS patients in this country result primarily from the lessened social value of gay people as determined by stateside, conservative religions. Similarly, Africans are blamed for originating AIDS, which supposedly spread to them from green monkeys. From there, in the bodies of laborers, it somehow disseminated to all Haitians, who were believed to be peculiarly attractive prey for promiscuous American tourists.

The social consequences of having a health and medical issue defined primarily as a social problem of (and for) outsiders are very real and serious. Evidently, in searching for an explanation of how AIDS evolved as a dismissable minority problem, one finds that social attitudes and political arrangements are the cause.

In this country, the disavowal of AIDS, the fear of gays, and the abandonment of PWAs are the result of heterosexism. For Africans and Third World people, the disease is ignored because of its racial and social class characteristics, made worse by the presumed association of the poor with promiscuity, venereal disease, and often illegitimate needle-sharing practices.

Given the worldwide demographics of AIDS, this situation is a frightening reality. The World Health Organization (WHO) reports that HIV infection, the putative cause, is spreading so rapidly that 40 million people could be infected by the year 2000. The former head of WHO's special AIDS program,

Dr. Jonathan Mann, believes that 110 million cases may be a more realistic projection, partially because blood is left unscreened for HIV in much of the underdeveloped world. By 1995, 10 million could be dead or dying from AIDS.

In 1990, WHO reported that there were about 700,000 known cases, and 6 million to 8 million infections worldwide. Now the Harvard School of Public Health reports that the number of infected people expected to develop AIDS by 1995 will exceed by far the total who have developed the disease to date (Mann, Tarantola, and Netter 1992).

The vast majority in this estimate are poor, Third World people living way beyond the direct reach of GMHC. As Jon Tinker, president of the Panos Institute, observed:

> The global underclass, those who live in rural and urban shantytowns, who cannot afford condoms and are not reached by family planning advice, who cannot read and therefore are least likely to be reached by educational campaigns, who have little or no access to health clinics, who may have to sell their own blood to buy food—this global underclass will likely bear a disproportionate share of AIDS misery. (Heise 1988:21)

This cataclysm has remained unheeded because gay people, minorities, and poor people (mostly Third World women and children) are still the most at risk. Worldwide, 2.5 million people have already died, nearly 13 million are infected (40 percent of whom are women), and 100,000 have AIDS. By 2000, Asia will have more infections than Africa, and in 1992, 80,000 new cases were expected in the United States alone.

Despite this scenario, what remains appalling is that the over 6 million African adults assumed to be HIV infected or already sick can expect no more than a few dollars' worth of attention or assistance in their lifetime. In contrast, most urban American gays can spend or have access to hundreds of thousands of dollars yearly of medical aid, if not from the government and in insurance, then from the community in direct support services. Even so, given the impassable horror and suffering of American PWAs, the plight of African, and now Asian, PWAs is unimaginable.

It wasn't until December 1988 that the World Health Organization and the United Nations were able to successfully sponsor worldwide AIDS awareness activities. "AIDS," Jonathan Mann points out, "will ... put our global conscience to the test" (Heise 1988:27). AIDS forces the world to recognize fundamental injustice and the evil consequence of discrimination. "The world is still handicapped in the battle against AIDS," Mann concludes, "by debating whether it is O.K. to distribute condoms, exchange needles, give sex education, whether people with AIDS deserve care that they obviously deserve" (Altman 1992: B10).

If morals and social status mix with medicine in this country, then politics, economics, and racism shape the contours of medical care everywhere else. It takes massive public relations efforts for GMHC and other fledgling AIDS organizations nationwide to redefine AIDS in medical terms—just so public interest can be fairly and objectively aroused. Rhetoric aside, however, in contrast to the gay community in the United States, the world has yet to show its concern and compassion in decisive ways.

If there was little concern for the welfare of gays when gay life was flourishing, it would be even harder to garner sympathy for sufferers of a sexually transmitted health problem, especially in an age of economic retrenchment and renewed moral scrutiny. GMHC's efforts could go only so far because if there were no public or institutional outcry about commonplace and everyday gay bashing and homophobic discrimination, then how could there be any now over the new oppression caused by AIDS? And these issues are fundamental to any resolution of AIDS. There is still little vigorous public discussion about gay civil rights or the wants, needs, and entitlements of homosexual citizens and neighbors.

The Moral and Social Determinants of AIDS

Aggressive "moralists" understand the significance of AIDS for their anti-gay or pro-family agendas. As Watney (1988) argues, they also understand the salience of AIDS to gay social, economic, and political life. Gays represent an alternative life-style and a competing culture at odds with establishment religion and the social institutions dependent on it for their legitimacy. What really threatens conservative, stateside religions and sends them into a reactionary and defensive posture, however, is their realization that a successful gay movement will eclipse their hegemony over sexuality and society. For them, AIDS is a blessing in disguise for restoring the balance of power.

AIDS-homophobia now has a medical basis that helps sustain both religiously sanctioned patriarchal sexuality and the present distribution of social privileges and rewards. Through its pervasive authority over the social order, the religious Right influences the way the issues of gay rights, public health policy, and social responsibility for AIDS are defined. This influence of the religious Right matters not only because the moralization of AIDS affects the definition and search for cause and cure but also because it has become the vehicle for tying social benefits to civic status, albeit in a pluralistic society.

"AIDS," Watney (1987:3) writes, "is effectively being used as a pretext ... to 'justify' calls for increasing legislation and regulation of those who are considered to be socially unacceptable." There are scandalous consequences for institutional arrangements if gays, minorities, and PWAs are treated with compassion or if AIDS is acknowledged as a political and ethical problem rather than as a punishment for sin.

Unfortunately, this hesitancy permits the virus to spread even further as the society continues to reclassify people or activities at risk in inconsistent and incongruous ways. It was September 17, 1985, when President Reagan first uttered the word AIDS. The second time he did so (April 1, 1987), he indicated that, in the equation between morals, medicine, and health, gays brought the disease on themselves and that science had no real obligation to be supportive or concerned. By then, hundreds of thousands of people had become infected, and hundreds more had died.

The very fabric of gay life was under siege by an unidentified microbe, yet homosexuality in and of itself was being posited as the cause of the disease. One perversion, moral entrepreneurs "reasoned," was simply and justly causing another. Civil rights for gays, long sought after and won, were again being challenged or denied. Gay community resources were being depleted by the need to reassert the legitimacy and worthiness of gay life. On the medical front, precious time was lost because politicians would not release the necessary research funds for fear of disturbing a public that believed that AIDS was a self-inflicted minority problem intended by their patriarchal God.

AIDS is uniquely problematic because it is a physical illness and viral infection that has been defined in terms of socially pejorative and religiously proscribed categories like homosexual, prostitute, or drug-addict rather than by specific modes of transmission. By shifting the cause of illness from a structural and empirical or scientific source to a purely social one, scientific objectivity is diminished and the investigative process disrupted. Prejudiced social arrangements thus remain legitimate and unchallenged, though they fuel the spread of HIV.

Arguably, it is preexisting social and environmental conditions that put gays, drug-users, and minorities at risk and allow the AIDS pathogen to enter and basically become lodged within these populations. Just as the specific nature and mode of operation of the biological or viral cause(s) of AIDS are not clear, the attitudes, conditions, and behaviors that facilitate its spread also are not yet fully known or understood (Farber 1992). In this sense, AIDS worldwide occurs in the presence of many cofactors, not the least of which are sociological or political in nature (Crimp 1988). Unsanitary environments and high-risk behaviors, preexisting health disorders and infections, and social disenfranchisement and stigma are all socially derived conditions.

AIDS is related to alienation and urbanization. From a social science perspective, it is the result of the intersection of genetic makeup, personal hygiene, sexual and drug behavior, social networks, stress, guilt, social isolation, loneliness, psychological well-being, and the unavailability of legitimate social and sexual options. What nearly all stigmatized People with AIDS have in common is disenfranchisement and social marginality. This sociological fact alone could sustain any number of conspiracy theories.

The social context of AIDS explains why some classes of people are infected and/or at risk and not others. This is especially significant, since casting HIV infection as the sole cause of AIDS affects research and policy development by leaving the social sources of AIDS unattended. It also leaves too many questions unanswered.

In his multifactorial assessment of AIDS, long-lived PWA Michael Callen (1988:37) points out that the specific biological reasons an urban gay man gets AIDS are not the same as why an IV-drug-user or hemophiliac or African gets AIDS. He believes that what others glibly refer to as "cofactors" may actually be the causes of AIDS: "The immunosuppressive environmental and lifestyle factors which some scientists say 'predispose' risk groups to infection with HIV may by themselves be sufficient to produce what we now call AIDS. They can destroy the immune system without having to invoke (yet) another virus to explain the damage."

The question of either microbic or social cofactors in AIDS causality introduces the previously ignored corollary phenomenon of racism in AIDS. Both the black and white media underestimate and misinterpret the frequency of AIDS among African-Americans and Latinos. It is even likely that AIDS existed unrecognized in minority IV-drug-using populations for some time, perhaps even longer than among gays, who brought attention to it through well-established political, medical, and media contacts. Because they were poorer and less organized, minorities with AIDS remained ignored. They may have been noticed early on had researchers bothered to look at the data, social systems, and health problems of IV-drug-users more carefully.

Attuned to the historical prejudices about minority culture, sexuality, and social behavior, the media unsympathetically notify African-Americans and Latinos of their role in AIDS fulmination. Conversely, much of the inability of these groups to politicize AIDS and to carepartner PWAs results from, in addition to social class issues, their denial, shame, poverty, and unwillingness to be identified as supportive of gays or involved with drugs.

This situation for minorities is compounded by sexism, racism, and the focus on gay AIDS. The symptomology and presentation of women's AIDS generally remains unattended, as do these women's particular medical and social needs (Ports 1988). Women, like minorities, have not yet been able to lobby effectively in AIDS because they too are divided by their own class interests. Quite simply, there is not a lot of sympathy for drug-users or their sexual partners.

Yet there are significant and particular socioeconomic factors that weigh heavily on minority group health. AIDS, for example, is compounded by and related to high unemployment, poor schooling, inadequate housing, and limited access to health care. Likewise, the high rate of drug use and sexual activity among impoverished black youths simply spins the virus off further into populations they are intimately in contact with.

Even though all African-Americans will eventually bear the burden of AIDS because of racism, only insofar as the black underclass is economically, politically, and socially linked to the larger black community can we say that all African-Americans are threatened by AIDS. In general, social class has proven an effective barrier to HIV fulmination. That blacks (Haitians, Latinos) are being stigmatized for AIDS is a function of racism. Prejudice has colored the recognition of any social or behavioral differences among and between minorities by social class, making it appear that all members of a minority group are ill or at risk by definition.

Prejudicing whole communities of people by making them solely responsible for a medical problem that actually victimizes them if not physically then socially is unfair, mean, and political. It also confounds further the analysis of cause and subsequent proposals for cure by erroneously shifting the focus of attention to a social category rather than a social condition.

That people don't know the facts of transmission is a function of how AIDS is defined in terms of "who has AIDS," "who is at risk for AIDS," and "what constitutes a risk" (see Chapter 4). If people believe it is limited to homosexuals and drug-users, then they may act in ways that might prove dangerous because they assess life-styles rather than the danger of specific activities with specific individuals and assume that AIDS has nothing to do with them. Despite the fact that it is women who have to be leery of men, well-intentioned humanist Elizabeth Kübler-Ross (1987:30) is dismayed because "we do not do enough to discourage young men to avoid prostitutes."

The way the causality of AIDS is determined (groups versus activities versus conditions) is also important because how this question is framed will affect who delivers health care, what help will be offered, and how PWAs will be defined and treated. "In this culture," Hammonds writes, "how we think about disease determines who lives and who dies." "The history of black people in this country," she notes, "is riddled with episodes displaying how concepts of sickness, disease, health, behavior and sexuality, and race have been intertwined in the definition of normalcy and deviance" (Hammonds 1987:29). It is this power to define disease and normality, outsider and insider, that makes AIDS, volunteerism, and AIDS education/prevention political phenomena.

Trapped by their own categories of analysis, early social science researchers missed fundamental facts about AIDS transmission. Generally, they failed to acknowledge the extent of bisexuality or recreational drug use, extramarital affairs, or sex for hire. In their identification of AIDS with groups, they did not recognize that people define themselves and their behavior differently from the way the professionals say they should or do. Consequently, these "objective experts" misunderstood the cause, severity, and extent of AIDS. By mixing together activities, nationalities, sexual orientations, life-styles, races, and occupations, they clearly relieved themselves of responsibility.

Because social attitudes influence AIDS research, many important questions remain unanswered. Why is it that the median age of AIDS cases differs in different segments of the population at risk? Why do nongays with AIDS rarely come down with Kaposi Sarcoma—the "AIDS cancer"? Given the amount of drugs consumed by IV-drug-users, blaming Kaposi Sarcoma in gays primarily on "poppers" becomes suspect. Why are the survival rates so varied for different risk groups? "How come," Callen (1988) asks, "the rate of antibody positivity among hemophiliac users of Factor 8 is so high while the rate of actual progression to AIDS is dramatically lower than in other risk groups?" Why do some people infected with HIV get sick or sicker while others stay well for years? And we are still puzzled as to why an infectious disease of the magnitude of AIDS is still found primarily among "outsider" minority groups.

The Real Issues

As a waxing and waning media event, AIDS news remains distorted as a medical, sociological, and human interest story. The news media delight in the exceptional AIDS infectee or infector rather than emphasize the politics of AIDS, the scientific scandal at the National Institutes of Health,[3] the problem of health insurance for gays and PWAs, the lack of experimental remedial therapies, the holding back of potentially helpful drugs from desperate PWAs, or the social costs to society of an unabated and growing health menace. Watney (1988) calls this "the spectacle of AIDS."

We know precious little about the human costs of AIDS and the overall psychological, social, and economic destitution of so many People with AIDS and their families and friends. What is the relationship of the deaths of over 30,000 gay New Yorkers to the city's faltering economy? We know virtually nothing, or care little about, the infolding of the gay community because of AIDS. All this avoidance of the "truth about AIDS" and the gay community has shaped the public consciousness, making it impossible to decide appropriate strategies of disease containment. Until very recently, little attention had been paid to the social and structural dimensions of AIDS and the loss to our society in personnel and talent. Rather, emphasis is on the cost of AIDS to the insurance industry.

At one time, media coverage created the impression that the heterosexual American public was a morally protected fortress, essentially immune to infection, hence, concern. The media ignored gay fears about AIDS, testing, treatments, and so on until ACT-UP, which identifies itself as a diverse, non-partisan group united in anger and commitment to direct action to end the global AIDS epidemic, forced them to pay attention (Bordowitz 1988). The established media had presented AIDS as a plague when it could have instead examined how discrimination and moralism affected the quantity and quality of AIDS research and health care.

The intersection of AIDS, homophobia, psychic brokenness, maladaptiveness, social status, and civil liberties has not been fully explored, exposed, and presented as an important consideration except by gay researchers. Rarely, if ever, is there any coverage of the remarkable contribution (financially and personally) of the gay community to the care of People with AIDS. There is little mention of the fact that hundreds, if not thousands, of carepartners of PWAs have failed to contract the disease. Following a long period of sporadic and irrelevant media coverage, journalists began to attract public concern for AIDS by using a sensationalist approach pandering to prurient interests.

Not until the *New York Times* reported in 1986 on GMHC volunteers working with children did a few stories appear about the hundreds of parents and friends who lovingly nurse PWAs. Human-interest stories had generally concentrated on the occupationally infected health care worker or the abandoned PWA at odds with his family. Even now, the media plays on the atypical heterosexual child who contracts AIDS accidentally, thereby creating the illusion of innocent victim and random infection.

GMHC and the "Morality" of AIDS Education

The question of educating and informing the public about AIDS transmission is distorted by the morality context of AIDS, though it is less so than in the past. The media are generally responsible for the pornographic obsession with the details of what they identify as gay male sexual behavior. Rather than elaborate on the political question of whether educational efforts should be directed at individuals or groups, the news industry simply reports the federal government's preference for testing and identifying HIV carriers. Conservative writer and statesman William F. Buckley actually suggested tattooing HIV carriers and PWAs. Yet no moral outcry prevailed.

Instead of discussing publicly whether education should emphasize safer sexual and social behaviors for everyone, reporters frame the issue in terms of either abstinence or social control (Crimp 1988). Until the publication in 1989 of Ronald Bayer's book on the social consequences of private acts in a health crisis becoming legal issues, few people, other than gays, publicly discussed the civil rights implications of policy proposals that did not answer questions of responsibility for public health and personal welfare.

Raising these questions became possible only after the heterosexual infection rate began to increase faster than that of gays. In 1990, reports Rasky, AIDS funding shifted after lawmakers suffered personal losses among friends and constituents that "allowed them to see it [AIDS] and address it as a public health issue rather than one defined by morality or life-style" (Rasky 1990:A22).

Yet the simplistic suggestion of the political majority that AIDS can best be managed by testing and/or quarantining people, rather than through education and social change, remained unquestioned and unchallenged by the mass media and by policymakers. If anything, these ahistorical, moralistic, and badly timed suggestions should have generated a public discourse. For a democratic society, the implications of using the legal system to control a medical problem are significant. Only the gay press consistently discusses these issues and raises these questions.

By operating within its own political economy, GMHC supported the idea that "safer sex" would be a better alternative to getting AIDS, to being quarantined or imprisoned, or to "civic death." Safer-sex education, however, remains challenged as inappropriate by those who prefer to emphasize abstinence as the only preventive. Abstinence, of course, would limit the spread of AIDS, but it would also end homosexuality (what the religious Right term "the sin of pleasure") and would legitimate the social control of sexuality by stateside religions. While condom commercials have appeared sporadically, they are beset with challenges by conservative "religionists." By summer 1988, they disappeared from the airwaves. Oddly enough, they were geared primarily to heterosexuals despite the fact that hundreds of thousands of gays are infected with HIV and are at exceptional risk. Although GMHC pioneered their use as an AIDS preventive for everyone, New York City did not produce condom ads for gays until 1989. These ads have yet to be aired.

The argument that gays have educated themselves within their own networks also misses the point. Millions of homosexually active men are not involved with the gay community, are bisexual, and/or do not see themselves at risk because they don't identify themselves as either homosexuals or as members of the gay community. Millions of others can't be reached through vanilla descriptions of safer sex. To reach these at-risk populations, GMHC (and HERO [Health Education Resource Organization] in Baltimore) published and distributed graphic "comix" illustrating safer sexual techniques. Unfortunately, these highly effective safer-sex comic books have been declared inappropriate and ineligible for government funding.

On October 14, 1987, Sen. Jesse Helms announced on the floor of the Senate that he might "throw up" after viewing these comic books. He succeeded in amending the Labor, Health and Human Services and Education Appropriation Bill, which allocated $1 billion to AIDS funding and research, to prohibit federal funds for any AIDS education, information, or prevention materials (such as GMHC's comic books) that "promote or encourage, directly or indirectly, homosexual sexual activities." He sees AIDS prevention and education programs as encouraging "safe sodomy."

In California, the state Republican party accused the San Francisco AIDS Foundation of distributing obscene materials. The charge was aimed at several safer-sex brochures and newsletters that the foundation had frequently distributed throughout the state. Sen. John Doolittle was quoted as saying, "All I know is that I like what happened today. We tubed the Surgeon General's report [on AIDS], which was appropriate. [And] we took off on that nasty, pornographic AIDS literature, which needed to be done." Fortunately, on May 11, 1992, a federal judge, at GMHC's instigation, declared unconstitutional any government ban on AIDS educational material deemed morally offensive.

Doolittle also proposed measures that would have led to the quarantine and denial of civil rights of gays. Yet the director of the San Francisco Department of Health has reported that in three different surveys of San Francisco's gay population, the rate of new HIV infection was thought to be essentially zero. He said, "That is remarkable. The rest of the world is asking us how we did it. It was done with these educational materials" (Linebarger 1987). Precious little attention was paid to these concerns by the mainstream press.

In the early years at GMHC, when policy was first being formulated, there was little known about the psychological profiles of at-risk individuals or the social settings that encourage high-risk behavior. Until 1987 and the publication of research reports on behavioral changes among gay men in San Francisco, neither the social nor the personal demographics of high-risk individuals had been clearly established. The conditions necessary for HIV to become destructively active have not been clearly determined, either.

Generally speaking, most information available about gays or drug-users remains inaccurate or not useful for the purpose of risk or illness assessment. These diversified populations have life-style differences so great in range that any generalizations about who is at risk, and of what one is at risk for, would have to be suspect. We still do not know how many HIV-positive people will develop AIDS and we still do not know how to accurately define either AIDS or the full range of HIV infection.

Since gay and minority civil rights are so erratically and sporadically guaranteed in the United States, transmission patterns cannot be correctly assessed or prevention programs developed if those individuals and constituencies considered at high risk cannot participate in the formulation of research and policy development because their social value and legal status is so tenuous.

4

Democratization and the Response to AIDS

THE QUESTION OF "WHO HAS" versus "who is at risk of" AIDS is important because it determines how AIDS is engaged as a problem and how responsibility for AIDS (care, treatment, resolution) is allocated. Likewise, from where help comes (private or public sources) and the form that it takes are important considerations. These factors shed light on why people volunteer in AIDS and point to the incipient meaning of gay/AIDS volunteerism as a unique political mobilization.

Policy debates about rights and entitlements in relation to AIDS are limited to those publics who can articulate their concerns in acceptable and systematic ways. Because the nongay homophobic public continually confused the virus with social groups rather than activities and has ignored class and ideological issues, gays and AIDS have become coterminous and the community both libeled and politicized. Concern remains, however, not about correcting the public's irrational fear and condemnation of gays or increasing AIDS education but about creating sympathy for "innocent" victims, like Ryan White and, now, Arthur Ashe.

Because AIDS is a metaphor for majority-minority relations and the assignment of health care rights by arbitrary social characteristics, social status determines our capacity to be compassionate and the people to whom our empathy as a society is directed. Thus AIDS needs to be demythologized so that it can be confronted directly as a scourge, that its human face can be revealed, and that the suffering it causes can be made known and shared.

Who or What Causes AIDS

Because homophobia determines perceptions of the cause of AIDS, the disease is presented as impersonal statistics and in terms of cities, life-styles, and sexual orientations rather than in human, let alone scientific, terms. Because

51

the real biological causes of AIDS remained unexamined for quite some time, a realistic discussion of its transmission through sexual behavior and improper drug use was delayed.

When social causes were posited, they had little to do with social arrangements but emphasized life-style decadence. Highlighting specific high-risk behaviors was thought to validate disapproved, though widespread, social and sexual activities such as recreational drug use, fellatio, anal intercourse, cunnilingus, and bisexuality. False, impressionistic "data" on minorities were collected from the venereal disease rates reported by free, public clinics and became the basis for policy proposals despite their biased unrepresentativeness.

Unlike heterosexuals, gay men are stereotypically presented as "disco junkies" who primarily engage in lots of anonymous and promiscuous anal sex. This view is the natural outcome of defining homosexuality as sexual acts and roles, as Greenberg (1988) does, rather than as relationships, emotions, and feelings. This emphasis leaves heterosexuals morally superior.

The same is true of the apathetic interest in minority AIDS. The question of how disease, drug use, and the social conditions of minority life interconnect is barely considered. "One of the reasons," write Marin and Marin (1990b:108), "why research on AIDS that directly affects Hispanics has been slow and inadequate is the limited number of qualified Hispanic researchers working in the field." Outsiders miss the texture of relationships and cultural expectations that have an impact on AIDS transmission and containment among minority people.

Disinformation about AIDS distorts its nature and character as a cluster disease. Instead of finding fault in social structure, those who look for a cause (and thus a cure) for AIDS blame minorities because Latinos and blacks are generally thought to use drugs and sleep around. Collectively they become hotbeds of AIDS transmission, as low-status people in general are assumed to be "natural" or automatic HIV carriers.

Blaming entire social groups for the disease *in a morally causative (political) sense* is dangerous and harmful. AIDS affects specific populations because of social conditions, not personal degeneracy. The vast majority of African-Americans and Latinos are not prostitutes or drug-abusers, and sexual activity is not the summation of gay life. Yet this is how AIDS sufferers are perceived and treated, and often as a result see themselves.

Unlike these other groups, prostitutes suffer a double stigma. Because they are considered sinful, sociopathic, and a risk to themselves, others think that they transmit AIDS to their clients, not that their work puts them in contact with carriers (Leigh 1988). Despite the evidence that hard-core drug-users have lessened sexual capacity, they are believed to automatically infect their prostitute-girlfriends, who then selfishly infect their "tricks" and children. Yet there is little proof that prostitutes are disproportionately infecting their male clients, though they seem to be getting excessively infected themselves, more because of drug-using habits. Nevertheless, they are being scapegoated as the "immoral" vector of AIDS into the heterosexual population.

Early AIDS reporting identified the disease in terms of nationality and race, making Haitians and Africans particularly suspect and dangerous. Prostitutes, however, are considered infected by virtue of their occupation, and gays and IV-drug-users because of life-style "choices." Consequently, as Shilts (1987) documents, it was not apparent that AIDS is a blood-borne disease that also puts children, those undergoing blood transfusions, and hemophiliacs at risk. It is still difficult to explain why or how African AIDS is largely heterosexually transmitted, although many theories tainted with racism are now being offered (Eckholm and Tierney 1990). Speculators fail to notice that sexual behavior and identities have different meanings throughout the world, which makes predicting AIDS in social categories impossible.[1]

These facts indicate the political nature of AIDS and the usefulness for the political majority of tracking this illness in an ethnocentric or culturally biased way that reflects only American prejudices and concerns (Gilman 1988). This way of tracking AIDS frees the majority of responsibility and dehumanizes minority experiences. Yet if classification categories were shifted, heterosexual transmission (from male to female in the vast majority of cases) would account for most of the world's AIDS cases. The whole definition and meaning of AIDS would thus change accordingly and so would the way it is resolved politically and responded to institutionally.

We can be sure that certain population segments located in specific social strata and engaging in specific behaviors are at higher risk of AIDS. Gay men and minority drug-users have socially constructed and identifiable boundaries that allow the virus to circulate within relatively closed social networks. Gay men were both experimenting with and enjoying sex in ways tried and true while an unknown virus circulated about. There was no knowledge of a deadly illness, infection, or disease being sexually transmitted and no real *medical* reason to change behavior.

At Risk of AIDS

Homosexuality is neither socially nor sexually maladaptive, except when expressed instrumentally, like any impersonal encounter. Rather, specific sexual acts become risky when a biological pathogen is present. The potential for maladaptive behavior increases, however, when sexual activities are depersonalized and profaned by institutionalized and internalized homophobia. Together, these conditions also retard the politicization process. Because gay men are not being afforded other options, sexual activity for many overshadows concern about relationships, agape, equity, and self-acceptance. Empowerment and impersonalism are mutually exclusive.

Stigmatized, many gays are unwittingly driven into sexual liaisons and activities that have now been proven to be maladaptive to individual health and collective social and psychological well-being. Maladaptive behavior is induced by the structure of society and results in the depoliticization of the individuals who exhibit this behavior. People at high risk of AIDS all experience social marginality, oppression, discrimination, self-loathing, and disempowerment. They are put at risk by social position, social behavior, and a variety of psychological characteristics, not by group affiliation per se. Low social status increases risk because discrimination and marginalization weigh heavily on the psyche of individuals in afflicted groups and often lead to dysfunctional social and sexual activity. For minorities, this situation results in alienated drug use and furtive sexual behavior.

The largest segment of minority patients with AIDS are IV-drug-users. Goldstein (1987:25) writes that "the prevalence of IV drug-use in minority communities is clearly why the rate of AIDS cases among blacks and Hispanics, relative to their numbers in the population, is three times that of whites." The fastest-growing number of cases of AIDS in this country is among women partners of minority IV-drug-users. Black women are thirteen times and Hispanic women eleven times more likely to contract AIDS than white women, and 91 percent of all infants with AIDS are nonwhite.

The determinants of risk, then, are social-class status, poverty, alienation, discrimination, underemployment, low self-esteem, lack of opportunity, social isolation, and political impotence. Only insofar as these factors weigh more heavily on minorities can AIDS be considered a black and Latino problem. At least in New York, certain groups are at high risk because of underlying social factors affecting behavior and not because of their race or ethnicity as such.

> And the behavior that is putting minorities at heightened risk is the sharing of needles by drug-users. The state Division of Substance Abuse estimates that three-quarters of the IV-drug-users in New York City are black or Hispanic: that's 150,000 people, most of them heterosexual men. At least half of the IV users are thought to be infected with the AIDS virus—and presumed infectious. Bisexual men represent another source of transmission, but in the nation as a whole, five times as many black women caught AIDS from sex with a drug-user as from a bisexual man. (Goldstein 1987:24–25)

The spread of heterosexual AIDS is no less free of sexist underpinnings. The disease among minorities can be traced to many social pressures, not the least of which are multiple partnering by men holding patriarchal beliefs about male sexual privilege. That the transmission of the virus from women to men is relatively uncommon (and unlikely) indicates that men bring the virus to women in and through a myriad of circumstances and activities, if not behavioral expectations. Because of identity issues and the life-styles of many bisexual males and some drug-users, women will consistently remain at high risk.

If groups rather than activities remain emphasized, AIDS in America could be defined as a disease of heterosexual IV-drug-users and their sexual partners and offspring. Regardless of the source of AIDS, if heterosexually identified men have infected blood, they bring HIV to their partners and, if they are bisexually active, to gay men as well.

In terms of activities, heterosexual males are at risk if they are anally passive when performing bisexually and/or are IV-drug-users. Their female sexual partners are likewise in danger. Because venereal diseases often appear in clusters and pairs, heterosexuals who are infected with venereal diseases other than AIDS are at risk because they have been exposed to individuals who might also be HIV carriers.

Gay men as such are randomly at risk only when engaging in specific types of homosexual behavior—primarily passive anal intercourse without condoms with someone already infected. Since the biological transmission of AIDS is often sexually derived, it has entered the relatively closed (although forever changing) gay community, thus putting all homosexual players ingesting their partners' body fluids at risk. This risk is likely because of the latency period in AIDS fulmination and the ubiquitousness of HIV. AIDS is a gay problem because gays live in social and sexual networks.

Using sexual orientation to determine who is at risk is inaccurate because sexual identities for heterosexuals are often fluid, changing with position taken and activity performed in the sex act. Such individuals drift in and out of sexual liaisons without considering themselves at risk because their identities do not come from the gender of whom they are having sex with. Heterosexuals as a group, nonetheless, are not at any greater or lesser risk than other populations. They are put at risk by what they do sexually and with whom specifically they do it. A similar problem exists relative to illicit and unsafe use of recreational drugs, an activity present among all social classes, races, nationalities, and sexual orientations. Using these categories, therefore, to determine who is at risk for AIDS misses the point.

The real issue of AIDS is not whether heterosexuals are at risk but whether the society will respond and support AIDS research and People with AIDS regardless of their social characteristics and personal behavior. Obsessing about heterosexual AIDS as a threat to the "mainstream" society masks the real political agenda behind AIDS hysteria. For Sikov (1988:15), it is "to define as a dark collective 'other,' men and women who differ from the majority, and to keep such an 'other' defined by a disease."

That more American heterosexuals are not infected with HIV is a function of the way the causative agent enters the bloodstream. The general consensus still remains that even close social contact with an infected person does not facilitate infection. Except, perhaps, for inner-city urban areas, it is also agreed that under ordinary circumstances neither female-to-male nor female-to-female transmission occurs easily (Solomon 1992). For all practical purposes, heterosexual transmission is a dead-end straight line going from male to female and ending with her and her offspring. If it were not, the whole society would be infected because the virus would be in a wider circular motion, going from male to female and back again.

American AIDS

In the United States, AIDS disproportionately strikes the socially and politically disenfranchised: gay men, blacks, Latinos, prostitutes, bisexual men, and IV-drug-users and their female partners and children. While Latinos compose only 8 percent of the population, they account for 15.3 percent of all AIDS cases. Since 1988 alone, the number of heterosexual cases has jumped to 40 percent of the total, the vast majority of these occurring among minority women. Nationwide, blacks are twice as likely and Latinos 2.5 times as likely as whites to contract AIDS.

Before the inclusion of blood-cell count as a determinant of AIDS, the New York City Health Department figures compiled for August 1990 indicated that African-American and Latino residents composed 44 percent of the city's population but made up 57 percent of the 23,840 reported AIDS cases. Eighty-four percent of the women with AIDS were black or Latino, as were 91 percent of the children with AIDS. As projected, with the wider definition of AIDS, by 1991 there were approximately 51,000 cases in New York City (Navarro 1991a:D21).

A half decade ago, it was estimated that New Yorkers were dying of AIDS at the rate of 200 a month, making AIDS the leading cause of death of NYC men aged twenty-five to forty-four and of women aged twenty-five to thirty-four (*New York Times*, July 12, 1987:30E). AIDS is now the sixth leading cause of death nationwide. Additionally, the number of Latino AIDS cases has been increasing at a more rapid rate than in the U.S. population generally. Navarro (1989) reports that the city estimates that there will be over 3,000 new Latino cases per year by 1993.

On Thursday, April 30, 1992, New York State health officials announced that the rate of HIV infection among black women having babies in New York City had actually risen since 1988 while that among Latinos and whites decreased. The rate of infection for non-Latina black women jumped 12 percent, but fell by a quarter for non-Latina white mothers and a third for Latina mothers. As reported in the *New York Times* (Dugger 1992:B3), "Between black and white women ages 25–29, the gap in infection rates was even wider. The rate rose more than a third for black mothers, to 356 infected out of 11,395 in 1991, and plummeted more than 50% for white women, to 30 infected out of 10,569." The rate dipped slightly for Latina women.

In terms of total numbers of Americans infected, the lowest estimate has been about 600,000 in 1986 to 1 million by the mid-1990s. As of June 1991, there were 182,834 cases officially counted through registration at the Centers for Disease Control (CDC). Including blood-cell counts would raise this figure by approximately 175,000. To date, over 120,000 have already died, the vast majority gay men. June Osborn of the President's Commission on AIDS now expects 45,000 new infections each year, "with the more likely number two to five times that—90,000 to 225,000" (Osborn 1990:15). In any case, most shocking is the expectation that the number of American AIDS cases will double in the next two years, an estimate that is more than the past ten years combined.

Obviously, AIDS especially victimizes American gays, if no longer in as high numbers as before then in peculiar and particular legal, social, psychological, and spiritual ways.[2] Statistically, as early as 1988 San Francisco had lost more men to the AIDS epidemic than that city lost in World War I, World War II, Korea, and Vietnam combined and doubled. While the overall rate of new infections has declined, according to former San Francisco mayor Art Agnos the word "decimates" best describes the situation. As he is quoted in the *Sentinel* (April 1, 1988:4), "The word 'decimate' means literally one out of ten. And in San Francisco, by the end of the year, one out of ten gay men in our city will have died of AIDS or will have been diagnosed as having AIDS. Within five years, it will be one out of four."

Unlike other American populations at risk, gays live in and with community, joined together by common interests, needs, and social and *institutional* networks. Gays then are collectively at risk and, as such, are distinguished from both other groups and the occasional homosexual player who lives furtively, disattached from himself and community. AIDS is a threat to the institutional stability and continuity of the community, not just to individual homosexuals and bisexuals and their partners.

Despite the presence of many "homosexualities" (Bell and Weinberg 1978) and the different modes of homosexual expression, gays share institutions, aesthetics, and expectations, and there is an identifiably gay culture, politic, and normative framework. Since AIDS can be sexually transmitted, the very fabric (emotion and desire) of a shared or collective gay existence is under siege. It goes to the heart of the matter of gay identity.

In AIDS, the most intimate dimensions of human existence, often the sources of our deepest pleasure, have been welded to the threat of lethal disease. As an epidemic with roots in private acts, AIDS forces into the social realm matters that liberal societies have increasingly sought to protect from public scrutiny and legal control. That in the United States AIDS is a disease of those who have sought the protective mantle of privacy—drug-users because of the illicit nature of their behaviors, gay and bisexual men because of the historical burdens of stigma and criminalization—had indelibly marked the epidemic. (Bayer 1989a:79)

Were it not for the growth and popularity of gay social and political institutions after Stonewall, the founding of GMHC, and the death of friends, AIDS would have destroyed the willingness to struggle together *for a common life* as a unique and gifted people. For all practical purposes, the magnitude and destructiveness of AIDS require a local, yet all-inclusive community organization for the disease to be contained and the needs of PWAs to be addressed.

The desire to survive and live together as a people and the need to address AIDS directly, quickly, and easily make GMHC the primary gay and AIDS social service agency in the city, if not the world. Government grants aside, even though GMHC is a local community organization, it draws on more people, has more volunteers and members, offers more services, staffs more positions, and collects more funds than any other gay and/or AIDS organization ever.

Risk and Society's Concern

The question of who is at risk is a central issue in the politics and resolution of AIDS because it affects whether the deaths of disenfranchised people matter. It is not even important how accurate the information, classifications, and predictions about AIDS causation and fulmination are because "AIDS hysteria" is affected most by people's impressions.

The response to and responsibility for many AIDS-related problems are functions of whether AIDS is seen as a "democratic illness," that is, one that places everyone randomly at risk. Whether the gay person is seen as a legitimate member of society, as an "everyman," is, of course, the question. If gays were seen this way, no voluntary community mobilization for AIDS would be necessary because citizen entitlements through established sources would be available.

That gays and almost all other PWAs are outsiders is a sociological reality that explains why AIDS had to be democratized for society to pay attention. That AIDS "is or isn't" or "has or hasn't" become heterosexual has always conditioned the mainstream response. Gay demands for both citizenship and the attendant health rights that accompany it are attempts at inclusion—outsiders have no medical or civic entitlements.

Because of this disassociation between society and gays as deviants or AIDS carriers, the only viable response is continuously active and vigilant voluntary community initiatives that can establish specialized programs and a system of implementation under community control. This exclusion, coupled with real human need, became the raison d'être for GMHC's existence. Gay/AIDS volunteerism in New York is shaped by little more than the lack of concern and compassion shown PWAs.

AIDS would have remained an ignored minority issue garnering only trivial concern unless another ground for involvement and compassion were established. This new basis, notes Poirier (1988:471), came from the exaggerated public fear about heterosexual AIDS advanced by a sensationalist media, the World Health Organization, and a conservative (though forthright) surgeon general rather than from direct and real interest in the welfare of the underclass. As people everywhere became convinced of their own vulnerability, a diffused, if not covert, social response to the needs of gays and other minorities at risk became possible.

Because of this new fearful interest, socially and politically disenfranchised minorities, social institutions, the individual PWA, "those at risk," the political majority, and the gay community were all brought into contact with one another, though in untried ways. It is ironic that while the disease has remained limited to identifiable subgroups and to those engaged in high-risk activities with them, public interest and hysteria about AIDS have actually increased, indicating the usefulness and necessity of fueling public fears to generate broad interest in AIDS, if not gay or minority AIDS.

Herein lies the crux of both the political problem and the gay response to it: Mainstream society abrogated its responsibility to address the civil claims of gays and the health care needs of PWAs until AIDS appeared to threaten those who were not "outsiders." Until then, resolving almost all AIDS-related problems remained a minority obligation, even though unsuspecting individuals would also be at risk because they would not be properly educated about modes of transmission and how the virus networks. Without democratization, many people would think that they are somehow immune (by not being identified with a risk population), and their unrecognized maladaptive behavior would continue as before.

Everything changed in 1986 and 1987 when AIDS hysteria swept the country and people with power became attentive, although often in a way that attempted to control gay life and people (Watney 1987:3). Fortunately, these generally unfounded fears about causal and possible infectability were able to generate interest and support from potentially sympathetic heterosexuals who could now show legitimate distress by claiming that they feared for society's well-being or their own safety. This help involved indirect support for gays and minorities, but only as PWAs.

The growing destigmatization of AIDS allowed creative and professional notables (e.g., Elizabeth Taylor, Dionne Warwick, Bette Midler, and Whitney Houston) to get publicly involved in AIDS care and fund-raising issues at no reputational risk six years into the crisis though being so helpful personally to PWAs from the beginning. It was their involvement that facilitated both increased public and private funding for AIDS and the destigmatization of the disease. Well-known Americans such as Liberace, Rock Hudson, Perry Ellis, and Alison Gertz (and now Magic Johnson and Arthur Ashe) had to get sick or die before AIDS became an acceptable, if not "respectable," cause of death. By 1990, fund-raisers for PWAs could be held without mention of gay AIDS or homosexuality.

Under the direction of socially prominent biologist Mathilde Krim, the American Foundation for AIDS Research (AmFAR) was able to diffuse "the mutual suspicion that exists between the gay community and the mostly heterosexual establishment" (Johnson 1988:30). Krim continually made the persuasive and direct argument that AIDS is a public health problem and not a gay disease. For her, "it is medically and morally wrong to dismiss AIDS as a gay plague or a scourge of the ghetto." Under Krim's tutelage, AIDS became the "fashionable charity" by late 1987 and gays and People with AIDS became human to the masses.

Countering this new, though suspect, magnanimity, writes Kateb (1988:458), "is the pity of rationalist, enlightened doctors, scientists, and lay people." Although it came after the risk to their reputations was diminished, "when they see a disease," notes Kateb, "they see only disease, see only its suffering. But when they observe that others in society are hostile to those who suffer, their vocational interest in healing may quicken; they may therefore work with an exceptional commitment."

The public conscience had finally been stirred, if not by compassion then at least by fear. Though she exaggerates the risk of AIDS (Farber 1992), Krim's contribution in the struggle against AIDS is immeasurable. While her approach is inclusive, its result or consequence is to make gays part of a larger mass of disabled Americans in need of sympathy. In a sense, gays become faceless because they are seen only as People with AIDS. Likewise, control of the field by gays is lost.

Unlike sex researchers Masters and Johnson (1988) in their epidemiologically weak publication on AIDS, Krim sticks to the facts, although she states over and over that everyone should be both cautious and concerned. Her objective is to arouse public support by keeping AIDS a public health issue. She believes that gays as citizens deserve attention and help. Krim constantly stresses the identification of modes of transmission and the regulation of high-risk activities that she believes are widespread. In contrast, Masters and John-

son fuel AIDS hysteria by claiming that the AIDS virus is already widely diffused within the American heterosexual population without offering any
proof or explanation as to why this might be the case.

In all fairness, Masters and Johnson do note that numbers of partners and
frequency of contacts are the critical links in AIDS transmission. For them, the
"AIDS virus" has established a beachhead in the ranks of the larger population because of the activity of large numbers of heterosexuals who have numerous sex partners and, assumedly, might also use drugs intravenously.
Given random and extramarital sexual activity among women, who put themselves at risk by not knowing their male partners' sexual and drug-use histo-
ries, HIV infection is spreading.

Yet only two months before Masters and Johnson's study was published,
the January issue of *Cosmopolitan* advised women not to worry about AIDS
because AIDS could not be transmitted through "ordinary sexual intercourse" with "ordinary people." In this article, Dr. Robert E. Gould, M.D., a
clinical professor of psychiatry, obstetrics, and gynecology at New York Medical College, argued his point empirically. His observations are true in one
sense but untrue in that unprotected multiple partnering by unsuspecting
women with infected males would spread the virus around. More significant,
however, is that his position unwittingly served the interests of the homophobic Right led by Norman Podhoretz.

The fundamentalist Right has interpreted Gould's article as meaning that
concern over heterosexual transmission of AIDS is really a political agenda
foisted by greedy researchers and gay rights activists upon a gullible general
public that need not worry about a disease that will never touch them. The
motivation is simply to get more money and support for gay rights and PWAs,
as if these were meritless goals in themselves.

The truth is that gays did not create this mythology, nor did the community
directly benefit from it financially or institutionally. The result was that gays
became indirect (or secondary) beneficiaries of societal largess. As a subgroup
of infectees, gays benefited as PWAs, but not because of acceptance as citizens
or worthy members of the "national community" (see Chapter 5). More accurately, the broader societal commitment merely helped to lighten the burden that nevertheless remained overwhelming.

For all practical purposes, recognizing and responding specifically to gay
AIDS remain hidden by democratization. This situation becomes a Catch-22.
Encouraging heterosexual or majority concern as it did, democratization was
done at the expense of gays and truly at-risk populations, since the specific social contours of AIDS would be ignored. There is now increasing attention to
pediatric and heterosexual AIDS even though (or because) they are not
rooted in the same social conditions as gay or drug-related AIDS. Emphasiz-

ing AIDS among the political majority disavows homophobia, alienation, and oppression as causative agents.

Heterosexualizing AIDS will result in gay concerns becoming secondary and educational efforts becoming skewed in favor of the majority. Abstinence will become recommended and be the preferred preventive technique. The control of AIDS education and prevention will be co-opted by homophobic moralists and heterosexuals who are concerned about transmission, testing, and quarantining and controlling homosexuals. Rather than being identified as living members of society, gays will be swept under the disease banner and dissected through the fulcrum of AIDS. Only as pathetic "others" will we be attended to.

The Gays Respond

Despite Fumento's (1989) persuasive analysis, we do not absolutely know if AIDS is festering among *all social classes* of heterosexuals. Yet predicting the demographics of AIDS in the future is made risky by the latency period, incidental sexual encounters between high-risk individuals and "majority" partners, and a reported increase of random sexual activity among heterosexuals. There is also the possibility that AIDS has many causes,[3] if not vectors, and that other population clusters might become contaminated in the future (Farber 1992).

What we are certain of, however, is that gay men have suffered the greatest generational losses from AIDS and that the gay response to it is the most awesome and overlooked. "Thus far," wrote Krieger and Appleman in 1986 (pp. 31–32), "the vast bulk of the cost of the AIDS epidemic has been borne by vast amounts of unpaid labor donated by community organizations founded by gay activists, as well as by private charities and a few local governments— and *not* by federal agencies."

This is still true today, from funding for social services to AIDS education and prevention. "In New York City and San Francisco," notes Arno (1987:190), "the magnitude of donated labor is enormous, conservatively estimated to be between 100,000 and 150,000 hours per year in each city." Today, given the number of people, agencies, and cases, the figure is closer to 200,000.

It is because of this gay mobilization that countless individual lives have been saved from despair and an indigent death on the streets. Of this phenomenon in San Francisco and New York, Kübler-Ross (1987:155) wrote years ago:

> Although this is rapidly changing, the largest group of AIDS patients is still homosexual men. They have carried the stigma of the disease for six years and have

buried hundreds of their friends. At the same time, they have educated themselves and have organized extraordinary support systems that now serve as examples to other cities and other countries.

AIDS, through PWAs, is embraced by the gay community, while for racial and ethnic minorities contracting AIDS often means further denunciation and isolation. This infolding of the gay community is important because accepting AIDS not only actualizes gay pride through community integration but also forces AIDS to remain in national consciousness, making possible the mobilization of other at-risk minority populations.

If anything is democratic about AIDS to date, it is the willingness of gays, at least in large cities, to fund programs and create protocols that assist anyone with AIDS. So exceptional is this support for PWAs by GMHC that resistance is now emerging about using private gay capital to support research efforts that should really be funded by pharmaceutical companies and the federal government. Demand for services from GMHC remains very great while the community's resources remain limited. AIDS has forced gays and lesbians to forgo other important communal concerns. Many question whether a gay organization like GMHC should be so democratic. Others feel the gay community should be an "AIDS community" and that GMHC should be totally inclusive.

This vast mobilization, nevertheless, has had an enormous and mostly positive effect on the individual and collective gay psyche. Had it not been for this ingathering, the attempts of the political majority to create and enforce proscriptions around homosexual activity as a way of preventing AIDS would have succeeded. The legitimacy of being gay, as well as the viability of the whole gay rights movement, would have been destroyed.

Poirier (1988) argues that mainstream society would be willing to rid itself of gays by letting AIDS fulminate. This would, in fact, resolve two social problems at once: the medical problem of AIDS and the problem of "sexual diversity," normally seen or defined as deviance. In the killing off of gays by neglect, the public ideology relative to family life would be validated, pressure on the scientific and medical establishments would end, and the public good or peace restored.

This situation of homophobic neglect is the general sociopolitical environment out of which GMHC and all other AIDS service groups nationwide were born. By owning AIDS, however, GMHC established another agenda that recognized that without fighting institutionalized and internalized homophobia, the longtime enemy, nothing meaningful or beneficial can be done. What better way of ending internalized homophobia in gays, that is, disempowerment, than a community-wide volunteer effort that embraced PWAs? The alternative was abandonment and collective death.

As accurately depicted in the 1990 American movie *Longtime Companion*, personal tragedy daily enters the lives of gay men. Friends, neighbors, community members, and past and present lovers are dying by the dozens, frequently in wretched physical and emotional condition. Often alone in the city, without supportive kin and perhaps few or no friends, young men become disabled or terminally ill, many times simultaneously losing their homes and employment. Many PWAs are still being mistreated by the health care system and in many cases by their families when their AIDS diagnosis coincides with the disclosure of homosexuality or drug use. It became GMHC's responsibility, if not by design then by default, to do what was necessary to comfort people until death came.

"The incredibly vigorous and sustained response of the lesbian/gay community to AIDS," writes theologian Kevin Gordon (1989:201–202), "in its generating of national, state, city-wide, and individual support systems and services ... is not an ordinary effort." It had to make up for the inadequate governmental response in education, social service, and patient care and prevention programs. It placed a tremendous burden on the already taxed gay community. He continues:

> The primal lesbian/gay experience of the world through the centuries, the moral geography around which lesbian/gay identity has itself crystallized, is that of knowing ourselves to be a "throw-away" people, dispensable and disposable to both Church and state. Collusion by benign neglect in the genocide of one's own by both Church and state was not unthinkable to the lesbian/gay community in this time of AIDS, because it was in no way novel.

Gay community initiatives filled the void in services created during the moralization period in the evolution of AIDS. Of necessity, People with AIDS learned to rely on their own for succor. In a very real sense, GMHC was founded to help gay people live fully and, if necessary, to later die with dignity. Remarkably, as AIDS spread further into other populations, GMHC maintained its commitment to children, women, bisexuals, drug-users and their families, and carepartners and friends, even though gay interests as such would, of necessity, be served less (see Chapter 11).

Despite this magnanimous gesture, however, there was resistance among drug-users to be identified with AIDS or GMHC because of the stigma attached to them both. "There is resentment, too," writes Goldstein (1987:26), "about sharing the epidemic with gay men—especially gay white men. Some of it is homophobic to be sure; but it also speaks to the differences between racial and sexual oppression." Drug-users and minorities also resent the social-class differences and the privileges that come with simply being a white gay man. The Latino response to AIDS has been particularly hindered by the lack of funds and the availability of informed researchers and health care providers.

The Minority Reaction

Looking at AIDS in terms of class rather than in racial, ethnic, or sexual terms actually explains AIDS's status as a low-priority social problem. For those communities and populations touched directly by AIDS, a class analysis would ideally encourage an integration of divergent concerns across class, cultural, and life-style lines because of shared disenfranchisement and a common fate. This integration is important because the African-American, Latino, and gay communities are distinct from one another in terms of their cultures, sexual behaviors, affluence, reasons or proclivity to use illegal drugs, and other factors. They are all touched similarly by AIDS, nevertheless, and the creation of an "AIDS community" is bringing them together in untried ways, often at GMHC itself.

The structural pressures for drug use and/or maladaptive sexual behavior among blacks and Latinos (and gay minority members and drug-users) make AIDS a different problem for them than for gays who are whites. Sexual behavior is an essential component of gayness and the natural and preferred vehicle of expressing emotions and relationships. In this sense, the "whole people," if not the whole person, is involved in AIDS and the subsequent re-definition of gayness and sexuality that AIDS demands. The population or community has the virus in it and it is spread sexually whether the contact is intense, long-term, or merely casual. Drug use, however, is not the central way minority groups identify or "become themselves." If anything, drug-users have their own subculture and a distinctive social status that crosses racial, ethnic, and class lines, often leaving individuals in opposition to one another. They do not have community.

Because AIDS was defined as "gay and drug related," African-Americans and Latinos resisted admitting to or identifying with the illness even though it was spreading rapidly among them, albeit among a subpopulation. Acknowl-edging AIDS would have been an admittance of bisexuality, homosexuality, and/or drug use within the larger collectivity. "To avoid the stigma of being cast with diseases of the 'other,'" writes Hammonds (1987:31), "the black media, as well as other institutions in the community, avoid public discussions of sexual behavior and other 'deviant' behavior like drug-use." It was not until the weekend of June 10, 1989, that leading African-American clergymen in New York City started a campaign to mobilize 600 black congregations to re-spond to AIDS. Another such call was issued in November 1991. In a sense, the minority community, unlike the gay community, disowned its own.

Minority resistance to being identified with AIDS stems from the African-American community's reticence to discuss black male sexuality and drug use. For Latinos, distancing from AIDS comes from multiple and competing community identities, loyalties, and social worlds. While white gay men have been able to foster a positive connection between sex and community, even in the face of AIDS, the minority communities have lived with the fear of even greater stigma than they already suffer if they acknowledge any of their own as gay or drug using. As Hammonds (1987:33) notes, the traditional association of disease and promiscuity with blacks all but ensured black disassociation from AIDS.

The social fact or reality of "illegitimate" sexual behavior and drug use has long been repressed or disavowed by African-American and Hispanic leaders, which indicates both their shame and rejection of these activities. Gays, as such, can never do the same because gayness itself is still the issue at hand. In the public's mind, "who had the problem" defined "what the problem was," and for gays this meant redefining AIDS in such a way as to avoid dissolving the community by negating the legitimacy of homosexual activity. This need to redefine makes AIDS a totally different issue for gays than for other at-risk populations.

While homophobia is central to minority disavowal of AIDS, social-class differences between white gay men, blacks, and Latinos are also another significant explanation. In the case of AIDS, like in most things, these differences were translated into the political ability to gain some social services. Even though these services seemed meager to gay activists, the minority community saw them as another form of white privilege and favoritism.

> As services became available, gay groups took advantage of them, partly because the community embraced its afflicted, marched with them and publicized their plight. As prevention programs were developed, they were targeted toward gay men, partly because talking about sex is hardly a problem in the gay community. … Now that the true contours of the epidemic are becoming apparent, some of the rage in minority communities is being directed at their rival for scarce resources—gay men. (Goldstein 1987:26)

From a political perspective, minority communities are not generally aggressive or organized and powerful enough to demand adequate programs and treatment protocols in most any area. AIDS only complicates their needs and desperation further. There are no organized constituencies of "sex partners of IV-drug-users." Advantaged Americans do not care about the health needs of the poor, the disinherited, or the "sexually promiscuous."

According to Mel Rosen, former director of both the New York State AIDS Institute and GMHC, "It's only in the last year that it has become acceptable for [the minorities] to say 'This is our problem. Give it to us and we'll handle it'" (Goldstein 1987:26). He continues: "Where were they when we went out and did outreach in their communities in '83 and '84? Where were they when we sent out our first contract proposals and not one minority organization bid for it?" For Rosen, the problem with government is that it can't respond ahead of what the public demands. "All the power comes from the communities. And from where I sit, I don't think the minority community was ready for this."

Why the gay community had to respond quickly is, of course, the starting point of this book and the context for understanding the direction this effort took. Gay people simply read the writing on the wall faster, and it was terrifying. We knew what had to be done and did it, virtually at once and together. Ironically, this response was similar to that of the majority population, who reacted only when the disease appeared to hit home. For us, it merely came home to roost earlier and more dramatically. As will be demonstrated in Chapter 8, altruism aside, had AIDS not been gay, community interest in the life and struggles of PWAs would, likewise, be at a minimum.

PART TWO

Ideology: Volunteerism and AIDS

Photo © Marc Geller

The "International Display" of the entire AIDS Quilt in Washington, D.C., in October '92. 400,000 visitors viewed 20,064 panels.

5

Volunteerism, Community, and Blaming the Victim

PUTTING STIGMA AND REPUTATIONAL risk aside for the moment, there is nothing ahistorical about responding to AIDS the way gays do: through community-based initiatives. Voluntary action is, for better or worse, the means through which Americans prefer to solve problems. Nonprofit volunteerism is now completely integrated into our social structure, making it a normative expectation rather than a random or insignificant social activity. Helping others in need is part of the ideological package that justifies our understanding of ourselves as a distinct, if not "chosen," people.

On coming to America in the 1830s, Alexis de Tocqueville was so struck by the American penchant to form and voluntarily join organizations that he said it "must be seen to be understood." In an oft-quoted passage, he wrote:

> Americans of all ages, all stations of life, and types of disposition are forever forming associations. There are not only commercial and industrial associations in which all take part, but others of a thousand different types—religious, moral, serious, futile, very general and very limited, immensely large and very minute. (Tocqueville 1969: 523)

Over a century and a half later, social historian Robert Bellah (1985:167–180) is able to identify this same strand in American life, albeit in more specific ways. For him, Americans are now *expected* to solve their problems at the local level through their own collective will. In "getting involved," they also settle the peculiar and growing American problem of feeling isolated, unconnected, and powerless.

While joining voluntary associations gives individualistic Americans a sense of needed attachment, it also fosters social integration by recognizing everyone helped as neighbors and worthy citizens. For this reason, nearly all American presidents verbally support problem solving on the local level and invoke the "golden rule" or the "love of neighbor" to justify their position that vol-

71

unteerism is patriotic. From both a dislike of bureaucracy and a sense of personal responsibility, ordinary Americans are cajoled into voluntarily taking responsibility for overcoming social ills, as if by biblical injunction.

Given the relationship of religious organizations to American institutions in general, it is not surprising that most volunteering is done under religious auspices and played out within these same communities. Today, volunteerism is supported by the state, whose charity is potentially more universal though often as limiting.[1]

This linkage of volunteerism to the religious imagery of patriotism and nationalism is now considered by many to be part of our civil religion and is central to understanding gay/AIDS volunteerism. Ironically, gays' taking the initiative to serve others in need reflects a value emphasized by all American religions and complements the country's Protestant and capitalistic character. Gay volunteers adhere, albeit unknowingly, to conservative and republican views of where responsibility for problem solving lies, while the growing AIDS industry demands more public support.

Though Americans offer help to needy neighbors freely, to have any merit, charity cannot be coerced, especially not by the federal government. This is why American ideology emphasizes solutions that can be managed by local groups rather than those that require one to join larger political parties, clubs, or organizations. In this regard, gay/AIDS volunteerism is traditional. Its distinctiveness lies in its unique political application in both creating and embodying a "community of interest" through the activity itself. With AIDS, GMHC became the responsible gay community.

Community and American Volunteerism

To understand gay/AIDS volunteerism, it is important to identify the different meanings that "community" can take in American society. There is a particular usage that Tocqueville identified as "self-interest properly understood"; that is, it is limited to people and objectives necessary to the preservation of the advancement of self. Implicit in this need to "get involved" with others "as a community" or even "in the community" is the peculiarly American notion of the relationship between self and society. This connection is central to gay volunteerism because epidemics as social tragedies can integrate private and communal interests. This, in turn, makes the community's response both possible and logical.

> Individuals are expected to get involved—to choose for themselves to join social groups. They are not automatically involved in social relationships that impose obligations not of their choosing, and social institutions that are not the product of the voluntary choice of the individuals who constitute them are perceived as illegitimate (Bellah 1985:167).

It is the essence of community that gays and GMHC be the carepartners and supporters of PWAs. Yet Bellah chooses to exclude gays from any recognition as either a community or as valid members of society. He renders gays invisible by suggesting that there is no shared, engaged, and enjoyed gay identity. Bellah prefers to see gays as living in "life-style enclaves" based on the "narcissism of similarity" in patterns of leisure and consumption. He ignores gay psychosocial identity across time and place, the presence of shared institutional networks, the reality of gay history, and the fact that gays are everywhere and therefore part of the public.

His position diminishes the fact that even before the trauma of AIDS launched major political and charitable initiatives, there was a longtime gay rights movement addressing commonly shared concerns. Gay people had been collectively involved in neighborhood, environmental, educational, and civil rights issues, to say nothing of gay institution building for decades, and principally since Stonewall in 1969. In terms of AIDS volunteerism, it is this collective and experienced gay consciousness, rather than the sharing or domination of public space, that has propelled the community beyond isolation and privacy into public, institutional endeavors.

Bellah's ignorance of gay history and his failure to recognize gay community life, expressly now during AIDS, result from his basic centrist views about society and family life. He thus speaks of self-reliant "congregations created and maintained by the voluntary cooperation of self-reliant individuals living in self-reliant families" as the American ideal and norm.

If this were indeed the case, voluntary activity in any form might not ever be needed. Moreover, many urban people living in relationships are not living by this family norm, especially gay and lesbian people. "Family" for city dwellers, gay people, single people, and others includes friends and neighbors and the right (and expectation) to depend on them in time of need. Being and living in community creates a bond between individuals, particularly gays sharing an event like AIDS.

Because charitableness is self-selective, volunteerism and public welfare projects clearly define social worth. Who is helped and acknowledged as in need not only indicates social acceptability but also tells us how the national society is organized and citizen entitlements distributed. Almost always, social status and social networks determine how Americans apply their volunteering "instincts." And this is also true of gays because AIDS volunteerism reveals the affective feelings we have for one another and is not purely altruistic (see Chapter 9).

Though a reaction to exclusion, the freedom and willingness to volunteer in AIDS reaffirm faith in gay community. It also reveals the biases of our social institutions. In a democratic society, positive pluralism requires that the majority system not only be open to minority communities but that the majority do what it can to encourage and sustain diversity. In a contemporary idiom, it requires that American society accept multiculturalism. This is precisely what has not happened in AIDS and why gay volunteerism needs to be celebrated as much for its historicity as for the peculiar structural and psychological barriers it overcomes.

Especially because PWAs, gays, and GMHC overlap so much, the issue of social status and the "common good" is central to our discussion of the political meaning of both AIDS and gay volunteerism. The questions now are, which community do PWAs belong to, who among them should be served, and by whom? Are People with AIDS part of the larger polis or are they isolated or separate minority elements? Are PWAs ever to be included in the common good or their needs addressed by government? If it is unredemptive to help the morally scourged, will minority people be allowed to die?

Crimp (1988:6) emphatically states that "scientific research, health care, and education are the *responsibility and purpose* of government and not of so-called 'private initiative,' an ideological term that excuses and perpetuates the state's irresponsibility." Terian (1986:26–28) believes that it is the duty of government to protect all its citizens since justice and concern with human-made evil should be government's primary objective, even if it requires a radical shift in consciousness and social arrangements. She claims that while charity on behalf of the needy is always necessary, it is good only when it shows respect for a person in the form of *agape* and when it works toward beneficence and justice. In the absence of such deference for gays, charity in AIDS takes the form of social movement involvement, political questioning, and direct helping.

There are different social consequences when help is mutually offered, done between strangers or friends, shared within a community, is organized, or is direct or indirect. It matters politically if the recipients are "blameless," one's own group, or just "others." Whether charity should be exercised to enhance the self-respect of the recipient or the donor, whether the church or state should be the responsible initiators and actors, and whether the goal is justice are all questions when community-based initiatives determine the conditions for their own largess.

Whether disenfranchised citizens have any claim to public support and compassion is the primary question in AIDS because social exclusion closes down democratic processes, and people die from marginalization. In this context, the common good is not served because it is limited to the self-serving interests of social conformists at the expense of legitimate human need.

Ideology and Volunteerism

In many ways, AIDS reveals that the common good is constrained by the boundaries of community. For this reason, the disease did not become a public concern until after the "innocent victim" category (e.g., Ryan White) was created and popular-culture heroes infected. Despite the massive contributions of gay talent to the creation and maintenance of Western civilization over countless centuries, it was not until the illness and death of actor Rock Hudson that the ubiquitousness of popular, closeted gay people, and AIDS, were brought to national consciousness.

The very reasonable debt that society owes to gays is not the issue here. Rather it is the debt that gays owe to one another that is significant. AIDS forces the living community to honor this obligation out of necessity since not paying it would mean communal and personal annihilation. For Bellah (1985:196–199), the ingathering of service to one another (as is the case in AIDS) is actually the way the good life is achieved because it solves the conflict between excessive individualism and competition and the human need for community, sociability, and meaning.

Gays who do not hide from or deny the reality of AIDS strike a balance between self-interest and the benefits of communal involvement, though this involvement generally becomes negligible for all segments of the American public when it is extended beyond the bounds of local community. Citizenship is virtually coextensive with getting involved with one's neighbors for the good of a particular group. Although gays, for the most part, have come to see minority PWAs as neighbors, many Americans do not consider gays as such. Nor do Americans understand "getting involved" to be either political in character or essential for democratic living as a mediating mechanism.

Bellah identifies this type of involvement as the "politics of community," which he claims stands in sharp contrast to the "politics of interest." This other form is the "pursuit of differing interests according to agreed upon, neutral rules." He writes, "One enters the politics of interest for reasons of utility, to get what one or one's group needs or wants, rather than because of spontaneous involvement with others to whom one feels akin" (Bellah 1985:167–180). It is normally undertaken by professionals and is related to power, alliance building, and interest bargaining.

If communal involvement is held together by affectivity and the politics of interest by practical need, the "politics of the nation," his third type, holds the country together through law and leadership in the "sense of uniting a disparate people for action" in the name of national purpose. While the mobilization of gays in AIDS is akin to both the politics of community and that of interest, it is the "politics of the nation" that concerns us here because AIDS, as a multifarious international problem, is not likely to be solved on the local level.

The control and management of AIDS nationally and internationally is best achieved by American support for international prevention efforts and through national institutional help and volunteerism—rather than one instead of the other, as battling advocates of the Right and Left maintain. This way communal and national interests will be kept balanced and equitably served.

AIDS suggests that the boundaries of citizenship are quite limited, while gay volunteerism indicates that the boundaries of community can be quite large if identification with the sufferer, both as person and outsider, is generated. Volunteerism has significant and broad political implications, most notably the creation of community and a thirst for citizenship among gays. Yet for many critics like GMHC cofounder Larry Kramer, ideological beliefs about community involvement merely justify government's reduced commitment and responsibility to AIDS, even though the community radically politicizes itself in response to the abandonment and compounded emptiness these beliefs create.

Kramer is only partially correct because government indifference to AIDS continues as part of a broader federal withdrawal from support for community-based initiatives. President Reagan's laissez-faire policy regarding AIDS, for example, was intended to decrease the federal bureaucracy so that government could save money. Despite the rhetoric, his policy was never intended to facilitate community development and political involvement.

Government hypocrisy is indicated primarily in the lack of comprehensive, integrated, and reasonable AIDS policy programming, both nationally and internationally. This programming deficiency, too, is a function of the social meaning of AIDS and the desire to maintain the distribution of power. Observe the interplay between morality and science in the membership of the first AIDS Commission appointed by Reagan. Gays wondered aloud about the members' sincerity, usefulness, objectivity, and qualifications; most members were appointed over the objections of gay activists. Cory Ser Vaas, a commission member appointed in 1987, told the *New York Native* that she hopes scientists will, instead of stopping the disease and virus, discover "the genetic predisposition to being homosexual so that we could minimize that behavior, thereby reducing AIDS."[2]

On July 31, 1989 (after a delay of seven months and well beyond the time limits set by law), President Bush's AIDS Commission was able to produce several hundred recommendations, the most useful being a ban on discrimination, yet no specific guidelines or strategies of implementation have been derived.[3] Despite improvements in member credentials and potential, little has been done since then and the commission is rarely heard of. In 1991, it said publicly that government and President Bush were not doing enough. Apparently, Magic Johnson felt the same about the commission when he resigned.

AIDS policy has remained generally vacuous until now because the federal government refuses to sanction homosexuality. Thus gay people are suspicious of all aspects of the official government's response to AIDS, including any recommendations made by the AIDS Commission. Desiring to maintain a presence in the debate yet remain independent of outside control, GMHC now has its own medical advisory board as well as a scientific review committee. Ironically, these acquisitions broaden its role in the nonprofit sector by making the agency, in effect, a "mediating community institution." As such, it is eligible for direct government support as outlined in a 1982 report issued by the politically conservative American Enterprise Institute.

AEI recommends support of problem-oriented "mediating structures" in American communities because they reduce direct government control of private life and community matters. The institute supports volunteer ideology (and republicanism) by stressing local problem solving rather than responses by large bureaucratized public or private social service agencies. After distorting this policy recommendation, the Reagan administration established a system of "Volunteer Action Awards," at least two of which were actually given to GMHC because it was a successful example of American ideology at work, dispensing millions of dollars of community services and funds and providing millions of hours of free labor.

By accepting these awards, however, GMHC unwittingly legitimated government distancing from AIDS, making the disease seem even more like a local, minority, or gay problem rather than a public health crisis. Ironically, although the social and demographic contours of AIDS are always changing, AIDS is not a looming threat to American heterosexuals. It is a public health crisis, however, and thus gays deserve help. Both the nonprofit sector in general and the federal government need to make commitments to AIDS sufferers because they are people and citizens and the need is so great.

Ideology and Reality

The government's shifting of responsibility for care and support of the disinherited blames the victim, even though gays, Latinos, and African-Americans pay taxes and deserve to be heard. The denial of entitlements tells us as much about homophobia and the way it is to be resolved politically and socially as about how the political system works and responds to diverse interest groups. Unexpectedly, government ideology and indifference facilitated gay empowerment, which is the solution to all politically derived and defined problems like AIDS.

At this very time, when the volunteer spirit has been loudly defined by Republican administrations as central to America's history, character, and survival, federal support and funding for community-based initiatives have been cut back. So ideological was President Reagan's belief that government is not the solution but the source of so many problems that he said at a White House luncheon on private-sector initiatives, "I just wonder if maybe God isn't waiting for us to do something [about the problems we face]. And while no one ... is capable of doing everything, everyone is capable of doing something."

It is this type of volunteer spirit that is, according to Reagan, the engine that drives our whole history: "The history of America is based on volunteerism." Expressing the same idea a year later, he said "America was built on the voluntary principle," which was "instrumental in our nation's advancement," making us "a strong and self-reliant people." It is our "most precious American resource" (Adams 1987:20–24). Basically, he sees volunteering as a moral and religious obligation for Americans.

According to Palmer and Sawhill (1984:271), though Reagan claimed he would "revitalize" the nonprofit sector, he actually cut "the equivalent of $115 billion in real terms" between 1982 and 1985. "The bulk of the cuts," they note, "would have come in the fields of social services, employment and training, and housing and community development."

In addition to discouraging philanthropy in the new tax codes, note Palmer and Sawhill, the federal government took a number of administrative actions that further eroded its relations with the voluntary, nonprofit sector.

> The first was the administration's decision to eliminate the government's principal vehicle for promoting community-based voluntary organization, the Community Service Administration. ... The second was to appoint as the head of ACTION, the government's voluntary action agency, a particularly ardent conservative who early on began an effort to stop funds from going to liberal, activist organizations. Simultaneously, as part of its budget program, the administration sought to eliminate or significantly scale back the postal subsidy for nonprofit organizations, which would have seriously hampered their direct mail fundraising efforts. (Palmer and Sawhill 1984:274)

Palmer and Sawhill note two other administrative developments that made a severe impact on voluntary charities. To counter a trend of federal money being given to advocacy groups, the Reagan administration drafted an executive order that would bar the distribution of funds to any charity that provided abortion or abortion counseling or that engaged in lobbying or litigation on public-policy issues, like AIDS agencies are wont to do.

The Reagan administration likewise advocated that organizations engaged in "political advocacy" would have to isolate all funds and resources used for that purpose from those used for the government contract if they received 5 percent of the operating budget from government funds. Despite its conservatism, AEI did not have this arrangement in mind when it advocated that "public policy should cease and desist from damaging mediating structures." President Reagan had actually cut back funds for community groups and voluntary organizations and services, making it both more necessary and more difficult for groups like GMHC to exist, unless their own communities could forever be continuously tapped.

Having inherited the Reagan agenda and ideology, President Bush maintained this outlook. On June 22, 1989, Bush made a proposal for a "national volunteer effort" to help the homeless, the poor, drug-abusers, illiterates, "AIDS victims" and other Americans facing severe problems. "From now on," the *Times*reports Bush as saying, "any definition of a successful life must include serving others." Asserting that "there is no problem that is not being solved somewhere in America," the president said: "You, you in this room, can prove that statement a thousand times over. It's in our hands" (Weinraub 1989:A6).

According to Clark Kent Irvin, associate director of policy, Office of National Service, in 1990 President Bush intended to reward individuals and communities for hands-on voluntary activity in the solution of social problems that his administration felt result from the decline of the family and religious values. His administration saw the solution to AIDS and homelessness in direct action by individuals in the private sector and not in any larger fiscal expenditures by government or private or public agencies.

However, in his March 29, 1990, address on AIDS, President Bush appeared to again blame AIDS sufferers for the disease. "We don't spurn the accident victim who didn't wear a seat belt," the president is quoted as saying (Hilts 1990b:A1). "We don't reject the cancer patient who didn't quit smoking cigarettes. We try to love them and care for them and comfort them. We do not fire them. We don't evict them. We don't cancel their insurance."

Translated to the gay experience with AIDS, his approach implied that gays should not be sexually active or should at least use condoms and that if they don't they will be loved anyway even though they are to blame by assumedly being promiscuous. Separatist and divisive categories like "innocent victims of AIDS," "gay AIDS," or "minority AIDS" were designed to divide and isolate people, making gays and drug-users appear even more foreign and reprehensible.

Blaming AIDS on PWAs supports societal disclaimers that AIDS is not a social problem. It shifts responsibility to individuals and their behaviors rather than the social arrangements that produce and make them maladaptive. If AIDS were a "majority" illness, social institutions would have responded with more immediacy and gay volunteerism and AIDS social service agencies would not be so necessary.

Blaming the "Sinful," Exclusion, and Community Integration

Moral exclusion legitimates violence against PWAs because gays do not live within the social expectations of the "new Right." Sex for pleasure outside of marriage encourages a "blame-the-victim" mentality and policies that reinforce oppression. Commission member John Cardinal O'Connor of New York shocked even his fellow bishops by disagreeing with their pastoral letter supporting the use of condoms as an AIDS preventive. He is quoted by Kateb (1988:455) as saying that "the church could not condone the public provision of condoms because the greatest physical harm is less important than the smallest moral harm."

The cardinal later refused to allow counseling on condom use at Catholic hospitals and social service centers, even though his refusal raises many legal questions about state funding grants to Catholic facilities. The New York archdiocese also opposes a recent decision by the chancellor of the New York Board of Education to make condoms available to students, the majority of whom are minority members.

For the sexually active, condemning condom use has serious, if not fatal, consequences. It also reinforces and celebrates sex for reproduction at the expense of gays, who emphasize pleasure, relationships, and feelings. As reported by Steinfels (1988a:A16), the cardinal goes quite far to undermine the gay psyche.

> In addition to the medical issue of condoms' effectiveness in preventing AIDS, he said, "psychologists and psychiatrists I have consulted tell me they are particularly concerned that there is little emphasis on sin or guilt." According to the Cardinal, "They believe it essential to help persons with AIDS accept and work through their guilt."

The message is that PWAs should feel guilty, confess, and repent so as to be "forgiven" and "saved." Because there is a strong correlation between religious imagery, internalized guilt, and maladaptive sexual and social behavior, it is not accidental that AIDS is most rampant in those cities and states with the most conservative and homophobic Catholic hierarchies. Both gays and drug-users live daily with stigma and social disapprobation. It is not surprising that outsiders would be most susceptible to a disease-causing pathogen like HIV, yet they are blamed for its occurrence.

Since religions committed to male privilege prohibit same-gender sex, the social distance and stigma that effectively "ghettoize" gay concerns are legitimated. In effect, gays, not being considered "real," normal ("natural") men, should die of AIDS because they are sinful "failures." AIDS will thus remain a minority/outgroup problem precisely at a time when help from the political majority is so crucial for gay health and survival.

Stateside religion's heterosexist commitments also help to fuel and sustain a virulent anti-gay violence that has become as epidemic as AIDS. "We are a community under siege," says Jill Tregor, acting director of San Francisco's eleven-year-old Community United Against Violence. "We are in a state of emergency" (Voelcker 1990:48). In New York City, and elsewhere, physical attacks against lesbians and gay men have greatly increased and fluctuate with AIDS hysteria. Queer Nation, a new gay civil defense group determined to "take back the night" and celebrate a hated label, was born in the summer of 1990, nine years into the epidemic, in response to increased street attacks on gays in Greenwich Village and throughout New York, especially at the start of Gay Pride Week.[4] Not a word of protest about these attacks came forth from any religious leader in the city.

Psychologist Gregory Herek believes that even homophobia does not go far enough to explain anti-gay violence. "It is very functional to be prejudiced," he writes. "It's reinforced by friends, by churches, and by society. They don't get any contradictory messages from the media saying its bad to gay-bash" (Voelcker 1990:49).

Although O'Connor once responded to the beating and murdering of several gay males in the city in a sermon at St. Patrick's Cathedral, which has been the site of many gay demonstrations aimed at sensitizing him to gay concerns, he fails to call gay bashings into question by denouncing their base and origination in religiously sustained sexism. He normally calls on the police to terminate these demonstrations whenever they occur.

According to Thomas Stoddard of the Lambda Legal Defense and Education Fund, an activist gay rights legal group, there is homophobic ambiguity in O'Connor's message. Because he made a general denouncement, he suggests that while gay oppression is alright, murder is too extreme a reaction. The cardinal's posture simply offers verbal compensation to the victims without attacking the social sources of homophobic violence and the role of religion in sustaining and perpetuating it.

In the same breath, O'Connor acknowledges his support of what he sees as his church's teaching on homosexuality and concludes that while homosexual behavior is sinful, "as in every other situation, however, the church never condemns the sinner, only the sin." In the words of gay activist Tom Nichols (1988:14), "How dare he preach against that which he has fought so hard to maintain on his home turf?" Because of the way O'Connor fuses sexuality with reproduction rather than with feelings and desires, his stand is the essence of theological pornography (see Chapter 12).

O'Connor's faulty systematic theology (Valente 1970) does violence to the psyche and personhood of all people not engaged in marital coitus and strictly reproductive sexual activity. It ignores the institutional sources of anti-gay violence by suggesting that such violence is a personal aberration rather than a learned, rewarded, socially induced, and expected behavior. In reality, a careful survey of urban gay bashing, at least in New York, would indicate that it is all too frequently carried out by church-affiliated, Irish Catholic males, especially from Brooklyn and Jersey City.[5]

Stateside religions, likewise, help AIDS proliferate by committing to the social and psychological conditions out of which maladaptive behaviors that spread AIDS occur. By condemning, they effectively exclude people from institutional participation, social discourse, and political power. This condition exacerbates the problems and violence faced by both PWAs and gays. It also sets the tone and balance of power in the debate on AIDS.

This strategy of blaming the victim neglects the deeper political nature of both AIDS and health care delivery from which People with AIDS and gays are excluded. It also diminishes the role of social structure in the causality of problems and ignores how exclusion from society affects personal behavior and identities, the potential for communal empowerment, and the willingness of public institutions to respond to the human needs of minorities. Placing blame on victims ignores the social sources of illness and downplays the responsibility of government in general to protect and serve the common good. This is especially true for AIDS because AIDS is not a disease of immoral individuals but, as Holleran (1988) maintains, of social structure and community. As a crisis, it affects whole classes of disinherited minorities, leaving gays and other citizens with few entitlements.

When institutionalized, AIDS-phobia is a problem rooted in homophobia, disenfranchisement, and discrimination. *AIDS-homophobia,* in turn, affects personal identities, social relations, communal integration, and support for gay civil rights and health benefits. Blaming the PWA is AIDS-homophobia at work. It also ignores the reality that specific interest groups, not the general public, have assumed the right to act as the public guardians of morals and medicine. Moreover, and less obviously, there are political and economic benefits in excluding the many people defined as "others" from entitlements within a stratified capitalistic economy. It is in the context of this continuous neglect and discrimination that GMHC and the AIDS service industry were born as supportive "communities of neighbors."

This phenomenon of community building and enlargement is important because in traditional political analysis, a social loss (like an AIDS death) is considered significant only if the victims are well placed and/or powerful or if social arrangements will be altered by their absence. This condition creates guilt and reinforces the notion that the loss of ordinary lives is not a significant concern. In reality, many families, friendships, relationships, social institutions, and professions are being decimated by the sickness and death of so many gay people and People with AIDS.

Until the meaningful allocation of national resources and will is separated from the moral ideas of the people who have power, thousands more will become infected and millions of people will needlessly die.

6

The Political Economy of Volunteerism and AIDS Prevention/Education

As DEMONSTRATED, THE FEDERAL GOVERNMENT'S negligible involvement with AIDS research, health maintenance, and prevention is a reflection of a whole system of beliefs about the nature and purpose of government and citizen involvement in (or responsibility for) problem solving. For Americans, it is better that an autonomous community voluntarily maintains public order, safety, and health. In reality, however, government's desire to "extend national service into every corner of America," as President Bush advocated, reinforces the belief that local communities alone should continue to supply and augment care for PWAs, despite the magnitude of the problem.

The Point of Light Initiative of the former president was a continuation and development of an earlier theme in American history, wherein citizens expressed their sense of social responsibility in religious terms by direct charitable assistance to the less fortunate. In this way, Bush was following the lead of his predecessor. "Helping others is just our way, part of our national character," President Reagan was quoted by the *New York Times* (December 27, 1987:27) as saying in a radio address at Christmastime that year.

> Perhaps it reflects that we as a people not only enjoy this holiday every year as a time off from work, but also take to heart the spiritual meaning of Christmas and Hanukkah. There is always much to improve. But I can assure you that the spirit of goodwill and benevolence—an aspect of our national character recognized since the early days of our Republic—remains a vibrant part of the American way of life.

Relative to AIDS, this "spirit of goodwill" is absent on the national level. People in general are disinterested in the plight of sick minorities. In addition to carepartnering PWAs virtually alone, gays now have the responsibility to

formulate policy, educate diverse publics about risk, staff prevention programs, fund-raise, and act as advocates on behalf of the poor and disadvantaged with AIDS. They have these responsibilities largely because the federal
government has, as a matter of policy, absented itself generally from the support and delivery of certain social services, especially in urban areas.

> From 1980 to 1986, social welfare programs lost federal outlays amounting to
> $58.9 billion, a 42 percent decrease; education and research funding declined
> $19.6 billion or 18 percent; and the arts and culture were cut by $5 million, or 15
> percent. In social welfare, the largest budget cuts were made in employment and
> training programs. Education was affected because social security benefits in
> higher education for adult students were eliminated, as well as other forms of fi-
> nancial assistance. (Odendahl 1990:60)

In June 1990, when both houses of Congress finally approved billions of
dollars in financial help to cities most hit by AIDS, the Bush White House, reports Hilts (1990d:B9), issued a statement that "the bill's narrow, disease-
specific approach sets a dangerous precedent, inviting treatment of other diseases through similar ad hoc arrangements." A good bulk of this money
would have been spent on preventive education, the area that conservative
public officials most resist addressing because it would bring to public consciousness the range of sexuality in human experience.

Supporting community AIDS programs in education and prevention also
means funding the gay organizations that propose them, and federal, state,
and local governments, relying on the old notion of the "deserving poor," according to Arno (1988:56), do not want to appear to be "helping gays."[1] As a
result, in many states newer AIDS projects not devised by gay people are
growing more rapidly with government support than the earlier, more established ones originated by gays.

The Bush administration intended to provide $870 million in Medicaid
payments for HIV disease in 1991 rather than give money to city agencies
themselves to manage. Congress, however, passed the Ryan White Comprehensive AIDS Resources Emergency Act of 1990 in memory of this brave and
"innocent" preteen with AIDS who caught the nation's attention. It also
amended the Public Health Service Act to provide cost-effective grants to lo-
calities that are disproportionately affected by HIV infection and to improve
the quality and availability of care for individuals and families with HIV. Nevertheless, the Senate Appropriations Committee "approved less than 20 percent of the money authorized for disaster relief to the cities hardest hit by the
AIDS epidemic" (Hilts 1990g:A1).

Because the need is so great and the populations affected by AIDS so specific, the gap in service delivery has been filled by volunteers, the vast (though
decreasing) majority of them urban, gay men affiliated with community agen-

cies rather than hospital organizations. These volunteers provide hundreds of thousands of hours of labor annually, in effect tremendously reducing the cost of AIDS care. In San Francisco, report Omoto and Synder (1990:154), the savings can be up to $120,000 a year per patient. According to health economist Peter S. Arno, by 1988 there were more than 300 AIDS-related groups around the country, most relying extensively on gay volunteers. At this point, the savings are incalculable.

As ideology, this issue of community responsibility and mobilization goes beyond just AIDS and gays. Former presidential adviser and attorney general Edwin Meese has succinctly expressed the low value that citizen participation was given in reality by the Reagan team. When asked if citizens would be encouraged to participate in the shaping of a government policy, he replied, "Yes, every four years" (Van Til 1982:207). This comment is significant because it points out that the federal government will respond to AIDS, but only on its own terms. In effect, the populace at large is allowed to be political only when permitted and when its concerns are expressed through public officials using official channels (as GMHC does) and who are presumed to represent the popular interest.

Reagan and Health Care Policy

Ronald Reagan came to office in 1981 publicly committed to a program of tax and human service cuts, an emphasis on volunteering, and defense program increases. The upshot, writes Odendahl (1990:68), was that "rich people now have more money in their pockets, poor people have less, and there are fewer incentives for redistribution." At the onset of Reagan's Economic Recovery Plan, not-for-profit organizations actually received more than one-and-one-half times more of their total funding from federal government programs as they did from all private charity. Reagan's budget proposals called for a 27 percent cut in 1985 in real-dollar support for nonprofit organizations.

This situation becomes far more severe when specific categories of nonprofit organizations are considered. Human service nonprofit organizations in particular could expect to find "a real dollar decline in federal support of 64 percent from 1980 to 1985" (Smith 1985:232). This decline equals an overall budget cut of about 25 percent for these organizations. In 1982–1983, rather than ask Congress to finance AIDS research directly, the Department of Health and Human Services (DHHS) took 95 percent of its AIDS research funds from already allocated resources for other health research projects. Other assigned moneys had yet to be allocated or spent. At best, in 1987 the federal government was willing to spend only about $85 million on AIDS.

While Congress eventually requested $234 million for AIDS research, federal medical experts Krieger and Appleman had concluded in 1986 that "by

1990 the government must commit at least $1 billion annually in new research funds" (p. 29). They noted that even this amount "may prove to be insufficient" to prevent the spread of HIV and to cure AIDS. Money aside, reports Hilts (1990e), the National Commission on AIDS told President Bush that "AIDS policy in the United States was like 'an orchestra without a conductor' because the Government had failed to lead the campaign against the epidemic effectively."

Diverging from the recommendations of Reagan's own national advisory committee, the budgets of both the National Institutes of Health and the Centers for Disease Control (the two federal agencies responsible for the nation's health) were actually reduced, forcing them to compete with one another for staff and AIDS funding. For Perrow and Guillen (1990:17), "a better indication of (funding) failure would be evidence that those who were most knowledgeable about the disease were unable to get anywhere near the funds they requested. ... And even after funds had been budgeted, they were deliberately not allocated."

Because of other budget cuts, federal support for nonprofit organizations has dropped about $17 billion below the level of 1980. Social service organizations have "lost $9 billion, or more than 35% of their federal aid" (Pifer 1987:125). This reduction in public support for voluntary human service delivery came during a period when Reagan was urging the independent sector to take on an even greater share of responsibility for social welfare. He claimed that charitable giving in the United States increased 77 percent to $88.2 billion from $49 billion from 1980 to 1986, making government assistance less necessary. In his assessment of this logic, Pifer (1987:125) writes: "Thus, paradoxically, just when more was being asked of the sector, its capacity to respond was severely weakened by a dramatic reduction of its chief source of financial support—government funding. On the face of it, this seems a curious contradiction in the pursuit of public policy objectives."

While it might actually appear that Reagan tried to stimulate voluntary initiatives through his 1982 President's Task Force on Private Sector Initiatives, the opposite is the case. In assessing Reagan's commitment, Allen (1983:23–25) concludes that while there has been a renewal in citizen involvement nationwide, it is more in the form of a general interest than real voluntary activity or even charity. Actually, the call for more voluntary commitments by communities came, notes Chambre, during a time when involvement in unpaid work was actually declining.

> About half of adults in the U.S. spent some time volunteering during 1981 compared to 45% in 1987. Although there was an increase in the proportion of volunteers who worked for the types of organizations that might have included some of those involved in AIDS work (education and social services), there was a substantial decline in health-related work. (Chambre 1989:13)

What is important, however, is the ideology used by Reagan to justify voluntary initiatives. Reagan encouraged a "charitable entrepreneurship" instead of a social justice agenda, as if charity were only another business within a free enterprise system. Yet the increase in private and corporate philanthropy to private-sector volunteer enterprises in 1987 was the lowest in twelve years. Recent figures show a decline in giving by the rich from 7 percent of the after-tax income to less than 4 percent (Barringer 1992:L16).

As a result of Reagan's much heralded 1988 Tax Reform Act (which made it less profitable for companies to donate to charity), the largest increase in charitable contributions came from individuals and not from the corporate sector, which showed no growth in donations from 1986 to 1988. Americans, however, notes Teltsch (1989:A16), donated $9.5 billion to health care in 1988, an increase of 3.2 percent, and $10.7 billion to human services, up 6.6 percent. The total donated in 1988 was $104 billion, which rose to $122.5 billion in 1990.

Baby boomers' contributions rose to 43 percent of all charitable donations in 1989 and constituted 55 percent of contributed volunteer time. In 1991, philanthropic giving increased by 6.2 percent to a record $124.7 billion, though nonprofit hospitals and human service organizations received only $10.6 billion, down from $11.8 billion the year before. How much of this was gay or AIDS related cannot be determined, but the generational increase by Americans born after 1940 partially helps explain GMHC's success.

Ideology, Gays, and AIDS

If modern gay-American history can be dated from the Stonewall riot of 1969, the second most important event in its evolution is that the fulmination of AIDS took place during the Republican presidency of Ronald Reagan. As important as the disinterest and moralization that Reagan generated was his policy on volunteering, private enterprise, and community involvement.

Reagan clearly saw volunteerism as a basic theme and ingredient in American civil religion. In effect, this attitude legitimates federal government disassociation from communal concerns and even those local problems that are as dramatic and shattering as AIDS. Volunteerism is now the justifying ideology for government indifference to the human tragedy of those who are exploited and disinherited. More important, it shifts the responsibility for cure and care from civic or public health agencies to individuals, local groups, families, friends, and communities. Reagan preferred to privatize AIDS rather than allow fundamental social change on the institutional level. In reality, government ideology became a justification for budget cuts in those agencies dealing with public health and safety.

When a government suggests moral and individualistic solutions for a social problem, it is making a political statement. Inaction is a social control strategy designed to target AIDS as a gay problem, remove gays from public life, and neutralize growing gay political and economic power. Since community responsibility was justified historically as essential for democratic living, the federal administration could claim that it was doing the right thing by not interfering with community autonomy or even gay life and health. Advocating popular testing for HIV suggested more than benign concern and neglect. It was a facade for intervention and control.

Because the issue of prevention is greatly complicated by the lack of consistent and meaningful civil protection for gays and HIV-positive people (clearly noted by the 1987 report of the AIDS Commission), the federal government considered mandatory testing and possible quarantine of all "high-risk" groups as a solution to AIDS fulmination. Had civil rights been in effect, the issue of mandatory testing would not have been so frightening, though it still would have raised serious constitutional issues.

However, because HIV has been found to hide in macrophage cells (which elude easy detection) and because many people with AIDS have produced no antigens to HIV (thousands of others who are HIV positive have yet to show signs of "official" illness), the whole issue of testing becomes somewhat less critical. Similarly, the continuous debate aired in the *New York Native* that HIV is not the only cause of AIDS but that another microbe works in tandem with HIV (as suggested by American researcher Dr. Shuh-Ching Lo and now being considered by Dr. Luc Montagnier, the co-discoverer of HIV), if true, makes preoccupation with HIV testing and tracing symbolic, if nothing else, though it does affect treatment.

Yet the suggestion to identify, track, and trace HIV infection persists. In California, misanthropic senator William Dannemeyer would have required doctors and health officials not only to report and identify their own HIV status but to reveal the names of all those who test positive for the virus so that partners could be traced. In New York, attempts by the city's former health commissioner to trace contacts of HIV-positive people have met with strong resistance from both gays and civil libertarians.

Since being HIV positive essentially means that one is either homosexually active, an illegal drug-user, or a sexual partner of a drug-user, the employment, housing, and insurability of HIV-positive people are subject to discrimination when their identities and social profiles become known through blood testing. Despite congressional bills barring discrimination, confidentiality of test results has never been absolutely guaranteed. Nor have the civil rights of homosexuals. More important, testing, tracing, and quarantining have less to do with AIDS prevention than with politically isolating, punishing, and intimidating gays.

There is another equally important variation of this testing issue that leaves at least the gay public confused. It has to do with whether community-based initiatives should recommend policy. In New York, this issue involved deciding if GMHC should recommend testing as a matter of course for all individuals perceived to be at risk. The argument in favor is that early detection can lead to early treatment. Supported by San Francisco's Project Inform, it had originally met with much resistance in New York, mostly because AZT (azidothimidine), the first approved treatment for containing HIV, is not tolerated well by many and is thought to be as dangerous and harmful as the disease itself.[2] AZT's effectiveness among all HIV populations had been brought into question and only became confirmed in November 1991, only to be devalued again in June 1992.

By 1988, with a state law in place protecting HIV antibody test confidentiality and the demonstrated efficacy of early intervention with AZT therapy, GMHC had no choice but to advise community members to determine their HIV status. To do this advising effectively, volunteers counsel hotline callers and supply them with reassuring information and referrals. GMHC holds rap sessions with the worried well and helps individuals interpret results, often referring them to sympathetic and knowledgeable doctors.

From the very beginning, one of GMHC's primary functions was to separate fact and science from fiction and homophobia. If particular behaviors by gays, bisexuals, drug-users, and drug-users' sexual partners put them at high risk for AIDS, then these populations need more targeted and accurate information. And there is no consensus about what these behaviors, other than anal intercourse, are. The certainty of transmission through unprotected oral sex has not yet been clearly established. Many experts feel that one exposure may not be enough to cause AIDS or even allow for effective transmission of the virus.

While heterosexual fear is exaggerated and misplaced, panic has a political function and serves two distinct purposes: (1) It permits heterosexual concern and involvement to develop and (2) it fuels the eventual desexualization of personal relations for anyone sexually active outside of monogamous marriage. Gays have survived this latest attempt at sexual "neuterization" through the adaptation and popularization of safer-sex techniques. Heterosexuals are only now attempting the same. Like gays, they are hampered by the same political morality that separates nonmarital sexuality from holiness. This anti-sex morality of government and the religious Right is evidenced in the debate over condom use versus abstinence as the more proper, rather than the more practical and humane, way of preventing AIDS.

The issue of abstinence is tied up with social control. It directs sexual activity into reproduction and marriage as if celebrating and enjoying the body for its own pleasure is wrong and sinful. Sexuality and sensuality are essential to

1

life and living ~~and are a free~~, natural, and personal gift. ~~Why limit~~ their exercise and expression to married heterosexuals?

For gays, the Reagan-Bush AIDS policy is as highly political as it is moralistic. It is thus very dangerous and misleading. In the words of Silin (1987:34):

> Can we really feel safe when President Reagan proclaims that all AIDS education must be done in the context of fidelity, monogamy, and the family, and when Centers for Disease Control guidelines repeatedly inform us that we should not have sex with "HIV-infected individuals"? Leaving aside for the moment the issues of fidelity and monogamy, I am sure that Reagan is not referring to the kind of families in which many of us live, nor can it be seen as anything but homophobic to suggest avoiding sex with "HIV-infected" people to a community where seropositivity rates may run as high as 70 percent in some parts of the country.

This is why AIDS is the "medical-political-moral" question of the century. At GMHC, AIDS creates its own social and political economy around the question of what must be done as a community of people to meet human needs. GMHC stands out in that it asks a fundamentally new question. In this sense, it goes beyond the concerns of organized community initiatives that grow and change and respond to parameters defined only by hostile or indifferent governmental agencies. When stressing (in the broadest sense) community needs, GMHC stays close to its mission and own sacred source, the community.

The Political Economy of GMHC and ACT-UP

Not only is GMHC able to bring together a disparate group of volunteers and PWAs to work on a common project within a formal setting, but it does so, seemingly effortlessly, by embracing AIDS and being identified with the community. GMHC offers an environment for the community to coalesce its commitment to service. The AIDS Coalition to Unleash Power (ACT-UP), in contrast, takes a decidedly aggressive posture to protect gay interests and keep them independent of government entanglements in the event that community leaders and representatives like those at GMHC become too complacent or co-opted.

Coming after GMHC, ACT-UP understands the politics of AIDS from a different, albeit more traditional, perspective, as something separate from economics in the broader collective or societal sense. ACT-UP, however, is effective only within a discriminatory system and only in a way that disrupts rather than replaces sexist, racist, and class biases in health delivery, medical research, and other areas of concern. In other words, in seeking citizen entitlements in an elitist system with purposely limited resources, ACT-UP doesn't directly challenge the fundamental inequities inherent in our for-profit scientific and health care systems, nor does GMHC.

This arrangement, wherein the entire medical and health professions pit one group against another to reward competitive inefficiency for private or personal gain, is left unquestioned. While they get attention and are dramatic, ACT-UP's strategies maintain the system. As exemplified in a recent news report by Kolata (1990b:A1) that an AIDS treatment was delayed for months (because professional considerations were thought more important than the collective needs of PWAs), this system generally works against the common good.

"[AIDS] battles," writes Byron (1991:26),

> pit the sick against the dying in a fight over money. Scientists and doctors, for example, are in a fierce competition for limited research funding: the scientists are focused on long-range goals to stop HIV with the development of antiviral drugs and a vaccine, while doctors are desperate for ways to treat people already infected. But President Bush and the Congress—which will spend a projected $800 billion on the S&L crisis and $2.2 billion a month in the Persian Gulf—have capped NIAID's [National Institute of Allergies and Infectious Diseases] AIDS research funding at $432.6 million and NCI's [National Cancer Institute] at $161 million for fiscal year 1991.

In the model of transformation, greed like this leads to defamation by turning research into property that can be negotiated for private gain or profit and common tax money into the machinery of war in the interests of corporate entities. This fragmentation leads to the actual death of real persons in the community.

In vain, ACT-UP's raison d'être is to ask why after ten years into an epidemic only one toxic drug had been approved for treatment. The organization stops at nothing in search of both an explanation and a cure. While GMHC's agenda and strategies as an agency appear mild by comparison, it remains the context within which the volunteer goes about creating an autonomous jurisdiction (a liberated zone) in which the work of nurturing and healing a dying people (the necessary work in AIDS) takes place. This is fundamentally political and radical because GMHC is holding together the fabric of life—human connections—for a whole endangered community and empowering it at the same time.

Given the prevailing moral meaning of AIDS (and its deeper meaning for gays), to force an interior change of attitudes and feelings about the self and the community is the ultimate political statement, not angry street demonstrations directed at institutions. Organizations can never be objective and fair because they represent self-perpetuating bureaucratic interests. Confrontational politics bring organizations into the politics of incoherence. They end up demanding solutions from without, in system-maintaining accommodation.

This is not to say that a cure for AIDS is not to be found in science or that researchers should not be pressured to do so. Rather, it is to suggest that we, in the meantime, must try to preserve and transform community in a way that transcends instrumentality so that, unlike in the medical/health profession, people are not processed as abstractions but are cared for with compassion.

In a sense, ACT-UP and GMHC are two players in a single drama, challenging each other in a continuous dialectic between science and human faith, politics and service, and the rational and affective. The big difference is not that GMHC can get the additional public funding that it increasingly seems to want while ACT-UP can't but that its volunteers remain in the service of transformation by bearing witness in a way that transforms and reconstructs social arrangements and institutional relations.

ACT-UP and GMHC are asking different questions. GMHC is attempting to build community as an alternative to the world of powerful fragments that feed upon each other at the expense of the poor and disinherited. ACT-UP takes this healed community energy and puts it to immediate and practical use, but within prevailing social arrangements. It uses rather than creates community.

In a very real sense, both the government and the gay community have something to gain from the present arrangement and agenda. The government's acceding to ACT-UP demands "cools out" the public and makes it appear that something is being done or even that gays have some power. Conversely, Republican party rhetoric on community self-help becomes validated. As an organization, GMHC delivers a service that impersonal government agencies could not and would not do.

The Political Economy of AIDS Research/Programming

Scientists and academics who are interested in AIDS suffer from the same homophobia that surrounds virtually any and all social-order studies of gay life. This homophobia is evident in contemporary efforts to control HIV fulmination in safer-sex education/prevention programs that depend more on natural science information and psychological assumptions than on an informed sociological perspective. This emphasis is troublesome because it obscures and underplays the social origins of AIDS in homophobic and racist discrimination. Today, gays are studied through the lens of AIDS with the focus on how homosexuality, not homophobia, causes the disease to spread. In this context, homosexuality needs to be controlled and reeroticized so that "sexually compulsive" gays can cease having unsafe sex. Maladaptive behavior is a psychological aberration because it is individually suicidal. It is not considered a problem rooted in social structure and low self-esteem even though it is destructive of community, depoliticizing, and instrumental in nature.

In the political economy of the 1980s and 1990s, programs offering individual therapy as solutions to social problems are both fundable and politically neutralizing. Such strategies are also easily measurable and understandable if not manageable. They also fit the personal experiences and ideologies of safer-sex program planners. These psychologists consider a transformation in personal relationships neither therapeutic nor useful. They do not see holistic relations as erotic, since "hot" though safe sex is thought of as the carrot that attracts gay men to undergo "reform" and remain that way. Encouraging safer, yet continually instrumental, sexual activities, thus, would be acceptable. For these reasons, changing the structural relations and conditions that lead to maladaptive behavior by creating community are normally passed over (even in gay-oriented safer-sex programs) in favor of individual behavior modification.

Government-supported AIDS education/prevention programs generally encourage depersonalized sexual behavior to continue unabated. Such behavior is thought to be popular, is tolerated because it tests the boundaries of sexual freedom, and is assumed more amenable to control because it is done by individuals. Because safer-sex programs depend on psychological intervention, they can be funded easily because they are less threatening politically to federal and state officials who have been pressured to do something practical about AIDS.

However, instrumental sexual activity, safe or otherwise, is always problematic to mental, spiritual, and now physical health. In state-supported programs, homosexuals (unlike heterosexuals) continue to be primarily defined by dysfunctional sexual activities. By influencing the subjective sexual activity of individuals, these projects, unawares, reveal homophobic conceptions of gayness. They reinforce gay stereotypes and celebrate a noncontextual gay eros that, in the long run, is destructive of community. In this sense, all AIDS education is political and needs to be so acknowledged, but in a way that empowers and serves the common interest.

From the perspective of community, what really matter are the quality and meaning of gay relations, not their quantity or mode of expression, as important as these might now be. Even though unsafe sex during AIDS is so terribly destructive, the continuation of maladaptive sexual behavior is also harmful because it depersonalizes relationships and has a negative impact on individual psychologies and community integration. Unsafe sex is maladaptive not only because it has an impact on communal life and health but because it is instrumental, springs from alienated sources, and retards the politicization process. Behavior is maladaptive, dangerous, and dysfunctional when it reinforces self-rejection and communal annihilation.

Yet if AIDS were not sexually transmitted, this masculinist or patriarchal sexuality would not ever be considered problematic, although the texture of gay relations is always affected negatively by impersonality. Referring to alienated gay male sexuality, Rosemary Kuropat (1989:17) writes: "Indeed, the gay movement has rarely been concerned with issues larger than the right (and the means and venues) of gay men to engage in the sex act. An exclusionary AIDS politics simply continues this sexcentricity; never in the twenty years since Stonewall has any force so completely intruded upon that right as has HIV."

In effect, safer-sex proponents operate conservatively rather than inventively in the approach, goals, and techniques they propose, such as eroticizing condom use. By devising solutions that promote safer sexual practices but that leave instrumental relations untouched, gay sexual activity will remain shaped by the heterosexist social order. The notion that "gay" means only furtive sexual activity is left unchallenged. Individual gay identities are ignored in favor of a harmful collective stereotype, which is then celebrated.

These programs pay little attention to the long-term consequences on community integrity of stressing methods of achieving safer sex that fit the political economy of government health agencies. These agencies believe that pathology primarily resides or emanates in individuals and is not the result of social arrangements. If an illness like AIDS, however, is defined as having social roots and collective consequences, it would be better to tie the personal interest to the collective need because such links are empowering.

Attempting to change gay male sexual behavior through sexual reconditioning leaves psychic and social fragmentation (the ultimate source of maladaptive behavior) intact. It serves the interests of the political majority, who see gays as sinful, deviant, and sexually compulsive. For them, engaging in unsafe sex becomes a treatable, individual distortion that leaves the social forces shaping behavior both blameless and in control. Actually, when cleavages between the self and the community are re-created, responsible sexual activity becomes less likely. Many individuals oppressed by homophobic conditions often take their anger and frustrations out on each other, especially when that which they hold in common (their homosexuality) is defined as illicit, problem causing, and troublesome.

Maladaptive sexual behavior is a response to social exclusion and reflects psychic and emotional fragmentation. It is the result of the institutional restrictions on holistic relations among men and between men and women that spring from sexism. Given the intertwining of religious and cultural values, masculinist gay sexual expectations are the product of the same authoritarian religious ideologies and structures that consistently deny the validity of women's experience. As Irvine notes, the reification of gender and sexual norms, and the stigmatization of difference are serious endeavors that maintain a social hierarchy of power. In patriarchal culture, the binary opposition of male and female forms the basis of the central organizing hierarchy. Phallocentrism enforces the notion of woman as deficient because of her lack of a penis. Similarly sexual differences like homosexuality, transsexualism, or transvestism are considered deviations that pose a treat to the heterosexual imperative. (Irvine 1990:20–21)

There is an important politic involved, then, in the attempt to redefine AIDS causation/prevention in terms of individual maladaptive behavior or even "collective life-style madness" rather than as a social-class or structural issue. At the very least, it "cools out" individual gays and affects community solidarity and gay political behavior.[3] Psychological solutions actually support dominant political ideologies and discriminatory social arrangements by not encouraging healthier sexual behavior through the cementing of psychic and social connections. By manipulating homoeroticism, present prevention programs make it safe to go on fragmenting social and sexual relations.

Working with individuals in rationalized, educational programs can only be done dispassionately and thus only further split the community by isolating sex from the affective. Indeed, safer-sex education programs assume that knowledge by itself leads to change even in something as emotional, personal, and self-defining as sexuality. Abstinence based on fear, likewise, cripples politically by denying feelings and connections to ourselves through others as valid sources of knowledge.

Even if possible, teaching grown men to eroticize the male body differently than what is customary would be useful only in the short run and would do nothing to empower the community. The strategies used to encourage safer sex are actually guilt producing and limit community integration, gay self-acceptance, and healthy interpersonal relations. The joy and pleasure of responsible and authentic self-discovery through connections are ignored as goals. This is why communalization is so important.

Community as Therapy

When guilt, sex, stigma, fear, and the God of orthodox religion are forced on an individual separated from community, the stage is set for the development of maladaptive social and destructive sexual behavior. Under these circumstances, both volunteerism and empowerment become impossible and dysfunctional sexual activities that confirm and validate a disattached individual's negative feelings of self-worth are likely to increase. As psychotherapist William Wedin (1984c) indicates, internalized homophobia (living away from and in opposition to community) is often expressed as a desire for anonymous sex, which is directly related to the spread of AIDS.

Frequently, choosing multiple and anonymous sex partners for instrumental purposes is a function of low self-esteem. "That's true of everybody, heterosexual and homosexual," says William Shattls, a psychotherapist with many homosexual and gay patients (Rabinowitz 1990:107). "Sex is tied up with their identity; to give it up is narcissistic injury. But choosing to do what their feelings dictate over what they know is good for them ends up causing the torments of hell." Dysfunctional sexual behavior during AIDS indicates ambiguity about the value of life and the depth and beauty of personalizing relationships.

According to *The Wellness Letter* of the University of California at Berkeley (Vol. 6:3 [1989]), "optimism and a sense of control over life's events seem to contribute to health, well-being, and longevity." These attributes are precisely what identification with or participation in the life of a community achieves and what happens at GMHC. Nearly 23 percent of our survey respondents strongly agreed that they volunteered to change their feeling of impotence regarding AIDS "by doing something for others" and 29 percent agreed that this was generally true for them as well. Fifty percent indicated that they became more self-assertive after they began volunteering and 75 percent said that their sense of self-worth increased as a result of their work on behalf of PWAs. In terms of safer sex, a full 40 percent indicated that volunteering itself helped "change their sexual behavior for the better." In effect, these individuals became empowered because they were helping others in need. In terms of gay/AIDS volunteerism at GMHC, the data indicated that when voluntary helpers or carepartners sense their beneficial effects on others, their psychological health is enhanced because feelings of helplessness and depression are diminished and replaced by a sense of self-worth, satisfaction, and even exhilaration.

These psychological benefits are important because identification with the community became synonymous with illness and death and needs to be redefined as life-giving. Isolation is increased and compounded when sexual activity is surrounded by fear and instrumentality. In AIDS, trust (the basis of relationships that have feelings attached to them) is violated and the experience of and the desire for community become suspect.

The solution to maladaptive behavior in general, then, lies in the canceling of guilt, shame, and fear about same-sexing. This is done by first choosing to be identified with the gay community, identifying with the larger collectivity, affirming personhood, and then bearing witness to others, especially PWAs who are experienced as extensions of the self. A community can thus lay positive claim to itself. Unlike with heterosexual AIDS, the social fabric of the gay community has been attacked, its basis for being undermined by AIDS. It cannot be restored as a sacred or valid source of identity through the teaching of safer-sex techniques that counter "sexual compulsiveness" as a psychological deficiency. To be contained, AIDS requires a fundamental reordering of relationships, so that persons no longer remain unknown to one another.

What is important is not the fact that anonymity often aggravates the spread of AIDS but that there can be neither a life-giving and empowered gay community nor positive personal identity when impersonality and individual need color social and sexual interactions. Homophobia, not sexual compulsiveness, prevents people from discovering their own inner, sacred sources and hinders their identification with the collectivity that their interests should be connected to.

In effect, when gays practice unsafe sex, they are acting homophobically; the unsafe sexual behavior becomes an anti-gay, anti-human act, not just an individual pathology. This attitude needs to be disestablished because it hinders public, political action and thereby retards a just and lasting solution to AIDS fulmination and the question of gay social, political, and medical entitlements. "You're talking about a victim here," notes Shattls (Rabinowitz 1990:140), "about men who are the products of cultural values that say it is not okay to be a homosexual. This is a homophobic culture." For him, "it's not surprising when someone who's grown up learning to hide and despise his sexual feelings goes out and behaves self-destructively." Yet because stressing only instrumental safer-sex practices in AIDS prevention hinders communalization, this emphasis will ultimately result in a return to the behavior and conditions that reigned before AIDS, however collectively dysfunctional they are.

Changing individual behavior, rather than the conditions out of which both apolitical and maladaptive sexual behavior spring, therefore, reinforces the structural sources of violence already present against the gay psyche. Emphasizing individual rights and needs, safe-sex educators and government funding agencies see the erotic desires of individuals as superior to the needs of the larger collectivity. However, because the gay community suffers more as a result of AIDS than do individual actors, HIV transmission needs to be controlled collectively for the sake of the common good.

AIDS is very much a gay disease, if not just physically then certainly socially and spiritually. "More precisely," notes Denneny (1990:16), "an epidemic is the occurrence of death as a social event." When this happens, "both the individual *and the community* are threatened with irreparable loss" (italics added). AIDS prevention can take place only with the deinstitutionalization of homophobia, the achievement of which requires political action by the community for the community. The bonds of affective community are established when the shared or common identity is accepted as positive, when people identify and feel a part of a larger whole, and when individuals see their future tied up with the fate of their group. This is why and how volunteerism heals the scars and compounded loneliness of both AIDS and self-rejection.

7

Who Volunteers: Minority Volunteerism and GMHC

AS A CITIZEN EXPECTATION, American volunteerism is rooted in history and culture. Yet the specific question of "who volunteers" in AIDS appears more related to "why people volunteer" and not to some cultural or social norm. This narrow question, however, leaves unattended different volunteering rates by social class, education, race, gender, and even sexual orientation. These different rates are especially important since HIV infection crosses several social boundaries while volunteers in AIDS generally do not.

If we are not certain why people do or do not volunteer for a cause, we are equally as uncertain as to what keeps them in volunteer organizations. Even the variables used to predict who will volunteer do not seem to indicate who will stay a volunteer over time. AIDS volunteerism burnout is a real phenomenon, occurring after about nine months of service. After a brief respite, AIDS volunteers return for a few more months of work but often do tasks other than direct carepartnering.

AIDS touches, in different degrees, white heterosexual males, gay males, African-Americans, Latinos, lesbians, hemophiliacs, children, and heterosexual women. There are structural and historical reasons why these populations do not readily mix socially, and now organizationally, during this time of AIDS. There are grounds for GMHC's demographic profile other than its identity and gay white male corporate culture that explain the large absence of nongay volunteers there or in AIDS care generally.

Racism in the gay community mirrors that of the broader society and is no less evident, although it often reflects a class bias rather than an ethnic one. Even a casual stroll down Christopher Street reveals that the next generation of gay men and lesbians in New York will be black and Latino, even Asian, should enough of them survive AIDS. Few, if any, gay organizations are actively seeking minority members and none have cultivated minority leaders as a matter of policy except the group "Men of All Colors Together." Only the

1987 gay and lesbian mobilization in Washington and New York's Gay Pride Week celebration have had significant and celebrated input by women.

The enormous gap in gay organizational continuity caused by the death of a generation of gay men is exacerbated not only by gender and racial issues but also by social class differences and by the various agendas each gay, female, and minority constituency wants addressed at GMHC.

That gays volunteer in AIDS is not surprising. But while we do know that women and minority Americans often volunteer informally, we do not know how sexual orientation affects rates and reasons for volunteering. Nor do we know the type of organizations in which they participate or the specific projects undertaken. Sexuality might cut across gender and racial differences, with gay blacks, Latinos, and lesbian women belonging to organizations ignored by social researchers. Gay contributions to the nonprofit sector are equally overlooked because volunteers are not asked about their sexual preference.

Women Volunteers

To understand the uniqueness and oddity of gay male volunteerism, it is necessary to compare it to that of other populations traditionally recognized as volunteer sources and, tragically, now touched by AIDS as well. Of all minority groups, only women are generally recognized as central to the volunteer enterprise. Yet the most notable characteristic of both the public and non-profit sector is that while women far outnumber men in nonprofit jobs, they earn even less money than they would in the for-profit sector. Although two-thirds of the staffs in nonprofit institutions are women, and there are greater numbers of women on the boards of human service and "expressive" agencies, men usually dominate and order these voluntary organizations to their values and interests.

Men control the directing boards of most service agencies (especially those that have large budgets), perform instrumental functions, and are regarded as vital to the community. "The most prestigious posts in nonprofit organizations," notes Odendahl (1990:117), "are less available to women, even those with old money."

Women are believed to possess qualities of instinct, intuition, and demeanor that make them appear, notes Chambers (1985:10–11), "more adept at softening the hearts of the poor and at leading those who had strayed from the path of virtue back to the way of righteousness." This heterosexist perception helps shape women's roles and strategies of adaptation to volunteer work and organizations. Nowadays, notable contributions by women are institutionalized in the social worker role; these women thus can gain respect as professionals. For decades, however, feminist women were free to develop and manage their own agendas professionally, free of male interference.

A study of involvement with voluntary fund-raising activities for philanthropic organizations showed not only that the men and women differed in their approaches to fund-raising (men borrowed methods from business whereas women relied more on the "manipulation" of personal relationships) but also that philanthropic work functioned as a career and major outlet for women's energies and talents. Men apparently had no vested interest (or need) in volunteerism.

Despite their skills and success, moreover, many women underplay their contributions because they have internalized the negative stereotypes about using social events as a forum for organizing activities and generating interest in a problem. Women use informal, not manipulative or rationalized, social networks. The work they do thus remains invisible and underevaluated because it remains hidden behind the facade of "party giving."

Early biases against women in public service or professional roles, however, unintentionally motivated women to capitalize on and utilize their own talents and connections to achieve collective ends. This seems to be especially true for urban married women of the upper middle class. Working-class women, having fewer options and less time and energy, tend to be limited to a narrow domestic housekeeping role and might not value participation in impersonal voluntary associations. Upper-class women, however, are expected to be both philanthropic and charitable, not only with money but with their time.

This class difference has to be understood within the context of sexist discrimination as well as the natural helping networks characteristic of women and other disadvantaged groups generally. These networks keep women's contributions, if not their altruism, uncelebrated. Personal contact groups render help and assistance informally and spontaneously rather than in, and through, formal, male-dominated associations and protocols.

Generally, the type of organization a woman volunteers for is determined by her family's status and the stage in the family life cycle she occupies. Frequently, many women belong to voluntary associations for purposes of impression and status management. In terms of class differences in volunteering, there are variations in expectations, settings, and values offered as explanations. As class-related hostility, anxiety, frustration, and anomie increase, women are less likely to volunteer. According to Odendahl (1990:117), however, women frequently serve "as a particularly important means of entree for self-made husbands into cultured society." As a rule, women have a less difficult time bridging class barriers because they "enter higher circles at a lower level."

The better educated a woman is and the higher her social class, the more likely it is that her volunteering takes on male characteristics, that is, becomes more overtly political, more instrumental, and more committed to the administrative goals of the sponsoring organization. These gender differences in participation result partly from structural elements in the family life cycle and from discrimination, although they may also result from differential male and female socialization.

Male commentators on women's networking systems tend to see them rooted in frustration and the need to socialize to share common experiences, despite their otherwise stated objectives. Minnis (1951:20) explains:

> The need to be on the center of stage sometime in her life, the need to be taken seriously, the desire to use talents developed in youth and now lying fallow, a strong wish to aid in a world of displacement and conflict, and a need of outlet for energies untapped at middle age—all these factors may make participation in a women's organization seem to be a stabilizing solution.

Researchers think that women involved in urban political work become involved initially for their own benefit, such as to keep busy or to obtain satisfaction from acquiring new skills. After women with resources have had many years of volunteer experience, their motivations for involvement supposedly shift to professional growth and education. Of particular significance is the fact that the vast majority of women volunteers obtain out-of-home employment within five years, which indicates that their volunteering is an opportunity for further advancement.

Male organizational models stressing instrumental goals and motivations clearly do not apply in the case of those women who simply may prefer to be with one another out of attraction, much like gay men do. Evidently, it is rarely considered that women are ever motivated to volunteer out of charity, altruism, moral considerations, or political concerns in general, that they want to nurture or show compassion, or that they want to exercise managerial capacities. Lesbians and feminists have certainly developed organizations that are efficient and timely and that depend on scores of volunteers with ideological rather than social concerns.

The Women at GMHC

There are now over 300 women at GMHC, but in 1986, when the survey research was conducted, there were only 172, at least 90 percent of whom were volunteers delivering direct services, the remainder being on staff. At that time, only about 17 percent of GMHC's staff and volunteers were not gay white men. It is for this reason and the fact that American AIDS was and still is disproportionately a gay male disease that this report concentrates on gay male volunteers. This fact makes the dedication and commitment of GMHC's women volunteers and staff even more remarkable.

The "AIDS virus" has been associated directly with gay male sexuality rather than with women per se. This perception is, of course, dangerous and erroneous since women are being infected by bisexual and intravenous drug-using men in ever-increasing numbers. This partially explains why the women at GMHC have identified with a problem and constituency normally assumed not their own. Since they are not at risk sexually from gay men as such, it is surprising, indeed encouraging, that their commitment is so strong, if not in numbers then in perseverance and determination.

GMHC's women volunteers, virtually all of whom personally know gay men and People with AIDS socially, want to do something to help their friends, while male volunteers generally see AIDS in larger political and communal terms. As should be the case, the women of GMHC are applauded and celebrated for their support. They perform numerous and significant, if not profound, acts of kindness.

At GMHC, women are in various positions of authority, from president of the board of directors (1989–1990) to heads of departments, often acting as spokespersons for the agency. They are also volunteers, staff, managers, educators, and advisers. Like their male counterparts at GMHC, they are gay identified though not necessarily lesbian. They are particularly humanitarian and important actors in AIDS because they nurture outcasts. Their presence and availability to the men is remarkably healing, if not enlightening.

While their positions at the agency are based on their skills, it is also true that for many women their social-class connections informally (and tremendously) help GMHC. As in all philanthropic organizations, it is often the social connections of the women that has prompted successful fund-raising. In AIDS, this allows GMHC to appeal to the heterosexual male establishment.[1] Ordinarily, however, like the men, most are motivated by humanitarian instincts to help a specific constituency they feel personally connected to. GMHC veteran volunteer and board member Barbara Grande le Vine (1990:5) explains her involvement in GMHC this way:

> Major illness was almost unknown in my life. So was volunteering for anything. I had been trained to be paid for my efforts. I'm a professional model and the slick fashion world where emphasis is placed on the relatively unimportant was not the breeding ground for serious volunteer efforts. ...
>
> The immediate cause for my involvement was a *Newsweek* cover story in 1983, "Gay America in Transition," that explored society's attitude toward AIDS. What resonated for me was the pain, fear, rejection, and isolation that persons with AIDS were suffering—emotions with which I strongly identify.
>
> I still hold vivid memories of the first months at GMHC. I remember the orientation interview in GMHC's first home, a ramshackle Chelsea brownstone, where I was encouraged to try crisis intervention. I remember my apprehension, wondering why I was seeking added responsibility and commitment. I remember

signing on as "a pair of hands" while waiting for crisis training—answering phones, collating and filing, serving refreshments at meetings—learning more about the organization. I remember then feeling a connection among sensitive people who quickly became an extended family to each other and to Persons with AIDS.

While men and women alike share the same tasks and objectives, women remain tangential, somewhat removed because of GMHC's central character as a gay male agency. As always, they are serving the needs of men. That they are doing an especially good deed by their willingness to give witness to people socially distinct from themselves and believed indifferent to them is not the point. Rather, it is the fact that they, like gays, are "wounded" healers in a cause that has no friends—only other gays.

Guggenbuhl-Craig (1971) believes that women are both allies of the oppressed and natural healers. Yet because their relationship to AIDS, or at least to gay AIDS, is qualitatively different from that of gay males, the political significance of their volunteerism is less salient for them. In terms of coalition building, however, it is an important first step.

Until quite recently, the energies of the women at GMHC were not typically directed at broadening women's understanding of AIDS or, for that matter, any sexually transmitted disease within a feminist context. Because of GMHC's inherent bias, they were adjuncts and supporters of the men's concerns about AIDS. Given the demographics of AIDS and the absence of pressure to do otherwise, it was only from 1987 on that the unique dilemma and relationship of women to AIDS has been recognized either nationally or at GMHC and program adjustments made accordingly. Women's perspectives and experiences are increasingly influencing GMHC policy at about the same time that the agency becomes more dependent on their support and HIV infectees become less gay male in numbers.

More than anything else, it is GMHC's name that accounts for its demographic character, which is now not only part of public identity and culture but also largely accounts for its success and relevance. Unwittingly, blacks, Latinos, and women may stay away from GMHC because AIDS was not presented as their issue; GMHC implies, by its very name, that it isn't.

The growing lesbian interest in AIDS is now justified by the growing need to defend homosexual civil rights generally and by the fact that lesbians and gays are often interactive and dependent on one another because they share social space and social networks, even some institutions. Lesbians are also at risk of AIDS because of drug use and bisexuality and need a home someplace, if not at GMHC, which recently inaugurated a "lesbian AIDS project." In any case, gay men and lesbians are often very good friends, share concerns, and are involved in each others' lives. It is not important politically that lesbians are now befriending gay men; it is important that men (gay or otherwise) would hardly have responded to AIDS had it somehow been a women's disease.

While the sample was overwhelmingly random in my 1986 survey, I made every effort to include women as respondents since they were the largest "minority" at GMHC. While twenty-one of the twenty-nine women respondents indicated that they were heterosexual, another four identified themselves as bisexual. My daily experience of the organization indicates that this is a valid ratio, even though there is an increasing number of heterosexual women who are volunteering and on staff.[2] This commingling of gay men and straight women is a reflection of a long-term alliance. Likewise, the absence of heterosexual men tells us something about traditional sexist hostility toward gays.

Since the women of GMHC are a minority within a minority, it is not necessary to single them out for special scrutiny. Moreover, preliminary reviews of their responses indicated that they varied little, if any, from the gay males in either the conscious motives for volunteering, their interpretation of AIDS, or what they hoped to accomplish. They were politically astute and more likely than not indicated concern that they too were at risk.

As with the black and Latino populations, it is important to remember that women's story in volunteerism was written when sexism was fashionable and racism and homophobia taken for granted. There is simply no feminist or liberated sociology of minority (women, blacks, Latinos) and gay volunteerism over time.

African-American and Latino Volunteerism

Understanding racial differences in volunteering is not an easy task because of class and ethnic biases. Given the social organization of American society, the whole phenomenon of volunteerism is seen as functional only when it is institutionalized. Formal organization makes volunteerism conscious and purposeful, hence, legitimate, if not respectable. An organized agency effort is useful for recognition and hence for funding purposes. As previously indicated, formal organizations are very different from what Collins and Pancoast (1976) identify as "natural networks"—the informal helping networks generally used by women and poor people living in community.

AIDS volunteerism is less attractive for African-Americans because it is done, for the most part, in and through formal organizations. African-Americans rely on one another when in need of assistance and therefore are unrecognized as doing volunteer work, especially if mutual help is expected. They are also underrepresented in voluntary organizations because of class and cultural differences. Minority AIDS volunteerism remains difficult and different because of the stigmatized ways AIDS is spread and because of who specifically is at risk in these populations (bisexuals, gays, drug-users and their partners). Blacks do help each other and join voluntary organizations, but they frequently do so in informal ways and in nonwhite settings, which biased researchers ignore.

While the agendas of many African-American organizations evolve around specific civil rights questions, a substantial amount of black energy is also spent volunteering on the local level, primarily in churches, in areas of communal concern. Participants in these informal helping networks usually are of the same or similar socioeconomic class, and the motivation for helping appears to be friendship, respect, and the implementation of communal values. Moreover, these informal systems normally carry with them the expectation of reciprocity.

Given these interpretations of black voluntary participation, it is quite possible that black involvement in mainstream American organizations is hindered by exclusionist practices, social distancing, and unaggressive or biased recruitment procedures. It is more likely, however, that black volunteerism is also affected by organizational typologies and goals as well as styles of administration.

Years ago, Yearwood and Weinberg (1979:313) noted that the reason black churches can so readily provide social services is that "their members prefer to deal with their brethren rather than with the personnel of impersonal public bureaucracies." Elsewhere, Yearwood (1976:120) quotes a black pastor:

> These people who are semi-illiterate or illiterate, they feel more at ease with the member of the church whom they know and trust, who maybe will have more time and patience to deal with them, rather than someone from the agency who has to go right by the rule, and ... they don't take time to deal with each person ... they have to process people. So these people feel better with somebody from the church, they have a better rapport with them. They can open up, they won't be laughed at if they can't read; if they don't understand they take the time to sit down and explain it to them. It makes a difference.

In the supposed absence of formal agency structures, African-Americans appear less involved in voluntary work. They are, however, deeply involved in helping networks. Yet Drake and Clayton (1945), in their landmark study of Chicago's black community, claimed that there is almost no participation among the lower classes, which they characterized as generally disorganized. For them, club activity among "Negroes" is associated with above-average educational attainment and economic status. In reality, participating in political and voluntary activity is widespread among poorer blacks when a community project is involved. Viewed through an ethnic community model, black organizational volunteerism is actually quite high.

Guterbock and London (1983:440) claim that ethnicity explains these differences in volunteerism. Basically, "race and class-conscious blacks participate to excess as a positive means of striving for social changes that could benefit the whole black community." This statement supports the view that among blacks, socioeconomic status is related to both political activity and voluntary association membership.

Like their white counterparts, African-Americans see their activity as community service. Drake and Clayton (1945:662) were the first to identify black volunteerism as both rewarding *and* socially expected—a fact that still rings true. They write:

> Throughout the world of the [Negro] middle class "right connections" are stressed, and this otherwise sprawling group of people with diverse incomes and occupations is given cohesiveness by an intimate and complex web of voluntary associations. These constitute the "markets" by which individuals symbolize their aspirations and the position they have attained in the competitive struggle to get ahead. They provide occasions upon which a middle class person can display his other symbols, such as clothing and correct public behavior, among people who, like himself, prize them. Middle class organizations put the accent on "front," respectability, civic responsibility of a sort and conventional recreation. Some of these organizations, too, become the means by which middle class people "on the rise" come into contact "above" them socially and by which mobile lower class individuals can rise from the class below.

As with other mobile ethnic groups, many formal African-American organizations are concerned with political issues and draw their staff and financial support essentially from the better-educated classes. These organizations, however, are generally supported by all classes, especially if their issues are relevant to the poorer classes, as, for example, in the black civil rights movement. What is important is how black middle-class respectability interferes with the genesis of black concern about AIDS.

These class biases are also central to understanding the Latino response to AIDS. While there is some evidence that Mexican-Americans have relatively high rates of participation in church and school organizations, there are no large-scale studies of Latino volunteerism in general from which we can generalize. Even so, Mexican-Americans' response to AIDS would inevitably be handicapped by an overall lack of resources, trained personnel, and openness to their involvement by institutionalized AIDS service providers.

More recently and despite grinding poverty, however, Latinos have formed many local and national AIDS organizations. They now can counter their own misinformation and fear of AIDS. Their cultural reticence about sexual matters and resistance to the impersonal deliverance of services by outsiders are real barriers to an effective Latino AIDS mobilization. High levels of drug use and underemployment among those most at risk do not usually or easily facilitate organizational participation, nor does the suppression of out-of-the-closet homosexuality.

African-Americans and Latinos at GMHC

Despite these class and ethnic differences, all minority groups share certain general attributes and evolve their political strategies and ideologies. Yearwood and Weinberg (1979: 303) point out that the strategies used by gay and black civil rights organizations overlap in many ways:

> At first, these early organizations took the position that they could best gain their ends by maintaining a respectable, moderate, middle-class image. They were oriented toward working within the system to educate the public and to change the laws. The early leaders of both black and gay organizations were middle class in their perspectives. They dressed in suits and ties and appeared as "reasonable men."

While true (in result, not motive) at GMHC, the politics of AIDS and the advent of ACT-UP have taken much of the "refinement" out of AIDS protests. GMHC does, however, primarily offer gays an opportunity to redefine their self-image as healthy and useful. It gives individuals a chance to be part of a good people doing good things. Minority organizations, write Yearwood and Weinberg (1979:313), "appear to enhance their members' feelings of self-esteem by allowing them to discover and to develop previously unrealized talents and expertise." As with women's volunteerism, minority volunteerism is not born out of frustration, marginality, or class expectations alone but also out of pride, determination, and humanitarianism.

Despite the need, perhaps even the opportunity, there are relatively few native Spanish speakers and blacks either on staff or as volunteers at GMHC. However, GMHC initially had Latinos in positions of authority, as grant writers and fund-raisers and in programming like crisis intervention counseling. There is a myriad of reasons that explain Latino absence at GMHC, many explaining black absence as well.

To begin, there is the simple issue of homosexuality. Because gay life contrasts with black religiosity and Latino social attitudes and family expectations, identifying with AIDS or GMHC is problematic for these minorities. Add drug use as a mode of transmission and poverty, and the social distance between GMHC and the minority community grows larger.

To be sure, there exist interracial and interethnic gay mixing and a community group called "Men of All Colors Together" that promotes integration, but there are also segregated clubs, bars, and resort areas. This distancing is as much a result of income and education as race or ethnicity per se. It takes a lot of money to get to Fire Island, Provincetown, or the Hamptons, somewhat less to Jones Beach, and considerably less to Jacob Riis Park in Queens, New York, where black and Latino gays now attend in larger numbers.

Another telling explanation is the fact that poorer people are often less organized and less trusting of formal organizations. And the minority segments at risk of AIDS in New York are, to say the least, generally impoverished and disorganized. Couple this with the moral and class concerns of African-American churches and voluntary associations, and the plight of minority AIDS patients becomes even more desperate.

At GMHC, there is also the problem of white corporate culture as defined by affluent gay males. GMHC's ambience is quite astounding, if not notorious, for a community-based service organization. It is well housed, professionally staffed, and remarkably well appointed and designed for a twelve-year-old social service agency.[3] One could argue that it takes a lot of money or class, if not anglicized social refinement, to feel comfortable at GMHC.

But the most likely explanation for the minority absence at GMHC is the simple fact that the needs of the minority populations at risk of AIDS are different from those of gay men. While it is probably better all around that each constituency manage its own affairs (which they increasingly are doing), GMHC cannot be a full "AIDS community" without minority input. All GMHC can do is offer encouragement and considerable financial and advising support to nongay AIDS organizations that, fortunately, have grown in number in the past few years.

In Contrast: Gay/AIDS Volunteerism

It is the interchangeability of client and carepartner and the self with the communal (the subjective and objective) that are the most telling characteristics of both gay and AIDS volunteerism. Nearly 83 percent of the volunteers surveyed at GMHC in 1986 identified themselves as homosexual men, the remainder being primarily gay-supportive heterosexual women.[4] Because of depleting recruitment sources, this figure today is down to around 75 percent.

In AIDS work generally, it is still white, middle-class men who are doing what sociologists call "dirty work," labor considered less prestigious because it is often done for free by women, who are typically the bulk of volunteers nationwide. Seventy percent of the respondents in our 1986 study, for example, indicated that "they identified with People with AIDS," even though they did not think that they were infected or at particular risk themselves at that moment.

This remarkable act of kindness that gays have shown one another springs from connections made (in the margins by marginals) with outcasts even more feared and demeaned than themselves. As described by Kübler-Ross (1987), "collective altruism" of this type in AIDS refers to unlikely works of mercy and charity done against all expectations and odds by a community for rejected others seen as the extended self.

This emphasis on linkages among and between gays and PWAs is significant because it indicates high self-acceptance and the presence of community. This indication changes the nature and meaning of both altruism and volunteerism. In the traditional models of volunteerism as humanitarian work, gay/ AIDS volunteerism seems too practical because of its collective, group nature.

As will be discussed in Chapter 9, even if the "doing of good is not so much for the benefit of those to whom the good is done as it is for that of the doers," as Atwater and Robboy (1972:4) maintain, this does not undermine its altruistic value because "moral sensitivity" to the needs of similar others is quite common in character and produces meritorious results.[5] The operative words here are "similar others." Moral behavior often arises from connections made to a community rather than from detachment from it. Famed sociologist Pitirim Sorokin (1950:211) likewise sees altruism as a nurtured form of love, frequently reinforced by particularly meaningful personal experiences in the context of community.

"An altruistic person," write Atwater and Robboy (1972:5), is one who is "unusually open to identification with others' suffering." This type of cooperative charity is situation oriented and is focused on the solving of a problem, often presented in the form of an emergency. "The needy person is in some kind of distress, and the charitable actor 'automatically' cooperates by helping him get out of it" (p. 7). Unlike other forms of altruism, in cooperative charity the recipient is an active participant in reaching a solution and is not just a convenient object for the doing of good, as in normative charity. Altruism has limits, and gay/AIDS altruism is no exception. If anything, this limitation generated volunteerism in the first place, defines its character, and now affects GMHC's future development, identity, and relationship to both AIDS and the gay community.

And, thus, community is found in gay/AIDS volunteerism and is not found in minorities, where HIV festers among their subpopulations.[6] Hence the response to AIDS differs organizationally, although given the philanthropic history of women and minorities the differences would have occurred anyway. For whatever reasons, the collective consciousness of gays is retuned daily, especially now because of AIDS. One would think that the same would have occurred for minorities and women, but it hasn't even though women in both these groups are at high risk of infection for reasons of sex and race.

Unfortunately, class and life-style variations, personal and political ideologies, education, and other factors all fragment female and minority populations, making their interests less compatible or uniform. Yet the way HIV spreads and who it touches brings all gays together into one interest group, automatically and immediately. Altruism aside, the event itself created the need.

Gay/AIDS volunteerism was really born of many reasons, many of them purely practical in nature. If we can assume that human behavior (including altruism) is rooted in social circumstances, then GMHC's response, despite its magnitude, is not so odd. Not only were shared concerns and attachments present, but homophobia created an urgency all its own, as did AIDS.

8

Gay Volunteerism Before and After AIDS

THE CONDITIONS THAT GIVE RISE to voluntary homophile organizations and the motivations to join them mirror the experiences of minority organizations generally, especially when social and political rights are at issue. Community-based initiatives are provoked by sociological circumstances that have an impact on individual psychologies in a collective way. With the presence of AIDS, the problems of stigma and homophobia create basic differences in the characterization and agendas of virtually all homophile associations and need to be highlighted as political phenomena to be fully understood.

Gay community organizations are characterized by the stigma imposed on a public homosexual identity, both before and during the presence of AIDS. While gays enjoy each others' company and the opportunity to control a social environment, gay ghettos exist because homosexuality also isolates. When community is absent, this isolation reinforces suspicions and negative beliefs about having stigmatized identities. And there are real negative consequences to having a homosexual identity.

Before the historic Stonewall rebellion of 1969, it would have been virtually impossible to identify oneself socially as homosexually active and not suffer employment discrimination, mobility limitations, and civil abuse. This mistreatment reinforces collective guilt and dissociation from the community as a sacred source. Without communal support, psychic strain becomes enormous. Plummer (1975:175) says:

> To be called "homosexual" is to be degraded, denounced, devalued or treated as different. It may well mean shame, ostracism, discrimination, exclusion or physical attack. It may simply mean that one becomes an "interesting curiosity of permissiveness." But always, in this culture, the costs of being known as homosexual must be high.

113

While Lennox Yearwood and Thomas Weinberg (1979:303) indicate that both black and gay organizations "developed as a response to perceived social isolation and discrimination" of this type, gays alone still generally lack civil protection when being openly gay. George Weinberg (1973) claims that in this context it is difficult to maintain favorable feelings about oneself. Such internalized homophobia, moreover, undermines community, and political behavior suffers accordingly.

Unfortunately, it is from this perspective (of stigma, shame, guilt, closetedness) that the earlier surveys of volunteerism among gays were done. This is, of course, also true of virtually all studies of homosexual life. Other than in the Kinsey report of 1948 and the work of Evelyn Hooker in the 1960s, not many flattering, objective, or accurate things have been or are being said about homosexuals.

Volunteerism Before Stonewall

Well-known sociologist Edward Sagarin (1966) describes the Mattachine Society, the most significant gay political organization of the time before Stonewall, as an "organization of deviants." This view is continued by Salsberg (1971), who adopts this deviance perspective in his study of gay volunteer groups. He believes that psychic distress, guilt, shame, and fear motivate "deviants" to secretly meet each other in gay organizations for "self-serving reasons."

Neither Sagarin nor Salsberg could imagine a communally identified, self-accepting, and politically active gay community volunteering in the public domain from a space of pride and dignity rather than a space of need, loneliness, or confusion. In this pre-Stonewall period, the prevailing view was that homosexuals wanted to be alone and left alone and that they would achieve this by staying in the closet.

In contrast, Humphreys (1972) sees the gay liberation phenomenon as another social movement in the long history of racial and ethnic civil rights struggles. D'Emilio (1983) also claims that there is an unrecognized historical continuum existing between the old "homophile movement" and the post-Stonewall era. What this means in effect is that the view of gays as meeting together only because of self-loathing or promiscuous sexual desires is not true and that gay volunteers in early gay organizations had substantial amounts of self- and communal pride.[1] Gays may differ, of course, in terms of goals, strategies, and ideologies, but they all share a desire to control their own social identity.

What do we know, then, about pre- and post-Stonewall gay volunteers? How are they similar to or different from gay volunteers in the AIDS era? Unfortunately, there is no information about gay volunteers in nongay settings because this information is simply not gathered. Much of what we know about pre-Stonewall volunteers comes from Salsberg (1971), who simply wants to identify what types of "gay deviants" join which types of associations. Although there are shortcomings to his study, he did find that the general joining patterns of male homosexuals was higher than those of the overall population. Most male homosexuals belonged to only one organization, but they were highly active within it.

Respondents who were *not* members of the gay civil rights group that he studied but who belonged to other organizations joined associations whose goals and activities did not appear to be concerned with homosexuals or their plight. Only 6 percent of their memberships were in other homophile associations; these individuals were more inclined to join professional and civil rights organizations.

In terms of the specific hypotheses he tested about volunteers at the Mattachine Society, Salsberg (1971:42) found that joiners were less vulnerable to social punishment. "Sensed vulnerability," he writes, "constitutes a definition of a social situation in which the actor anticipates being the recipient of negative sanctions if the others with whom he interacts learn something of his personal identity." Of the homosexuals he surveyed, 71 percent of those who did not join voluntary associations were concerned with the possibility of disclosure of their "deviant" sex-role behavior, whereas 47 percent of those who joined voluntary associations were concerned about disclosure. The remaining 53 percent of association members worried very little or not at all about disclosure of their homosexual roles, in contrast to 27.3 percent of the nonjoiners. Among those who feared exposure, 56 percent still joined voluntary associations (p. 77).

After acknowledging that the Mattachine Society of New York is one of the most militant civil rights–oriented groups in the long history of the homophile movement dedicated to changing society's norms to an acceptance of the homosexual way of life, Salsberg goes on to say that its membership possibly betokens "a central preoccupation with their deviant sexual role" (p. 72). He perceives the society as providing "ego-strengthening experiences" and quotes Sagarin as saying that this organization attracts a large percentage of rebels and nonconformists who relish a battle with the world of respectability. Volunteering, in his framework, is done by disrespectful deviants for selfish reasons.

Rather than acknowledge that many homosexuals have always been proud, political, and not necessarily or solely sexually obsessed, he concludes (pp. 132–133) that gays spend most of their time cruising and then hiding to avoid being vulnerable, which, he feels, increases with promiscuity—the only public role gays are believed and depicted to play. Concealing identity becomes, therefore, the major preoccupation. Salsberg assumes that social relations among gays involve a guilt-ridden, furtive promiscuity filled with shame based in social rejection. In reality, however, any hiding is not from guilt but from real economic fear regarding loss of employment.

Given the demographics of his respondents, it might be wiser to conclude that low vulnerability is inversely related to education and income rather than to multiple partnering and the ability to hide. The relatively high level of personal achievement of his sample might also explain which gays volunteer. Yet Salsberg never considers social class as an explanation for volunteering or as a determinant of vulnerability. Instead, he sticks to a psychological vocabulary that stresses the therapeutic effects of gay organizational membership. He concludes that "male homosexuals who are members of voluntary associations are less likely than nonmembers to regard themselves as being more emotionally disturbed than the general population" (p. 135).

The data do support his hypothesis that male homosexuals who volunteer recognized themselves as homosexuals for a longer period of time and are more likely to read literature published by homophile associations than nonjoiners (pp. 137–138). Joiners are also found to be of "higher socio-economic status than non-joiners and Protestant or Jewish rather than Catholic." This finding, he speculated, is "due to the styles of living associated with upper levels of socio-economic status and the specific influence of these religions as they shape the attitudes, values, and behavior of their adherents" (p. 139).

His other hypothesis, that male homosexuals who volunteer are more likely to be involved in exclusive sexual relationships, is not confirmed. He argues that "these findings tend to substantiate the prevalent view that most sexual relationships among homosexuals tend to be short-lived, impersonal, and promiscuous in nature" (p. 140). He attributes the high attendance rates at meetings shown by volunteers to "an attempt to compensate for a lack of primary relationships in two areas—contact with relatives and an exclusive sexual relationship" (p. 144).

In this model, volunteering is nothing more than compensation for emotional deprivation and is rarely done out of conviction or altruism. Never does he consider gay volunteering to come from a positive source. Apparently, it is never done by people who are happy being single or proud of their sexual identities and bonds. As illustrative as his findings are, they are biased and severely limited in time and place. Moreover, they are determined by unfounded theoretical assumptions and the homophobic, sociopolitical atmosphere of the period in which he wrote.

Contemporary researcher Joel Brodsky (1985) starts with the assumption of institutional inequality and the reality of institutionalized homophobia and paints a different picture. He also acknowledges the effects of the Stonewall riot on the consciousness of gay people and assumes that community pride, commitment, and activity are normal and normative. Altman (1982a),

Marotta (1981), and Humphreys (1972), among others, also discuss the enormous changes in political, organizational, and social behavior that followed in the wake of the gay liberation movement.

The urban gay volunteers studied by Brodsky tended to be younger than typical volunteers and reflected the immigration of young and educated gays and lesbians to Capitol City, a midsized city in Nebraska. While participation in local and formal voluntary work could be spread between a dozen or so organizations, his respondents are identified as either belonging to or not belonging to the Coalition (a civil rights organization), first formed in 1981 specifically for the purpose of testifying on behalf of a gay rights ordinance. Of the gays and lesbians who answered, 44.7 percent of the males, as opposed to 32.1 percent of the females, indicated that they participate in the Coalition. According to Brodsky (1985:35), "This implies that while, on the one hand, the homophile voluntary association may attract both lesbians and gay men in its struggle against institutionalized stigma, it is unlikely to wage a struggle against sexism that the lesbian community as a whole can consider adequate."

If education is positively correlated with participation, its significance is somewhat diminished by a tendency among the most educated women to report less-than-regular attendance. Participation, Brodsky found, is greatest and most intense among those in city residence less than four years or between ten and fourteen years. Neither full-time employment, marital status, nor living arrangements show any statistically significant correlation with participation. Likewise, "the currently married and those who live with parents or children were less likely to be participants. In seeming contrast to such expectations, the fully employed were more likely to participate than, for example, students" (p. 59).

Unlike the explanations offered for "under-volunteering" among African-Americans, the most frequently cited reasons given by both genders in Capitol City was "not enough time/energy" followed by "not enough awareness of opportunities" (p. 60). In terms of the Coalition, however, the homophile organizational volunteerism is compounded by its gender mix, wherein gay men and lesbians share responsibilities. Among women, the lesbian/feminist collective attracts more members who participate more frequently than do the women of the Coalition, indicating that agendas, social organization, and environment affect gay participatory rates. Homosociality might be a significant issue for homosexuals and not their heterosexual counterparts unless they are specifically gender oriented in their purpose.

Finally, since "being out" is a central component of gay activism, it is surprising to learn that only 57.4 percent of Coalition members are open to all of their friends and that another 41.6 percent are open to some of their friends. Only 23 percent are open to all of their family, 44 percent are open to some of their family, and 33 percent are not open to any of their family. Only 9.5 percent are open to all their co-workers, 56.3 percent are open to some, and 34 percent are not open to any of their co-workers. Only 4.2 percent are always able to be open in public (pp. 68–69). Apparently, gay volunteering is tempered more by the perception of employment risk than by the problem of stigma, guilt, and self-loathing.

Gay Volunteerism in the Context of AIDS

In general, why people volunteer and who volunteers are influenced by sex, race, class, education, occupation, and sexual orientation. On an organizational level, the act of volunteering is affected by social needs, goals, administrative styles, accessibility, urgency, cause, and the time period in which it arises. The preceding data on gays were all collected in a pre-AIDS setting and reflected two different periods in gay history, namely pre- and post-Stonewall.

AIDS has created a third period and politic in gay history. Coming out is now no longer a private or arbitrary choice. It is a social, personal, and political necessity, demanded by the need and desire to survive both individually and collectively. Gay politics in the 1980s and 1990s, therefore, is inherently different and represents, for all practical purposes, the potentially last or final stage in the gay/lesbian civil rights movement. The politics of sex is now the politics of relationships.

Hoffman (1968) wrote that "walking into a gay bar is a momentous act in the life of a homosexual, because in many cases it is the first time he publicly identifies himself as a homosexual." If this statement was true in the 1960s, then the Stonewall riot and AIDS have permanently changed this perception and everything else. For the first time in history, gay people are going public in massive numbers, not only as individuals and couples, but institutionally.

Altman (1982a:77) notes that gay men are now "developing new forms of sexual relationships that make it possible to reconcile [the] need for commitment and stability with the desire for sexual adventure and experimentation." This also is true of lesbians, and according to Bravmann the changing patterns of interaction are much more than just sexual.

> Particularly since the beginning of the AIDS epidemic have lesbians and gay men forged new alliances across gender, built new community institutions for emotional support, health care, and social interaction, as well as continued to experiment with new forms of sexual play. What is important to recognize in all of these changes is that they have taken place very much in "public." (Bravmann 1987:18)

If it is true that gay men and lesbians have different political agendas, both the now infamous *Bowers v. Hardwick* case (which outlawed both private heterosexual and homosexual sodomy) and the general attack on gay/lesbian civil rights because of AIDS have brought these populations together, as never before. These two issues are central to understanding the meaning and significance of three different but historically related community mobilizations: the massive October 11, 1987, march on Washington, GMHC as a unique type of political association, and the AIDS volunteer as a special kind of activist and gay person.

While the contemporary gay/lesbian movement is too complex to allow for too many generalizations here, Bravmann (1988:3) notes that the October national march "tellingly indicates a shifting attitude within the movement ... [indicating] a rather substantial (if incomplete) broadening of the assumptions behind lesbian/gay political action."

The Supreme Court's decision in *Bowers v. Hardwick* to uphold a state's right to criminalize homosexual acts performed in private by consenting adults democratized the gay movement, opening it up more than ever before to women and racial minorities who saw the issues raised by the court in terms of sexism, fascism, and reproductive rights. The problems of women with AIDS, especially minority women, led them to ally with gays, who are learning much from women's oppressive experiences in the public health system. Having some privileges as white males, gay men are somewhat shielded from issues affecting other populations.

The October 11 march and the demonstration of civil disobedience at the Supreme Court on October 14 represent the first time that lesbians were overwhelmingly in control of a gay demonstration that, for all practical purposes, was an AIDS protest march focusing on better treatment of PWAs. At the Supreme Court, hundreds of men and women were arrested for their opposition to the Bowers v. Hardwick decision and federal indifference to the needs of People with AIDS. It is virtually impossible to look at these events and issues separately; they all impinge upon one another.

The GMHC Volunteer

The overlap of civil and health issues also explains both the character and nature of AIDS volunteerism and supports the general assumption of this study that if AIDS is a collective illness of a stigmatized minority, then volunteerism (as a political activity) would be undertaken only by people who live somewhat guiltless (or healed) lives.

To test this hypothesis, a special category or classification was created in the 1986 survey to measure how different in attitudes about their own rights and dignity as homosexuals AIDS volunteers are from pre-Stonewall homophile organization members. The study was based on the assumptions that volunteerism heals homophobia and that volunteers by definition are already predisposed to bear witness at a community-based initiative because they do not internalize negative or homophobic images of themselves.

AIDS volunteers at GMHC are considered *healed*, that is, identified with the community and with PWAs, if they are unconcerned that volunteering at GMHC identifies them as an AIDS worker (79.4 percent), a supporter of gay rights (77.2 percent), and as a gay person (72.85 percent). Healed volunteers' families know of their involvement in GMHC (78.3 percent), that they are very involved in the gay rights struggle (11.5 percent), or that they are some-what involved in the gay rights struggle (60.1 percent). These volunteers also agree or strongly agree with any of the following statements: that they volunteer because people in their community were getting sick and need help, that they feel a sense of communal responsibility as far as AIDS is concerned, that GMHC best represents and articulates the community's needs and that they identify with People with AIDS, and that their imagery of god is feminist in quality, that is, accepting, forgiving, and supportive. They also accept any component in their personality that emphasizes equality and the capacity to forgive.

All in all, 118 respondents, or 64.1 percent of the volunteers, meet all these criteria and are considered healed. The GMHC/AIDS volunteer, then, is generally drawn from a very specific segment of gay men. In terms of the project's hypotheses, GMHC volunteers are, in fact, less homophobic, more political, and more humanitarian (or altruistic) than either the gay community or society in general. For the most part, they are guiltless.

GMHC volunteers are also *nurturers*, even though they are men socialized into instrumental roles. Perhaps they are this way because they are feminists (at least ideologically) or because they are healed, filled with self-accepting pride. The nearly 70 percent of the volunteers who are identified as nurturers indicated that they like helping people in need, find satisfaction and rewards in traditional supportive or caring roles, are not interested in power and control over others, enjoy contemplation, meditation, and even prayer, and are nonrevengeful. In gay life, to be truly healed is to accept the feminine (the anima), to accept nurturing by doing it.

Nurturing dispositions are related to images of "the sacred" as accepting and supportive. Virtually none see god as a law giver. Nearly 55 percent think it very true for themselves that god is compassionate, forgiving, and loving. In their subjective understanding of religiosity, 75 percent of the volunteers recognize the sacred as a positive force in their own lives, even though, as a group, GMHC volunteers are not supportive of or identified with institutional religion. Only 16.3 percent indicated that they participate with any regularity in organized religious events, about the same number who participate, at least occasionally, in gay religious groups like Dignity or Integrity.

Twenty-seven percent prefer not to be identified with an organized religion but consider themselves believers, while nearly 23 percent practice religion privately. Thirty-three percent of volunteers indicated that they occasionally participate in organized religious events. Most, however, find the locus of sacredness in themselves, nearly 45 percent stating that it is very true for them that they do not care what a patriarchal God thinks of their sex life. Likewise, their religious attitudes are reflected in their egalitarian values. Questioning authority is very important to them, as is placing a religious vocation into service for others (58.7 percent).

While it is always difficult to gauge the relationship of educated Catholics to Catholicism, sociologist Andrew Greeley (1974) claims that Catholic lay people generally hold liberal attitudes on issues of interest to gays and women and that they increasingly do so today. Unlike Salsberg's findings, my survey results showed that at GMHC the bulk of volunteers (49 percent) were reared as Catholics (slightly less than half still identify themselves as such). Nearly 17 percent were raised as Protestants and about 15 percent as Jews. Being gay superseded any sense of religious community membership or loyalty.

I did not expect to find, however, such a homogeneous group of gay volunteers in terms of education, values, motivations, and general sociopolitical attitudes and interests. The gay men willing to identify with AIDS at GMHC are rather established, relatively wealthy, institutionally irreligious, politically sophisticated, egalitarian, democratic (both politically and socially), and highly compassionate or humanitarian in orientation and beliefs.

When asked to describe their political activity, nearly 74 percent of the respondents indicated that they are voting Democrats and 4.9 percent that they are voting Republicans. However, nearly 29 percent identify themselves as left of center. What is important, however, is the overlap between those volunteers who see AIDS as a political issue for the gay community (91 percent) and the 64.1 percent of the same group who see it as a political issue for only themselves.

It is quite possible that the gay GMHC volunteer is the crème de la crème of the community and that the organization attracts and absorbs its most energetic, dedicated, and conscientious members. This belief is not idle speculation. There has been considerable discussion in the gay press as to whether GMHC and/or AIDS siphons off too much gay money, energy, and talent. Being a GMHC volunteer is a resource allotment requiring energy and time.

That the AIDS volunteer is out of the proverbial closet is indicated in the response to several questions, the most telling being that over 75 percent surveyed lacked concern about being identified as gay or associated with AIDS or gay people and issues. Only thirteen respondents (7.1 percent) indicated that they are *not* aware that identifying with AIDS or GMHC might stigmatize them.[2] Several respondents noted in the margins that they are proud to be known as GMHC volunteers and that they are honored to be gay identified.

There is one area, however, in which volunteers indicated some apprehension about public disclosure of their gayness and it seems representative of virtually all gays not self-employed. When asked who knew about their sexual orientation, 97.8 percent indicated most of their friends. Only 45.1 percent are out to their employers and 65.2 percent to their co-workers. If anything, these data underscore the economic basis of oppression. Loss of employment is the great gay fear and underscores the need for legislation protecting the employment and housing rights of gays, never mind PWAs.

Given the general belief that gay people live in terror of their families knowing them in their fullness, it is instructive to learn that 81 percent of the volunteers are out to their families. An indicator of the need to be discreet about GMHC, AIDS, and/or gayness, however, is that while 63.6 percent generally acknowledged their involvement at GMHC, only 33.2 percent indicated that their employers know, 57.6 percent that their co-workers know, and only 29.9 percent that their employers accept their involvement at GMHC.

It is important to note that 78.3 percent of these same volunteers intend to continue to volunteer over any employer disapproval of their activity. And 90.8 percent indicated the same for co-workers' disapproval. As expected, the number of volunteers who would not cease their involvement with GMHC rises to over 95 percent if disapproval came from family or friends. Generally speaking, volunteers care little about what friends or family and, to a lesser degree, employers think of their volunteer work. For them, this work is a vocation for which they are willing to sacrifice very significant relationships to bring to fruition.

It is rather obvious that AIDS volunteers are very independent and free of certain inhibiting social constraints that would impede volunteerism at a gay agency. Perhaps this attitude results from their demographics. As a group, they are well educated. A full 74.9 percent have college degrees; 38.8 percent of those surveyed have undertaken graduate studies. Another 19.1 percent have some college education. Only 10.5 percent of the volunteers are unemployed (.5 percent are students), while 20.4 percent are self-employed. In a survey of AIDS volunteers in the Midwest, Snyder and Omoto (1991) likewise found that collectively these AIDS volunteers were highly educated, with 91 percent having attended some college and 67 percent having earned a college degree.

At GMHC, 68.5 percent of the volunteers are institutionally or organizationally employed: 23.6 percent are business managers, accountants, analysts, real estate brokers, or in similar professions, and 21.8 percent are artists, actors, writers, designers, or models. A surprising 13.8 percent are lawyers, architects, and editors. Respondents in social services (counseling, mental health, health care) make up 13.2 percent, and another 11.5 percent are in academia as teachers, educators, and librarians. Only 4.6 percent are in sales, and another 9.8 percent are secretaries, attendants, and service representatives.

As a rule, volunteers are working people who make the time to volunteer, averaging about eight hours a week. Time spent volunteering varies, of course, by assignment. Some in-house volunteers donate a few hours a week at the office, while others give several hours a day counseling, conferring, or just checking on the needs of their carepartners. However, when asked, "If time in general became a problem for you, would volunteering remain a priority?" 87.2 percent indicated that it would. Quite remarkably, nearly 37 percent of the volunteers are also the carepartners of friends and neighbors *not* assigned to them by GMHC.

While it is true that well-educated people do volunteer work in the United States, it is not typical that well-placed and well-paid professional males do the kind of "dirty work" and nurturing that AIDS patients require. And the volunteers as a group *are* well paid: The median income is over $30,000 a year. Fifteen percent indicated incomes approaching $35,000 and another 15 percent over $50,000; 7.1 percent make between $35,000 and $40,000, 8.2 percent between $40,000 and $45,000, and 2.7 percent between $45,000 and $50,000. Another 17.6 percent have incomes between $25,000 and $30,000, while about 25 percent made between $15,000 and $25,000. Less than 9 percent of GMHC volunteers make less than $15,000 a year.

Income, of course, will vary by age, which is the case at GMHC, where a substantial number of volunteers are over thirty years of age. GMHC was started by the age cohort precisely touched by AIDS the most (those thirty-five to forty-five years of age). Across the board, and by all measurements, this age group is also the most healed, most political, most community identified, and most activist on its own behalf. It also was the most affluent and best educated and, in the early years, the most involved and committed to GMHC and volunteerism.

Volunteerism and Gay Pride

There are, of course, many people who participate in or identify with homosexuality, but who are not accepting of being homosexual or are not involved in gay community life. They may also be caught in a particular subculture of gay life that is maladaptive or they may simply be having only homosexual sex with a person and feel that it is a private matter. Likewise, there are people who are proud and comfortable with their gayness but don't engage in any recognizable communal activities. Perhaps they have life partners, live in isolated communities, or simply prefer socializing with heterosexuals.

However, the 1986 research project discussed here is based on the premise that AIDS volunteerism does, of necessity, attract people with ties to the community. To identify these volunteers, I measured community pride among volunteers. Community pride was defined as self-acceptance and some identification or participation in community life. Those who indicated that they are *not* concerned that volunteering "might identify them as a gay person" (72.8 percent) are considered high in self-acceptance. To be included in the category of having community pride, named COMPRIDE, these respondents also had to indicate that they thought that "gays should in general" collectively identify with AIDS issues and/or People with AIDS (53.8 percent) *or* that gays should do so because "AIDS is often presented as a gay issue" (39.1 percent).

Another condition for being classified in COMPRIDE was that volunteers "see their participation in GMHC as a reflection or extension of their community identity and pride" (51.1 percent) *or* that in terms of their present sexual behavior they practice "safer sex" now because of their "sense of community pride and responsibility." Nearly 12.5 percent of the respondents indicated that this attitude is their primary reason for not engaging in sexual practices that transmit the AIDS virus, while nearly three times as many said that it is a somewhat influential factor.

Given the fusion of collective and individual interests in AIDS, 60.3 percent indicated that the most influential reason (23 percent think somewhat influential) for now practicing safer sex is their instinct for self-preservation. I assume that they meant self-preservation as a gay person. However, only 34.7 percent of the respondents indicated that community pride and responsibility have no influence at all on their sexual behavior (17 percent say it is the least influential).[3] Yet in "saving themselves," they are, in effect, saving the community.

Volunteers were considered to demonstrate community pride if they indicated that their feeling that "no one else outside the 'community' was going to help PWAs" significantly (23.1 percent) or very significantly (24.7 percent) relates to their reason for volunteering *or* that volunteering significantly (11.5 percent) or very significantly (9.3 percent) relates to the fact that their "friends were gay and they wanted to help them do something about AIDS."

Another indication of community pride was that their motivation for volunteering significantly (25.7 percent) or very significantly (38.8 percent) relates to the fact that people in their "community were getting sick and needed help" *or* that they agree (46.2 percent) or strongly agree (22.8 percent) that before they joined GMHC they "realized that AIDS was an issue central to the survival of gay people" *or* it is somewhat true for them that "they identified with People With AIDS for the most part" (53.3 percent) *or* that this is very true for them (16.9 percent) *or* that it is very true for them that AIDS makes them "realize that the survival of 'their people' was at stake" (41.7 percent).

A total of sixty-four respondents met all these criteria. This number represents slightly more than 35 percent of all volunteers.

On a superficial level, this datum by itself seems contradictory to our thesis. But placed in the context of the political economy of AIDS (homophobia, abandonment, stigma), it is an error to see the individual and collective interest as distinct and in opposition. In reality, community pride exists on a continuum (by meaning different things to different people) and is expressed in multiple ways.

There is, for example, a group of gay politicos who immediately know what AIDS politically means and who come to GMHC for communal reasons. They represent one extreme of the community. In reality they exemplify the unarticulated feelings of a substantial number of volunteers. Gay politicos, whose volunteering is a natural extension of their overall political beliefs and understanding of the democratic process, are communal leaders by definition. As such, they articulate policy for the larger community.

Gay/AIDS volunteers at GMHC are considered politicos (GAYPOLS) if they claim that "their involvement in GMHC is a political act or statement" (47.4 percent) *or* think that gays "should collectively identify with AIDS issues and/or people with AIDS because AIDS is often presented as a 'gay issue'" (39.1 percent) *or* see their participation in GMHC as "a reflection or extension of their political philosophy and/or insights" (47.8 percent). To be gay politicos (involved with the community), respondents also have to have a homosexual orientation (82.6 percent) *and* be either a voting Democrat (73.6 percent) or voting Republican (4.9 percent) *and* be either very involved "in the struggle for gay civil rights" (11.5 percent) or "somewhat involved" (60.1 percent). A total of seventy-six respondents (41.3 percent) fulfill all these criteria.

At the other end are a small number of volunteers (forty-two) who are thoroughly apolitical (APOLS). These respondents (22.8 percent) indicated that their involvement with GMHC is *not* a political act or statement (52.6 percent) *or* that they do not care what gays do or do not do regarding AIDS because they are "involved for purely humanitarian reasons" (22.3 percent) *or* that they saw their participation in GMHC as a reflection or extension of their "desire to socialize in a gay context" (32.1 percent). However, they also need to have indicated that they "were not involved at all in the struggle for gay civil rights" (28.4 percent).

In addition to meeting all these conditions, APOLS must have indicated that they do not "see AIDS as a political issue for themselves" (35.9 percent) *or* that they disagree (24 percent) or strongly disagree (19.7 percent) with the statement that their motivation for volunteering is "a way of protesting the mistreatment of PWAs" *or* that they disagree (16.4 percent) or strongly disagree (21.3 percent) that they volunteer "to defend the rights of PWAs through a collective effort" *or* that they disagree (21.2 percent) or strongly disagree (19 percent) with the statement that they volunteer "because AIDS is seen as a gay issue and that they want to help protect the social, legal, and political rights of gays."

Another characteristic of APOLS is disagreement (44.5 percent) or strong disagreement (18.7 percent) with the statement that they were motivated to join GMHC "because their friends were gay and that they wanted to help gays do something about AIDS." Given these conditions, forty-two respondents, or 22.8 percent of the volunteers, are not political.

Apparently, APOLS are not consciously viewing AIDS in either political, collective, or even "gay" terms. Like virtually all the volunteers, they claim to volunteer for essentially humanitarian reasons, even though GMHC is a gay agency, AIDS a gay disease, and volunteerism a gay cause essentially limited to helping gays.

While the vast majority of the volunteers at GMHC are identified with both the community and GMHC and see AIDS in political terms, they do not generally root their activity in the political and social reality of AIDS and being gay. This does not mean that gay/AIDS volunteerism is not political work, because it most certainly is, if not in intent then at least in consequences. Only highly communally identified gays volunteer for specifically and consciously political reasons.

For the most part, volunteers are political, communal, and humanitarian at the same time, but they also often separate these attributes. For the most part, they even understand the politics of AIDS, but political change is not usually a motive to volunteer. In many instances, there is high gay pride and communal identification but the presence of either of these do not necessarily generate volunteerism, even though its absence, if resulting from homophobia, certainly makes it unlikely.

On a sentient level, the substantial majority of volunteers think of themselves as simply responding as people or individuals to other people in crisis (even if these others are members of the same community, people whose lives they institutionally share). Many eschew the label altruist or humanitarian. Yet there are a substantial number of volunteers who say that they would not be involved at all with AIDS if it were not a "gay problem and a gay issue."

As will be demonstrated in Chapter 9, these apparent contradictions are resolved through the identification of a typology of volunteer motives and hence types of volunteers. Even if the volunteers begin with their own sets of ideas, beliefs, and motivations, it is unlikely that the experience of working directly with PWAs and GMHC will not affect their political consciousness. In fact, about 42 percent of the volunteers claimed that volunteering helps them "come out" to themselves and to their families, friends, and co-workers. That only 13 percent indicated that they are now no more willing (after joining GMHC) to identify themselves as either a gay person or a supporter/friend of gays generally means that they already had a high degree of "gay consciousness" before joining GMHC or that they are truly humanitarian, truly apolitical, or truly unsophisticated. In any case, they represent a minority of volunteers.

9

Gay/AIDS Volunteerism: A Question of Altruism?

WHILE THERE IS A relatively consistent profile of people who volunteer, there is no such unanimity about why they actually volunteer at voluntary associations. What we have instead are sensible, though obvious, suggestions that logically posit a wide spectrum of possible reasons for doing volunteer work. These explanations are similar to what sociologists identify as their positive or manifest functions for both the individual and society. To even a casual observer, however, they appear more like reasons for, than consequences of, volunteering.

Volunteering may serve to plug the gaps when one is between jobs, it can serve to fill leisure hours, and it is one way of maintaining self-esteem and an active life during retirement. By filling a void, the voluntary organization supposedly prevents personal disorganization, mental breakdown, suicide, delinquency, crime, corruption, and general disorder. Likewise, there are implicit social pressures and professional rewards in a democratic society that also make volunteerism both likely and necessary.

> It is largely through the activities of the voluntary groups, be their objectives economic, political, educational, religious, recreational, or cultural, that the urbanite expresses and develops his personality, acquires status, and is able to carry on the round of activities that constitute his life career. (Wirth 1951:46–47)

Identifying all the determinants of volunteerism is a complex process that is compounded by how the activity is operationalized and measured, both psychologically and sociologically. The word "volunteerism" is often applied to simple acts of charity, grand philanthropy, and deliberate humanitarian behavior, though these behaviors differ in meaning and motivation. Volunteering is considered a worthwhile activity because it has individual rewards and socially sustaining functions associated with it.

129

In the old parlance, however, before the "doing of good" became professionalized, willfully and individually helping others was how "being charitable" was expressed. As with AIDS volunteerism, such activity was believed to spring from a deep sense of connection and duty to others. Charity was seen as an obligation or expectation of ordinary people living in a world in which they and those around them had faith. Although charity evolved into formalized philanthropy, it remains altruistic behavior for Pifer (1987:121) because it indicates concern for the welfare of others.

Yet charity and philanthropy are not the same. "Charity," notes Hammil (1986:37), "in most cases is given to the poor or unfortunate citizen ... but the aim of philanthropy in its broadest sense is improvement in the quality of human life." Whatever motives animate individual philanthropists, the purpose of philanthropy itself "is to promote the welfare, happiness and culture of mankind."

Until recently, a positive function (reward) like this was thought to detract from any value that such generosity might have, especially if the motive or result was personally beneficial. Smith (1982:25–26) claims, for example, that self-interest seems to be the major component in volunteering. For him, however, this automatically negates its altruistic qualities.

Volunteerism as Altruism

Even though volunteering and personal gain often work in concert and more than likely even generate altruistic behavior, it is generally argued that if such behavior is not spontaneous it lacks any spiritual or redemptive value. For others, however, including a personal benefit as part of a motivation for volunteering begs the question, as it makes volunteer activity inherently selfish, though more likely.

Miller (1982:45) circumvents this problem of definition by identifying a volunteer simply as an individual engaging in behavior "that is not bio-socially determined, nor economically necessitated, nor socio-politically compelled, in which he or she carries out activities that have a market value greater than any remuneration received." Likewise, many contemporary students of altruism believe that virtually all such acts are rooted in specific circumstances and almost always have either subjective or collective rewards attached to them.

Although there might be an altruistic personality or altruism might be a biological imperative (perhaps a survival technique), altruism is rarely thought to be free of practical motivations. To be charitable is even considered part of human nature. However, it is generally agreed that these qualities do not detract from its merit. In fact, Piliavin and Charng (1990) conclude that rewards are now considered not only as complementary to altruism but at its very source.

This question of rewards in altruistic voluntary activity is important to our discourse on AIDS because of the collective nature of both the disease and the response to it. With the presence of AIDS, a community became altruistic to itself, for its sake and for that of the stranger. That there are high risks and few obvious rewards and benefits, for both the collectivity and the individual, does not detract from the fact that men nurturing other men is an extraordinary, philanthropic event. If altruism is "action taken for another's good," as Auguste Comte believed, is the value of AIDS volunteerism any less humanitarian because it is done by gays for PWAs, the majority of whom are also gay?

Is gay/AIDS volunteerism less altruistic because it has both a market and personal value—restoring the community and the individual to themselves and to each other as living entities? Or is this actually the ultimate act of selflessness, since under such trying loss and personal risk, it need not have been done at all—either individually or collectively? Private solutions are always possible. Therefore, the temptation to be free of AIDS makes bearing witness a constant struggle, a chronic choice to remain whole as both a person and community.

AIDS volunteerism is a high-risk activity with little chance of reciprocation (a traditional expectation), dubious psychic rewards, and little public appreciation. As AIDS volunteer Phyllis Townly (1989:26) notes, it is a personal and emotional experience not without cost: "My first encounter with the death of someone I cared deeply for at Bellevue was a disaster. ... For a few days, I was hyperactive. Doing anything, so I wouldn't think or feel. I was no good to myself or to anyone else."

Isn't it also possible since charity generally has boundaries, "do-gooders," and special or particular interests that gay/AIDS volunteerism is distinctive and highly altruistic precisely because it serves collective interests by empowering? As Badcock (1986) claims, altruism can be based on the identification of people with some group for survival purposes, which is the case with AIDS, which puts the whole community at risk of annihilation. Nowadays, similar linkages characterize corporate philanthropy. Odendahl (1990:52) notes that "corporate giving is an expression of enlightened self-interest," and Bellah (1985:167) feels that "most people say they get involved in social institutions to achieve their self-interests or because they feel an affinity with certain others."

It is only on the surface that volunteerism appears as a purely benevolent and generous act done selflessly and with humanistic intentions. For example, although 95 percent of GMHC volunteers think their work with PWAs is "primarily a humanitarian act or statement for them," in reality they exhibit a wide range of mixed motives for coming to GMHC and carepartnering PWAs. Among the many psychosocial motivations explaining volunteerism that could easily be applied to gay/AIDS volunteerism are the desire for social prestige and power, a social life during retirement, a learning experience, personal satisfaction and development, and job preparation.

The desire for involvement in "in" activities, a concern for others, an opportunity for emotional associations, and a service focus are often cited as reasons for volunteering and are true of gays at this time. This benefit aspect has been identified by Naylor (1967) as learning, self-actualization, and increased status gains. Many programs have increasingly become identified by how they help the volunteer rather than the client or recipient. However, GMHC volunteers rarely claimed these rewards as their primary motivations, though these benefits were certainly the result.

This theme of self-interest is reiterated by Schwartz (1982:73), who suggests that women especially volunteer to test out possibilities of returning to work; teenagers generally are looking for experience; men might be thinking of secondary careers; and a growing single population is seeking relationships and opportunities for socializing while doing something they consider worthwhile. Still others, she writes, "are using it for credit references." According to Haeuser and Schwartz (1984:25):

> In the past few years, awareness has increased that the quest for self-actualization as an individual requires becoming involved in altruistic endeavors as well as in self-centered activities, and that a sense of belonging to the community as well as to the self is essential for self-esteem and growth as a social person. Volunteering offers an opportunity for self-actualization and personal growth that may or may not include some skills and development with the potential for future employment. Whether or not this occurs, the process of involvement as a volunteer may prevent such personal problems as alcoholism, anomie, depression, and spouse or child abuse. Volunteering also mitigates the impersonal relationships between people and the organized agencies and bureaucracies with which all must deal.

In terms of voluntary associations, the consensus is that all such organizing for publicly beneficial purposes is usually the product of other motivations and human characteristics besides altruism—individualism, self-reliance, distrust of government, or, with AIDS volunteerism, impatience with public authority and eagerness to get on with the job. Yet as Phillips (1984:139) points out, although there are many motivations for volunteering, the most frequent explanation given is altruism.

This question of altruism in AIDS volunteerism takes on significance because of the uniqueness of PWAs' circumstances and the response to them by gays. Generally, PWAs need to be restored to a sense of their own value as human beings and this can be done only in the context of unconditional acceptance, like that offered by gay volunteers. This relationship between individual and collective interests and empathy and the will to help is variously described as "kin altruism" (Margolis 1982), "collective charity" (Atwater and Robboy

1972), or simply "prosocial behavior" by many others. Such behavior is attributed to either personality development, socialization, social and cultural expectations, modeling, experiences, empathetic skills, or moral training.

As found with AIDS volunteers, people who feel they have some control over events in their lives tend to do volunteer work, as do people with high self-esteem. London (1970) and Rosenhan (1970) found that voluntary altruism was related to a spirit of adventurism, a strong identification with a model of moral conduct, and a feeling of being socially marginal. Lerner (1971) emphasizes that the personality characteristic most related to helping is belief in a just world.

In their study of rescuers of Jews in Nazi Europe, the Oliners (1988) found that the rescuers' readiness to care was apt to stem from childhood. It emerged from just and nonviolent discipline that stressed reasoning, which helped them to develop a sense of personal competence and integrity that facilitated their identifying with others' pain. They found that many rescuers were reacting to an internalized universal ethic of caring or justice that demanded equality and respect for all. This ethic was often learned from a parent or significant other. The Oliners' rescuers did not see Jews as others; rather they acknowledged responsibility toward them as toward all people.

Basically, the Oliners argue that altruism is a behavior best explained by an interaction between personal and external social or situational factors. Most of the rescuers they studied, however, were characterized by a "normocentric expectation": They responded to the appeal of an authoritative other, usually a minister, a resistance group, or a helping network.

Thus some would consider gay/AIDS volunteerism altruistic and others would not. The difference between gay volunteerism and other kinds of volunteerism is that gay volunteerism is a collective effort rooted in relationships and social circumstances, motivated by informal, personal networks and role models who are friends and with whom they are living and dying daily. Because this environment is so encapsulated, gay/AIDS volunteerism retains a distinctive political and spiritual character.

Because Chambre (1991) sees gay/AIDS volunteerism primarily as part of a pragmatic subculture responding to uncertainty, she doesn't see its role in the communalization process as politically significant, although it is the only antidote to real annihilation. For her, citizen care of the dying is "one of several unique features" of AIDS. This is true only because gays are not citizens. It was in the process of bearing witness that the community rediscovered itself.

Humanitarian Motives in AIDS Volunteerism

Despite GMHC's commitment to all People with AIDS, gay/AIDS volunteerism indicates a strong community bias, a humanitarianism limited to friends and neighbors, despite public posturing to the contrary. While 69.4 percent of the respondents and 20.2 percent respectively agreed and strongly agreed that volunteering has given them the opportunity to demonstrate their "own values about helping people," they are, as a rule, generally drawn to AIDS because it is a gay problem. At the very least, this attitude is an example of a mixed motive for volunteering or a less-than-universal altruism. Whenever I tried to factor out a pure humanitarian motive for volunteering, however, I found that volunteering was almost always related to some other, more practical, fact. For this reason, I constructed a typology of humanitarianism that ranged from the somewhat pure to the self-serving.

Given my objectives and the design of the questionnaire, it was neither necessary nor possible to have tested for (or to have found) purely humanitarian volunteers who were at GMHC for purely altruistic reasons. In general, volunteers are not that single minded, and when they were given the opportunity to state why they volunteered it became evident that the motivations of AIDS volunteers ran the gamut from self-serving reasons and results to social ones. For example, at GMHC, 63.6 percent and 11.4 percent of the volunteers respectively agreed and strongly agreed that as a result of their work on behalf of PWAs their "sense of self-worth has increased."

In this survey, no respondent had only one reason to volunteer. All had a complex motivational system that became evident only after all the responses were analyzed. As an ideology to justify their behavior, however, nearly all volunteers consciously saw themselves as humanistically motivated. Nevertheless, there were trends and stresses. Like the humanitarians, politically motivated volunteers, for example, had different levels of political consciousness and different degrees of integration into the community.

Overall, the volunteers' identification with AIDS, PWAs, and GMHC evidenced traditionally understood political qualities. For example, they agree (40 percent) or very strongly agree (14 percent) that AIDS is a civil rights issue in the need of the communal response that GMHC offers. Nearly 48 percent agree and 44.6 percent strongly agree that AIDS threatens civil rights. While volunteers were also inclined not to see AIDS in apolitical terms before they joined GMHC, 67 percent indicated that since they joined their political awareness of gay rights issues actually increased. Seventy-seven percent indicated that AIDS caused a rise in political consciousness.

Ironically, while the volunteers' participation in other gay institutions was not particularly impressive, their involvement in AIDS was intense, perhaps even extreme. Many felt that if volunteerism was their first identification with community life it might also be their last. But because the political dimension of AIDS volunteerism is, after all, only a construct and not readily apparent to many volunteers, it was not surprising that barely half (47.4 percent) consciously volunteered to specifically make a "political statement about AIDS."

Apparently, the relationship of volunteerism to the politicization process remains unconscious.

I tried to identify as many subgroups of volunteers as possible but found that this did not necessarily shed any light on why people volunteered, what AIDS means to them, and how they understood their experience at GMHC. Because of the generally similar backgrounds of most of the volunteers (gay, well educated, relatively affluent, informed, community identified, and self-accepting), answers to questions measuring attitudes and knowledge of AIDS and gay political behavior were quite similar.

As previously indicated, there was a small minority of volunteers who fitted none of our assumptions. They were somewhat guilt ridden, unhealed, apolitical, and not overly involved in the community. Yet they volunteered, saw themselves as humanitarians, and were very concerned about AIDS and the care that PWAs were receiving. They simply wanted to do the right thing. Surprisingly, in terms of their motivations, they did not differ very much, if at all, from the bulk of volunteers.

Ideally, of course, it would have been beneficial to compare our findings and test our assumptions with a sample of gays who did not volunteer at GMHC. Questions of time, funding, resources, sampling, and so on made this impossible, especially since virtually all New York gays knew someone with AIDS and probably were in some service relationship to them. Instead, I interviewed fifteen gay carepartners who were not at GMHC and asked them why they did not formally volunteer even though their politics were quite activist and their demographics similar to GMHC volunteers. Their answers are informative and underscore the argument that no gay person in New York has been untouched, directly or indirectly, by AIDS.

Nearly all these interviewees said they were involved with AIDS work but preferred to witness alone, informally, and outside the confines of GMHC. Many were kept busy simply helping friends, and others claimed a general distaste of formal organizations. A few disliked the atmosphere of "death and dying" that GMHC is engulfed in. Still others mentioned that they were interested in preparing PWAs to die rather than merely comforting them while they lived. Some felt that there were needs not being met by GMHC that they could supply on their own.

For a few, GMHC programming was too narrow to capitalize on any unique skills that they may have to offer. Virtually all, however, were involved with the care of someone who was sick with AIDS and nearly all used GMHC's client support services when necessary. All praised GMHC and the work the volunteers were doing. As a group, they were astonished at the resilience of the GMHC volunteers even though they themselves were doing very much the same thing. Anyway, until the establishment of other AIDS service agencies, there was hardly an AIDS worker/volunteer in New York (if not the whole country) who was not aware of GMHC or who did not use its services, publications, staff, educational programs, and legal department at one time or another.

If it can be assumed that "do-gooders" need supportive, informal networks that help with loss, then GMHC volunteers, likewise, need such support, if not in more systematic ways. Was it possible that GMHC volunteers were lonely, lived with fewer social contacts, had a void in their lives that volunteering or GMHC filled? For some, maybe, but the majority were not social isolates. Virtually all volunteers delighted in GMHC's embracing of gays and PWAs, even though they confronted death, dying, prejudice, and discrimination as a result of being there. Nurturing and respect for individual differences became a personal expectation and requirement of GMHC volunteers, even though their empathy for gay PWAs was the strongest.

Many other questions about the typicalness of GMHC volunteers (in terms of rewards that were outlined earlier) were also raised in the questionnaire. I needed to know whether they were different from altruists who never joined either voluntary organizations in general or AIDS agencies in particular. Was it possible that the GMHC volunteer's reason for volunteering was to be part of GMHC rather than to help with the cause? I even considered the possibility that the most pertinent question might be why people joined an agency to help out rather than just help out on their own as the need emerged, like in the beginning.

Even at GMHC people came and went as the times and their needs dictated, making volunteerism and membership there a fluid category. Yet 50.5 percent of the respondents agree and nearly 15 percent strongly agree that "volunteering informally, say with friends for friends, would be good, but not as effective as working through GMHC."

Because AIDS's scope, relationship to gay people, and political dimensions made GMHC a logical and reasonable institutional response, the psychological question of whether GMHC volunteers had a particular personality trait that made organizational volunteering especially attractive became irrelevant. Rather, the question became (in light of the high 65 percent response rate) whether volunteers were so dedicated to GMHC that they would do anything asked of them (such as filling out a fourteen-page questionnaire). For a time, the agency was perceived as doing anything the community asked and as doing it well. Because volunteers were overly identified with their carepartners' suffering and predicament, they expected a community agency to relieve it. Were the respondents' answers biased as a result?

It soon became apparent that to ask why gay men volunteered in AIDS meant evaluating hundreds of hypotheses ranging from altruistic motivations to a relatively pure selfishness. For example, the volunteers may have suspected that they had AIDS (despite reality, only a minority thought they did) or that they were too isolated and without support systems if they themselves would need help and were preparing themselves for the inevitable. Yet only 38 percent said that if taken ill they would have to rely greatly on GMHC before friends or family. Forty-one percent said they would be able to rely primarily on family for help and 60 percent indicated that even though they could rely on their friends they might have to eventually use GMHC services sometime in the future.

In searching out their motives, I also needed to know if each volunteer wanted to help a specific friend. A surprising 87 percent indicated that it was primarily of no significance and 6 percent said that it was of low significance to help someone they already knew. More than 63 percent said they had not volunteered in response to a death of a friend. Nevertheless, family, friends, doctors, social workers, and individual PWAs frequently call GMHC for some advice or service.

I think of participation at GMHC and volunteering there as "high-risk altruism" because it reflects basic, yet extraordinary, humanist values. Why not say, then, that the community is altruistic toward the stranger, the "other," the biblical *anawin*, and that this makes gay/AIDS volunteerism even more meritorious than it is pragmatic or even selfish. It is a difficult effort to bear witness because volunteers have to subdue their fear of exposure and recognition, not just subdue their selfishness. When volunteers overcome barriers, volunteerism becomes altruism. It is true, however, that many volunteers thought they could bargain for either grace or time by doing good works.

AIDS can ultimately reach even a well person, but, it is argued, fear for oneself and the welfare of the community, which inspires one to volunteer, is more powerful than the fear of exposure as a gay person, especially if volunteering bought needed time. Yet 75 percent of the volunteers surveyed indicated that it was of *no* significance as a motive that they came to GMHC with the hope that doing good works would prevent AIDS.

Given the horror of an AIDS death, it seems particularly dated and biased to suggest that gay male volunteerism is done primarily to escape a hostile society, to fill a void in life, or to find a lover or sex partner. AIDS offers little respite from a mean world. Of the respondents, only 15 percent significantly and 9 percent very significantly indicated that they volunteered to have a focus and purpose in their lives and another 21 percent said that they came to GMHC to keep abreast of AIDS news or medical updates.

Clearly, ordinary theories to explain either volunteerism, philanthropy, or altruism do not apply easily to AIDS volunteerism. Most voluntary action studies do not deal with populations that are as identified with their clients as the GMHC volunteer is. They also tend to be too descriptive and heterosexist in assumptions to determine both what causes collective altruism and how it is effectively demonstrated. There are few available theories capable of explaining why affluent and professional gay men choose to change the bedpans of impoverished and deteriorating patients. To say that better-educated people are more altruistic or that they volunteer more does not tell us why they do or what it means—just that they do volunteer.

Nor is there any real literature on how collective altruism is affected by organizational contexts. Personal altruism is not the same as collective behavior for the common good, and the social science literature concentrates more on the subjective and psychological dimensions of altruism than on its communal attributes. At GMHC, 64 percent of the volunteers saw AIDS as a political issue for themselves, while 90 percent considered AIDS a political issue for the community. All benefit because both individual and collective interests are seen as one.

As I have indicated, the concern in AIDS here is not the subjective dimension of volunteering. Nor is it the organizational development of GMHC as an agency. The focus is on the emergence of pragmatic altruism, which is evident in behavior that an outsider observer would define as self-conscious altruism but would be seen differently by the volunteers themselves. GMHC volunteers indicated that they felt it was their duty to extend themselves and that it was natural to do so. As a rule, the volunteers (nearly 50 percent) described their activity in terms of compassion and concern and as something that had to be done because "no one else outside the 'community' was going to help PWAs."

These points are significant because whatever psychological theory exists about the roots of altruism does not go far enough to apply to GMHC volunteers. Contradicting expectations, nearly 20 percent of these men did not consider their families altruistic, no matter how liberally we defined the term. Less than a quarter had families that belonged to organizations or groups helping those in need. While 50 percent indicated that their families personally help people in need or in distress, 42 percent said that their families merely talked about those in need.

The Typology of AIDS Humanitarianism

A typology of humanitarians that includes subgroups of volunteers is central to the understanding of gay/AIDS volunteerism at GMHC. The following categories are indexes of humanitarianism along a continuum. To be included in any category, a respondent would have to be minimally identified as humanitarian in general and then agree more specifically with the questions indicative of each grouping along the continuum. This requirement did not preclude being in more than one category since none of the questions were mutually exclusive. Other than the desire to do some good, volunteers join GMHC for a myriad of reasons.

The Purely Humanitarian Volunteer

If a respondent answered the following questions about AIDS and volunteering affirmatively, then they were considered "pure humanitarians." Again, this did not mean that they also did not have other reasons for volunteering or that they did not also appear in other categories, because they often did. It just means that they met all the conditions of this construct.

PURHUMAN, like all the other constructs, was operationalized in terms of certain questions that were assumed to be complimentary and indicative of a purer humanitarianism. The construct stayed constant, and those who fit its requirements became characterized as such. What these respondents have in common is a pattern of highly humanistic attributes. While nearly all respondents in other categories saw themselves as humanitarians, these particular respondents had additional qualities that tempered the purity of their altruism.

In addition to indicating that their involvement with GMHC was a humanitarian act or statement for themselves (95.1 percent of the respondents did), volunteers were considered PURHUMAN if they first came to GMHC "because they saw AIDS as *primarily* an opportunity to help someone with AIDS" (58.2 percent) or if they claimed that "they did not care what gays did or did not do regarding AIDS because they were involved for purely humanitarian reasons" (22.3 percent).

They would also have to indicate that volunteering "because people with AIDS needed help" was significantly (32.6 percent) or very significantly (58.7 percent) related to their own motivations for volunteering at GMHC and that they significantly (19.6 percent) or very significantly (21.2 percent) felt the need "to get directly to People with AIDS quickly and efficiently."

A total of twenty-nine respondents fulfilled all these requirements, indicating that about 16 percent of the volunteers can be considered to be "pure" humanists by these measurements. I had thought that if the 95 percent of the volunteers who thought of themselves as humanitarians were fully or totally so, that they would have answered these other questions in equally large numbers. Apparently, however, when defined or operationalized by the individual, humanitarianism takes on different meanings.

The Politically Humanitarian Volunteer

It is inconceivable that any gay person not see working with PWAs as a forthright political act related to gay civil rights specifically. According to activist playwright Larry Kramer (1987a:14), "*There is nothing in this whole AIDS mess that is NOT political.*" While involvement with community is political, volunteers generally didn't recognize their identification with PWAs as political. Even though they were politically sophisticated and informed (most voted in elections and over 70 percent were at least somewhat involved in gay rights struggles), they didn't have direct or conscious political objectives when they volunteered. Yet over 70 percent of the respondents indicated that "since joining GMHC, they have become more supportive of gay rights."

While the interconnection between AIDS and gay rights is a real one, only 41.7 percent of the volunteers surveyed felt that "GMHC should take a more public advocacy role on the rights of gay people generally." While this response reveals a range of political understandings among volunteers, "the doing of good" is their overall conscious motivation and objective. Apparently, these volunteers feel that GMHC should primarily take care of PWAs and that other gay agencies should address political questions.

It is not that volunteers are not generally political in their views of AIDS or gay rights, because they most certainly are. Eighty percent claimed to have volunteered to "collectively protest the treatment of PWAs." If some volunteers were never part of any concerted, organized gay political effort, joining GMHC was for them *the* supreme political act, outweighing all other expressions of political behavior. Fifty percent of the volunteers indicated that they feel "more self-assertive" (more assertive about speaking about themselves) now that they are volunteering.

For respondents to be considered political humanitarians, their actions had to have some practical, political dimension that indicated an awareness of the political nature of AIDS. Ideally, they would indicate that their involvement in GMHC was either a "political act or statement" for themselves (47.4 percent) or that their participation in GMHC was a reflection or extension "of their political philosophy and/or insights" about AIDS and gay rights (47.8 percent). Politically humanitarian volunteers (POLHUMAN) would also have to indicate that their participation was a reflection or extension of their "own humanitarianism and ethics" (87 percent) at the same time that they saw AIDS as a "political issue for themselves" (64.1 percent).

Respondents in this category would, likewise, have to indicate how significant at least one of the following options was for their reason for volunteering: "Because AIDS is seen as a gay issue and I wanted to help protect the social, legal, and political rights of gays" (significant 23.4 percent, very significant 13.6 percent); "Before joining GMHC, I realized that AIDS was an issue central to the survival of gay people" (significant 46.2 percent, very significant 22.8 percent); or they had to agree that "AIDS issues cannot be separated from general gay rights issues" (significant 36.1 percent, very significant 15.3 percent).

Sixty-five people (36.8 percent) consistently met these criteria and are considered political humanists. Significantly, when crossed with the pure humanists, only four respondents met the criteria necessary to be included in both categories. While it is too soon to determine, it is possible that there may be a subgroup of volunteers who are altruistic in some basic sense.

The Personally Humanitarian Volunteer

As the research progressed, it became evident that at least some volunteers were not drawn to GMHC or AIDS volunteerism as a health and community issue in the abstract. Rather, they had some specific experiences relative to AIDS that made them aware of the crisis and the need for voluntary help. I labeled these respondents "personally humanitarian" (PERHUMAN). They would be so considered if they indicated that someone close or significant to them had been diagnosed with AIDS or AIDS-related complex before volunteering and whether this fact "*directly* influenced" their decision to volunteer.

While 38.6 percent of the volunteers indicated that the former was true, only 28.9 percent of this group indicated that this precipitated their involvement with GMHC. PERHUMAN respondents also indicated that they first came to volunteer at GMHC because "a friend/lover had died of AIDS and they needed support and help to take care of him/her" (13.1 percent).

If these conditions were met, these personal humanists would then have to indicate that volunteering "to help a specific friend who was sick" was either somewhat significant (3.3 percent) or relatively significant (2.7 percent) or very significant (1.1 percent) *or* that their "volunteering in response to a death of a friend from AIDS" was somewhat significant (8.2 percent), significant (6.6 percent), or very significant (12 percent) for them as a motivation. Forty-two respondents (22.8 percent) fulfilled these requirements and can be considered personal humanists.

These responses tell us that the volunteers are very proud of who they are, that they want to survive, and that they are identifying with the community for this reason. This attitude is exemplified by their willingness to help relative strangers, especially gays, live with AIDS. Had there been no identification with the community or had AIDS not been a gay male disease, there would have been little involvement with GMHC and/or AIDS volunteerism.

The Self-Serving Humanitarian Volunteer

This category was devised to see how many volunteers were actually getting some personal and practical reward or benefit out of volunteering and actually came to GMHC for this reason. It is not meant to disparage any volunteer or to suggest that they are any less effective, dedicated, or altruistic than those who are in some other arbitrary category. It is just that I have chosen to juxtapose certain beliefs and attitudes about altruism with the motivations actually stated by gay male volunteers.

Respondents were "self-serving humanists" if they indicated that any of the following options were either significantly or very significantly related to their reason for volunteering. They were asked to indicate the degree to which their volunteering was "a way of preparing themselves for a potentially serious illness" (significant 12.6 percent, very significant 3.8 percent) or if they felt that volunteering "was a way of helping themselves" (significant 22.8 percent, very significant 11.4 percent).

Of the volunteers who indicated that they volunteered to "keep abreast of AIDS news," 16.4 percent said this was significant and 4.9 percent that it was very significant as a motivation. Another 15.8 percent indicated that the need "to have a focus or purpose" in their lives contributed significantly to their reasons for volunteering, while another 9.3 percent said it was a very significant consideration. About 5 percent of the respondents indicated that they volunteered "in the hope that if they did good work, they somehow would not get AIDS."

In an insightful piece on the relationship of "AIDS Professionals" (A.Ps.) to wishful protection, Sal Lacata wrote shortly before his own death in 1991 in an issue of the *PWA Coalition Newsletter* about what it is like to be someone working in AIDS on either a paid or volunteer basis.

> There is an optimistic or positive attitude which abounds among A.Ps., when it comes to their own health status. That attitude works on the assumption that AIDS will not strike A.Ps. The vast majority know better and even admit their vulnerability but somehow, go on hoping they are earning "points" or "credits" in some cosmic equation which will translate into keeping them healthy. ... We knew A.Ps. were not specifically immune to AIDS, but we still did not or could not accept that AIDS was striking those of us who were helping and providing services for PWAs. We were the knowledgeable experts. We did not get AIDS.

These were the unarticulated assumptions of many volunteers. In constructing this humanistic type, no cases appeared, however, when an "and" condition was placed between each option. In other words, there is no die-hard or consistent group of "self-serving humanists" who volunteer only for the same "selfish reason." Rather, there simply are people who hope to do some good, perhaps gain something at the same time, and who are not perfectly altruistic all the time and in all circumstances. Since responses in this area were not cumulative, it was interesting to find that 110 or nearly 60 percent of the respondents had "not-so-pure" motives for volunteering on this variable alone.

When self-serving humanists are analyzed in conjunction with the social humanists described in the next section, it is reasonable to conclude that virtually no one volunteers without some personal benefit being derived. Indeed, simply volunteering at GMHC means the community, and hence the individual, will be helped. There is no real opposition between doing good generally and deriving some reward personally from doing so.

The Socially Humanitarian Volunteer

Despite the horror of AIDS, it is possible that a certain number of volunteers are at GMHC because of their desire for or need to create an exciting social life for themselves. GMHC and volunteerism would simply be a way to meet people—good people, at that (54.3 percent agreed and 22.8 percent strongly agreed that joining GMHC allowed them to network with other dedicated people). Socially oriented volunteers (SOCHUMAN), however, are *not* defined as those who enjoyed or participated in the social events sponsored by GMHC for its volunteers. Rather, SOCHUMAN are those who indicated that they joined GMHC because it was a "gay organization" and would offer them an opportunity to be with other gay people doing something significant together for the common good.

Respondents who indicated that they saw their participation in GMHC as a reflection or extension of their "desire to socialize in a gay context" (32.1 percent) *or* that their motive for volunteering was significantly (11.4 percent) or very significantly (3.8 percent) related to "meeting gay people and socializing with them" *or* that they volunteered to benefit "from the social life that volunteering might supply" (significant 8.2 percent, very significant 1.1 percent) were considered social humanists.

A total of sixty respondents, representing about 34 percent of the volunteers, can be considered social humanists. Many volunteers see GMHC as a gay community organization dealing with a gay health problem (56 percent). To the statement that "GMHC allows me to be myself and feel at home," 43.5 percent agreed and 20 percent strongly agreed. These volunteers wanted to help out and were attracted by the opportunity to work in a gay setting. In any case, they did not have to do it, so they are reaching out beyond themselves to do some good, and this is what constitutes their work as altruistic.

The Organizational Volunteer

Of the reasons given as to why people volunteer generally, status concerns are frequently cited as salient. Volunteering for a high-status organization would reflect on individuals' social awareness and commitments.[1] GMHC has more staff, more volunteers, and a larger budget than any other gay organization anywhere or at any time in history. Could it be that gay New Yorkers simply wanted to be part of it, to share the limelight?

In the words of a former board member, "it is amazing how many people and organizations outside the gay community marvel at GMHC's success." It now easily attracts support or acknowledgment from social luminaries in the scientific, artistic, and political world. However, while no one would argue that it is not doing essential work and doing it well, it would be inaccurate to claim that it is never criticized. To be sure, there are some serious detractors, like the disinherited Larry Kramer, whose disenchantedness will be addressed in Chapter 14. But for the most part, complaints are usually about specific personnel, procedures, or perceived program deficiencies. Unlike the Shanti Project in San Francisco, it has been remarkably free of scandal.

Given GMHC's reputation, is it likely that volunteers are drawn to it because of its status and reputation? There are other gay and/or AIDS-related organizations that use volunteers and need help and support, so why are volunteer energies not expended on them to the same degree?

I believe that volunteers come to the organization because their peers and comrades are being abandoned and need GMHC. Perhaps other gay agencies are too specialized, formal, and perhaps (at least, temporarily) irrelevant, while GMHC's objectives and ambience are well known and applauded. The agency has panache.

GMHC is worth the effort for its competence in capitalizing efficiently on volunteer labor. It is the right organization for the established middle-class gay whose sense of urgency fuels GMHC's budget and growth. Given GMHC's reputation and acceptance, volunteers were thought to be organizational volunteers (ORGVOLS) if they indicated that a significant reason (31.5 percent) or very significant reason (22.8 percent) for volunteering was because GMHC "represented the needs of PWAs the best" or because they significantly (33.7 percent) or very significantly (27.7 percent) thought that GMHC articulated community concern about AIDS effectively.

To be included in this category, respondents also had to indicate a response of "significant" or "very significant" to at least one of the following statements: "I volunteered at GMHC because the organization was so popular" (5.5 percent and 1.1 percent respectively) *or* "because they believed that GMHC would be doing important and significant work that they wanted to participate in while they had the opportunity" (42.4 percent and 33.2 percent respectively). Respondents also disagreed (31.9 percent) or strongly disagreed (4.4 percent) with the statement that "joining GMHC had *nothing* to do with the high esteem with which it is held."

A total of twenty-nine respondents or 15.7 percent of the volunteers fell into this category.

The Communally Humanitarian Volunteer

Being so central an issue in gay communal survival, the epidemic did more to galvanize gay people into political behavior on any and all levels of meaning and activity. I thought, however, that this communal concern would be a motivating force. It was quite possible that the "doing of good" by an AIDS volunteer emerged precisely and/or only because AIDS was a gay issue. Such volunteers would be communally humanitarian (COMHUMAN) and not necessarily humanitarian in general. I considered volunteers COMHUMAN if they were identified with the gay community and were carepartnering because gays were primarily at risk for AIDS or because they wanted to help a gay Person with AIDS. It is a narrow altruism, then, that is bounded by this consideration.

I also assumed that being involved and identified with the gay community was tantamount to being political, to making a political statement about identity and relationships. It was a contradiction in terms that someone be a gay politico and not be involved with the community and its institutions, especially at this time. The difficulty was in operationalizing "community involvement." Would this mean going to gay clubs and resorts, or just socializing in a gay context? Does it mean being knowledgeable of gay history, a constant reader of the gay press? If so, which gay press? If organizational participation is a significant measure, the memberships of GMHC volunteers are telling.

For example, only 26 percent of the volunteers "support" Senior Action in a Gay Environment (SAGE), a New York service organization for gay senior citizens. Approximately 20 percent support both the Lambda Legal Defense Fund and the Gay Rights National Advocates (GRNA) and New York's Gay/Lesbian Community Center. Less than 15 percent support the National Lesbian and Gay Task Force, a key gay advocacy organization. The largest number, 34 percent, indicated that GMHC was the major organization they supported.[2] However, many volunteers are involved with other AIDS service organizations, like the PWA Coalition and the AIDS Resource Center (ARC).

It is quite possible that these respondents were not too identified with the community's formal institutions because the political agendas of these institutions have always been relatively conservative, if present at all, or because they were seen as nothing more than socializing contexts. Undoubtedly, these older organizations drew members familiar with earlier gay rights issues, causes, and modes of socializing. Fashionable thirty- to forty-year-olds (who established the gay aesthetic of the 1970s and who were also being hit hard by AIDS) were not interested in their specialized agendas. After Stonewall, many also assumed that gay oppression was over with.

By the indexes I used, most volunteers were not aware of gay history or aware of or identified with communal institutions. In fact, only 33.3 percent indicated that they had first come to volunteer through information they had received from the "gay media," which in New York is quite substantial. Likewise, less than half of the respondents read the gay press (the *New York Native* [31.8 percent] and the *Advocate* [7.2 percent]) in addition to numerous specialized magazines such as *Honcho* and *Christopher Street* frequently, while another 29 percent and 23 percent respectively read them only sometimes. Since the *Native* had been acknowledged as doing exceptional AIDS reporting when the disease was first identified, one would have thought the number higher.[3]

It is also possible that many gays were communally involved only socially or recreationally. There are gays who may have never experienced social discrimination, perhaps because they were out of the closet, educationally or occupationally secure, or were well protected or insulated. The presence of informal gay networks and grapevines meant, in effect, that news traveled fast and far among individuals, making the passing of AIDS information easy.

The variable COMHUMAN was intended to measure volunteer motivations that were bounded by communal considerations. In terms of AIDS, this means that volunteers defined as COMHUMAN were involved in GMHC and volunteering because it was a gay issue *and* because they saw AIDS as a primarily communal health problem *or* because it is presented as a gay issue *or* because their participation was a reflection or extension of their own "community identity and pride" (51.1 percent) *or* because they volunteered (significant 18 percent, very significant 11.5 percent) to "defend the rights of PWAs through a collective effort." Communal altruists also had to have volunteered to make a political statement about AIDS and the treatment of PWAs (47.7 percent).

Respondents in this category also had to have indicated that they volunteered either because they significantly felt (23.1 percent) or very significantly felt (24.7 percent) that "no one else outside the community was going to help PWAs" or because they thought (significantly 25.7 percent, very significantly 38.8 percent) that people in their "community were getting very sick and needed help" *or* because they agreed (46.2 percent) or very strongly agreed (22.8 percent) with the statement that "AIDS was an issue central to the survival of gay people." Respondents could also have chosen the option that they thought the statement that "no one is going to help gay people in distress except other gay people and their friends" was very true (29.9 percent). Forty-six percent thought this statement somewhat true.

The sixty-eight volunteers (36.9 percent) who were COMHUMAN most likely also constitute a highly "healed" or pride-filled segment of volunteers. Of all the respondents, fifty-six (30 percent) of the total were both healed and high in community pride.

In addition to the aggregate answers given earlier, there are responses that also reflect the relationship of AIDS to GMHC and the relationship of both AIDS and GMHC to the gay community. Over 25 percent of the volunteers helped out at other gay organizations, splitting their time with GMHC. Even though GMHC siphons off the human capital of other community organizations, the volunteers' split loyalty helps deflate the criticism that GMHC is too big. A full 37 percent indicated that they would not be volunteering for other organizations if AIDS (and thus GMHC) did not exist, but 34.2 percent said that they would be doing so now at another gay organization. Twenty percent, however, indicated that GMHC was their first and last experience at volunteering.

No matter what the findings were, many GMHC volunteers did not want themselves identified or labeled as either humanitarians or altruists because they felt that they were simply doing what needed to be done. In their own minds, they did not volunteer to be (or because they were) altruistic or humanitarian, even though this was the nature of their contribution. It is unlikely, however, that these volunteers would simply have picked to help out this cause rather than some other. Indeed, there is an emerging view that similarity in attitudes, personality, political opinions, and national identifications between a victim and a carepartner promotes helping behaviors, and this is certainly the case in AIDS. The pleasure of working in a gay environment made it likely that AIDS would attract the communally identified and humanely committed. Like others elsewhere, GMHC volunteers picked their causes selectively and personally, if not communally.

Since this study of gay/AIDS volunteerism is done within a sociological frame of reference, our concern, in any case, is with collective altruism, or that behavior of a community that derives from identification with it. Given American ideological beliefs about volunteerism, then, GMHC represents an expected response. That it was given under such trying circumstances, against all odds, by the people at risk themselves, is why AIDS volunteerism is so unique and why GMHC is the primary voice, statement, and politic of the community. The question now is whether it will remain so as the demographics of AIDS change and the AIDS industry increases in size and complexity.

10

Volunteerism
and Voluntary Associations

WHEN PURITAN JOHN WINTHROP sailed into New England in 1630 to build a "city on a hill," he advocated that charity be a norm because it was consistent with Christian scriptures. The early colonists were the first Americans not only to form mutual aid societies devoted to doing "good works" but to surround them with religious meaning. These voluntary associations have since come to constitute the third major ingredient of a "Christian-American" republicanism. The involvement of citizens in voluntary associations is considered a potential deterrent to the excessive accumulation of power by the federal government.

Charity and good works, of course, have effects beyond their immediate utility. In addition to reinforcing beliefs about responsibility, they are often effective instruments of social control, supporting ideological explanations for problems like disease and poverty. They are also vehicles of socialization and a way of warding off protest over the distribution of wealth, thus making the social-class system more palatable.

Voluntary organizations are considered the means to a harmonious society, protecting traditional social values and relationships. Voluntarily helping neighbors has become the basis for a moral community and reflects social commitments and ties. Sorokin (1950:9–11) claims that volunteerism provides a "solid moral foundation of good deeds"; that is, it offers role models for others to emulate and it is this socially useful quality that also makes it altruistic. For these reasons, it is considered a "sacred imperative" for citizens to voluntarily offer assistance to those in need and deemed worthy.

Encouraging independent private initiatives is also thought to strengthen the nation's administrative, legislative, and even judicial processes. Conversely, volunteerism and human service delivery by voluntary organizations is often the way government evades its real responsibility for the public's welfare. Community-based initiatives let government off the hook even though a

149

majority of Americans seem to agree that government has a basic responsibility to take care of hapless people.

Historians Oscar and Mary Handlin (1961) argue that volunteerism, and the bureaucracies that it breeds, have entailed "heavy social costs" in terms of waste, inefficiency, and the duplication of effort, even though voluntary organizations usually aim to act or react to certain types of action undertaken or not taken by public institutions, that is, to fill some recognized yet unfulfilled human need. Like the Handlins, Reisman (1954:114) also sees voluntary associations negatively. For him, they are inadequate substitutions for the family and clan that pressure individuals to submerge themselves in an impersonal collectivity.

This is not the case in AIDS volunteerism because the gay community has had to duplicate already established social services. Because legitimacy, entitlements, and access to public institutions remain lacking, gays re-create the community by establishing organizations. Even though gay initiatives leave government absolved, unlike other voluntary groups, the whole point of the gay mobilization is to get the government involved in AIDS, but in a way that resolves the disease rather than dissolves the community. In this sense, the gay response is less to ideological pressures than to sheer need, fueled by a powerful and shared sense of worthiness. For many PWAs, GMHC substitutes for the family that has been lost upon diagnosis. The gay AIDS service sector is not an outside, unfriendly force but a collective ingathering.

AIDS and the Private Sector

Given the destitution of People with AIDS, the spread of AIDS beyond its early parameters, and the fiscal bankruptcy of the city of New York, representatives of seven foundations began meeting in New York in 1986 to address the AIDS epidemic. Their general goal, reports Carol Levine (1991:330), was to "urge philanthropy to play a significant role in expanding and broadening private sector leadership" in educating the public about AIDS and planning a "reasoned response."

In New York City, private-sector activity in general already added "over a billion dollars in charitable donations" to voluntary community initiatives, and "hundreds of thousands of people do volunteer work for the approximately 2,500 nongovernmental agencies that provide health and human-resource services in the city," reports Hammil (1986:36) in his review of charity in the city. Only gays, however, responded to AIDS. And this is not all that unusual because when charity is involved, or when community initiatives seek help, they almost always relate to the self-interest or benefit of the benefactor.

Contrary to popular opinion, notes Odendahl (1990:3), philanthropy disproportionately benefits private universities, the arts, and high culture rather than "community health clinics, legal aid programs, or other projects of the poor." A 1985 report of the Independent Sector (a nonprofit coalition of corporate, foundation, and voluntary organizations) reveals that even when money is available, only about 10.7 percent of the funds are given to social services, even though 15 percent of Americans volunteer their time and energy to these activities.

Despite their democratic appearance and integrative functions, philanthropic foundations are generally narrowly focused and intimately related to class, racial, and gender interests. They reflect and re-create the distribution of power. Philanthropy interacts with business and government and "cannot be understood outside of this context," writes Odendahl (1990:44). And because of the way government policy contextualized AIDS, broad philanthropic and social disinterest in AIDS were legitimated for some time.

Despite the destigmatization of AIDS, when the Citizens Commission on AIDS was founded in 1986 to assist New York City and northern New Jersey in responding to the disease, it nearly dissolved because it could not find a highly qualified and prominent CEO "or any other private sector leader" (Levine 1991:332) to chair it. With the heterosexualization of AIDS, it was only able to gain corporate support to end discrimination against PWAs (not gays) in the workplace. Eventually, the commission addressed health care issues in general (seeking more hospital beds, for example), lobbied for increased government funding, and increased support for drug prevention. Its greatest problem was getting sponsors and broad corporate support for its efforts and policy proposals.

In this context, GMHC was a response not to social anomie but to social isolation. AIDS was a real collective threat and GMHC was the way the gay community chose to protect itself from annihilation. Volunteerism was a new event in the lives of urban gay men, who were, for the most part, not tied to a history of philanthropy or wide support for gay institutions. It brought the gay community head on into the nonprofit sector, making it an important player in its ideological renaissance.

In more ways than one, GMHC was a product of the times, both following and reshaping a long tradition. Even though its advent occurred when involvement in unpaid volunteer work was actually declining and government supports for it lessened, the gay community was able to mobilize itself almost immediately. Despite a decline of over 1 million people in the number of volunteers in that field since 1986, gay volunteerism not only bucked this trend but did so with astonishing immediacy, magnitude, and unexpected success.

Why Voluntary Associations?

While directly helping friends and neighbors is still an American expectation (and greatly practiced informally by women and minorities), collective, direct, and personal aid to whole populations in need is a new phenomenon shaped by both urbanization and industrialization. In modern America, being generous in times of crisis no longer remains a part-time activity of the upper class. As the country developed, Americans systematized their charitable efforts in the name of fairness and efficiency. Voluntary associations now cover every social cause and personal need across the political, communal, and occupational spectrum. As professionals entered the picture, a wide range of programs and goals developed and a whole new industry, commonly known as the "independent," "third," or "nonprofit" sector, was born.

Given the range of volunteerism, voluntary action researchers make an analytical distinction between the charity shown or done for and between public, profit, and nonprofit organizations and that offered informally and spontaneously between private individuals. All community-based initiatives, however, share the general myth that private, informal, nonprofit voluntary organizations are somehow more effective, efficient, humane, empathetic, creative, and responsive than their public counterparts.

Voluntary associations are believed to have arisen out of spontaneous acts of free will in response to a perceived problem. They are considered reasonable, if not rational, answers to inadequate social or institutional arrangements, helping individuals adjust to social problems. In this sense they are both socially and politically conservative and very American.

Because voluntary associations perform such invaluable services, only their system-maintaining functions are emphasized and assumed significant. Americans tend to think of voluntary associations as indexes of how democratic the society is. By mediating between the individual and the state, voluntary associations unintentionally help integrate minority groups into the larger society. Likewise, they offer a legitimate focus for the affirmation of citizenship, govern (in the sense of making policy decisions and providing citizen services), initiate social change, and distribute power. Volunteerism is thought peculiarly American because it delays the development of a welfare state.

Community-based initiatives in this country have been noted to increase their participants' sense of political efficacy, becoming pressure groups that influence city, state, or national government. Generally, voluntary associations are thought to reduce both social and psychic tensions by promoting a sense of sharing, responsibility, and community, often acting as a form of social glue. They are, therefore, important because they intersect with all major social institutions—the family, education, the economy, religion, government, and social welfare—in a way that sustains their legitimacy.

Voluntary associations are believed to develop their members' organizational skills and to develop and cultivate their human capital. They also supply an opportunity for members to learn social norms, acquire information, and combat loneliness. While it is possible that there is an inverse relationship between conjugal family solidarity and rates of voluntary associational growth and participation, people claim that they volunteer to "feel empowered" and that they join voluntary associations because they believe that they work effectively to resolve problems.

Voluntary Organization Types and Functions

While general understanding of GMHC and gay/AIDS volunteerism might be enhanced by the theoretical frameworks found in the popular literature of the nonprofit sector, the uniqueness and complexity of AIDS as a social, medical, and institutional problem render classical approaches to voluntary organization types somewhat irrelevant, at least in terms of their emphasis and concerns.

In general, there is no commonly accepted taxonomy of voluntary organizations that easily distinguishes between volunteerism as a justifying national ideology and volunteerism as an activity. Nor is there much empirical data on the evolvement of voluntary agencies from social movements to specialized organizations, as is the case with GMHC. There is little information on how these two concepts intersect and on how changing staff, client, and volunteer demographics influence voluntary agencies and volunteer morale over time.

Virtually nothing is known as to how all these factors might hang together in an epidemic and at an organization where staff, volunteers, and clients overlap so much that they are intimately and continuously identified with their work as a cause, even when at home. Volunteerism is not typically analyzed in political terms, that is, as a movement that empowers.

There is little, if any, literature on collective altruism as a response to disempowerment and there are no studies of the role of volunteerism in the communalization process. Nor has there been any interest in the psychological and identity changes that occur among volunteers in a collective crisis like AIDS. Until now, we know little of the drama of self-discovery when a volunteer and an AIDS sufferer identify themselves as one another. The consequences of this recognition on organizational development, volunteer efficacy, and overall political behavior are not well understood.

What we have instead are fragmented theories on different aspects of volunteerism, such as its political dimensions, its relationship to the public social service sector, its effects on the welfare system, its manifestations in various voluntary activity, its organizational roles, and its consequences on communal and personal life. Many other studies concentrate on the social, demographic, and psychosocial characteristics of volunteers. Little information is available on how personalized volunteerism or collective altruism relates to the politicization process.

Although some researchers have focused attention on how voluntary associations are organized, what is missing is an overall unifying theory of volunteerism. The theory that does exist is normally taken from the sociology of organizations, bureaucracy, or small groups. To be sure, volunteerism is a complex phenomenon. It can be either formal (organized) or informal (spontaneous, accidental). There are individual and collective voluntary efforts, instrumental (goal- or cause-oriented) and affective (emotionally charged) volunteer organizations, and there are differences between the subjective and objective purposes of volunteer work. No single theory can explain all these variations, especially at GMHC, where they are all simultaneously experienced and where volunteerism is a collective effort and a communal expectation.

Some models of voluntary associations, however, are applicable to gay/AIDS organizations like GMHC. Blau and Scott (1962), for example, divide voluntary associations into four types based on who the recipient of the service offered is. In mutual-benefit associations, the membership gains; in service organizations, the prime beneficiary is the client; in commonwealth organizations, the public at large benefits; while in business concerns, the owners benefit.

A voluntary association is generally considered a private, nonprofit organization not purposely or centrally committed to sustaining an already established social system, that is, not directly producing goods or supplying a universally needed service. This is true of agencies serving dominant institutions, of those serving the interests of a significant minority, and of those mediating between institutional segments. In this way, voluntary associations basically function as interstitial social mechanisms. That is, they fill the gaps between major institutions by easing the strains between them.

Community initiatives can also be grouped according to the consequences they have on their sponsors. While some associations supply rewards in the performance of the tasks themselves, others offer these activities as vehicles for communion or sociability. Community organizations are also symbols or ways of evoking and reaffirming a collectively shared and valued belief system, often for the purpose of producing social change through the delivery of needed services.

Generally, social scientists have concentrated on the relationship of voluntary associations to the democratic process, emphasizing, for example, their "power-distributing role." Rose (1954:50–71), for example, maintains that voluntary associations, particularly those that are nonexpressive (that is, that are not directed at fulfilling members' emotional needs), serve to protect and sustain democracy by offering groups of individuals an institutionalized manner of having their voices heard in influencing social and political action and by acting as intermediaries between society at large and a specific category within that society. Many believe that citizens can gain power over their lives through voluntary associations.

Because voluntary associations express the wishes of their members, they are considered to revive the participation of citizens in the governing process. "Only through the action of non-political, voluntary associations," writes Oscar Handlin (1954:97), "could men check the state's power without directly opposing it. As long as men are free to act, they cannot be reduced to the blankness of the subjects of totalitarian regimes."

Basically, there are only two types of voluntary associations: expressive groups, which act to satisfy members' emotional needs, and social action associations, which are directed to solving a problem rooted in intergroup relations or in institutional arrangements. This type of instrumental organization differs from the expressive because its activities are immediately gratifying to the participants; in instrumental associations, a service or product is produced to maintain or change a normative condition.

By suggesting a third type of voluntary association, Gordon and Babchuk (1966) create a useful typology for understanding virtually all gay/AIDS social service agencies. For them, an association can be "instrumental-expressive" if it supplies a framework within which both types of activities can take place. In addition to using this functional distinction, they classify voluntary associations in terms of their degree of accessibility or openness of membership and the status-conferring capacity of the association.

All these characterizations are true of GMHC and the gay/AIDS service industry generally. However, because of the collective character of AIDS, this intermingling of the instrumental and expressive is the source of their success. For the gay community, these two, often contradictory, functions are vehicles of change and protest. They reflect and express the communalization of the disease and the community. They are also a way of promoting social cohesion and confidence in the democratic process. The collective nature of AIDS minimizes the disintegrating effects of single-issue or interest-group conflict among gays. All gay organizations have some agenda relative to AIDS.

In a community, the most serious conflicts come about where there are no overlapping memberships and with the presence of clearly isolated or divergent goals and objectives. While it is possible that different AIDS and community organizations will over time develop competing agendas that will become more definitive, insistent, and autonomous, it is unlikely that the gay community will soon bifurcate over this development. Although gay resources are limited and becoming more and more depleted, the complexity and diversity of AIDS issues and the presence of social networks and overlapping personnel in so many AIDS organizations keep information and connections flowing. And GMHC is still willing to generously fund "the competition," perhaps because they have different but not divergent or competitive agendas (see Chapter 12).

Also, because any involvement in the AIDS industry is an educative process—it exposes gays to inadequate social arrangements and the government's role in maintaining them—any AIDS work unifies interests and experiences with both emotions and personal identity.

While AIDS service agencies fill a gap and intersect with other social institutions, they also help participants determine their own needs and priorities by teaching them about democratic processes. Ironically, the result is that the gay response has uniquely political overtones that are disruptive of system maintenance because they empower in a way that destroys both ideologically justified indifference and homophobic self-denial.

In the establishment of GMHC, gays became autonomous rather than co-opted political actors. In this sense, the agency acts like a buffer against individual and collective anomie. By creating community autonomy, GMHC checks the state's power to control and define both AIDS and gays. Odendahl (1990:66) writes, "One of the greatest strengths of voluntary organizations is advocacy, the monitoring and pressuring of government to safeguard and raise the quality of public services." Community-controlled AIDS social service agencies are the way that gays now bargain from a position of strength with the rest of society.

GMHC as Voluntary Association

As an organization, GMHC now has a history, a reputation, a program and planning board, task specialists, boards of directors and trustees, managerial consultants, and a complex bureaucracy. This is now the overall setting within which a newly diagnosed HIV-positive person is welcomed, nurtured, and brought into primary contact with a carepartner and other GMHC services. It is also the context in which the gay male volunteer is recruited, trained, and ultimately connected to himself.

For former GMHC executive director Richard Dunne, this organized and efficient assignment of personnel and predictable delivery of services allow for long-range planning, the logical allocation of resources and assets, and the implementation, over time, of numerous service, educational, and prevention programs (Katoff and Dunne 1988). GMHC's primary and overt institutional role, however, is as service provider, because it delivers benefits not tendered (or, for that matter, intended) by government. It thus has nearly all the qualities of a "mutual-benefit" association combined with a "service organization" ethic. The public at large benefits, as do the clients, staff, and community whose bonds it must sustain.

In its vanguard role, GMHC innovates, pioneers, experiments, and demonstrates alternative community-based programming that educates and mobilizes various communities and populations. As an PWA advocator, it serves as a critic and watchdog, pressuring government agencies to improve or supply services. The organization reflects and sustains American ideological beliefs about volunteerism and community, thereby performing a value-guardian role.

GMHC is, on the one hand, an informal, empathetic, personal, and activist group of volunteers. On the other, it is a complex social service agency performing a multitude of functions and roles rather than specializing in one over the other, like most other agencies do. GMHC offers carepartnering, advocacy, and educational and mediating services to PWAs, families, public institutions, private organizations, and the gay community alike.

According to AIDS volunteer specialist Suzanne Kobasa, GMHC is unusual in that it poses a proactive challenge to singular authority and the presumed knowledge of professional and governmental agencies about service needs.

> As it assesses what policies and programs are needed to deal with the epidemic, GMHC rejects the common notion of the volunteer as mere auxiliary to established authority. It directly contributes crucial services and demands others, criticizing, for example, the directions of the original HIV presidential commission and the proposals for mandatory testing, name reporting, and contact tracing. (Kobasa 1990:285–286)

In this sense, GMHC is more political, though in less traditional ways, than the typical American voluntary association. In a word, it is a radical community mobilization because it creates a community of interest by shifting the locus of legitimacy from "the system" and from institutions to itself. This is how it facilitates communalization and hence politically reinvigorates the decimated gay community. Volunteers carry the torch in a dark period, breaking the silence around both AIDS and being gay. By connecting the two, bearing witness creates a new gay politic.

Caught between promises of help and hostility, AIDS service groups generally act like interstitial social mechanisms, both cooling out and channeling gay protest. With the terror of AIDS requiring a continuous renewal of priorities and commitments, GMHC becomes a mediating institution within the community and between itself and the outside world.

Social linkages allow the organization to be trusted, and in this way it stays relevant. With these connections, the community is made both whole and "holy" at the same time. When asked, 60 percent of the respondents in the 1986 survey claimed that GMHC's overall environment is a "liberating" one and that they enjoy its "at-homeyness." This "coming home" is the genesis and essence of politics because it reinforces both connections and identity in the context of need.

Part of GMHC's raison d'être is to advocate improved service delivery because public institutions are simply indifferent and because gays, as a rule, do not know how to use the social service industry to their benefit. Many simply assume that as white males their demands for service would be met immediately and attentively. Waiting for emergency room service for hours and days is out of the experiences of almost all gay PWAs. In the early 1980s, when the community's "social elite" began falling ill, there was no patience for service delays from public institutions, hospitals, or GMHC itself.

Coupling class privilege with a life-threatening disease causes gay PWAs to expect immediate service and attention, even though it remains virtually impossible to perfectly match staff, volunteer carepartners, and PWAs with one another randomly, all the time, to the pleasure or satisfaction of each. Gay PWAs expect personalized attention from their peers at GMHC, yet what is necessary for GMHC's survival is organization, but only to sustain and maintain its stamina, not just to routinize it.

Because AIDS-homophobia forces the agency to perform multiple tasks, GMHC is as distinctive an American voluntary organization as American society and the gay community are different from their European counterparts. It is continuously being reshaped by the overall sociopolitical environment gays live in and the nature and evolution of AIDS as both a disease and a social problem. As an organization, however, it faces all the political, managerial, funding, and institutional dilemmas common to all minority, nonprofit enterprises. In response to, or as a result of, this reality, GMHC encompasses virtually the whole range of organizational problems, interests, and characteristics generally attributed to voluntary associations, however paradoxical or impractical this may seem. It is, for example, social, purposeful, democratic, and affective as well as pragmatic, instrumental, bureaucratic, and efficient.

For these reasons, it is not easy to singularly type GMHC. Voluntary associations differ among themselves in terms of their legal status, responsibilities/liabilities, constituencies, and social linkages, and GMHC is no exception. Community-based initiatives generally vary in terms of their professionalism, social organization, clientele, recruitment procedures, funding sources, accountability, and public images.

Even though these differences make unilateral predictions about GMHC's future hard to gauge, such community associations do share many things in common that point to GMHC's future. For example, they normally depend on goodwill for support and generally share unique administrative and funding issues, especially as they relate to federal and state government. Outside funding sources take power away from the local community because community associations normally tie grants to administrative efficiency, thus fueling bureaucratic growth and conservatism.

Ralph Kramer (1981:107) writes of voluntary agencies in general that they "seem to retain their freewheeling, pioneering and loose organization for only a short time during the early formative states, while they struggle for identity and to establish their domain." Eventually (and inevitably), they become corporate, formal institutions, normally at the expense of services and clients. For him, the greater the division of labor and complexity of organization, the less useful and desirable is the presence of affective and personal satisfaction in the work performed.

On the internal level of the voluntary agency, formalization normally leads to regulations in accordance with administrative rather than client needs. On the organizational level, "voluntary groups," writes Odendahl (1990:66) "are vulnerable to institutionalization, goal deflection, minority rule and ineffectuality," especially when the division of labor increases. With the unabated organizational growth of these community-based cooperatives, their administrators are replaced by professionals rather than by organization or community members. Eventually this installation of specialists produces a fuller institutionalization of services and organizational procedures that deters community control.

Not only will professionals protect their own interests at the expense of clients, as Perlmutter (1984) and Wolf (1985) maintain, but only problems they can manage will solicit concern. In this context, volunteerism itself becomes just routinized activity, affectively neutral, with carepartnering being done disinterestedly, as if in an obligatory manner.

It is generally believed that bureaucratization destroys affectivity and creativity and eventually weakens the ability of an agency like GMHC to effect meaningful social change through the way the volunteer role is played out there. David Sills (1968:368) sees it this way:

> Some voluntary associations have goals and programs that are oriented toward the gradual improvement of the existing order. Their members therefore bring a relatively low degree of affect to their participation, and the organizational structure is relatively formal and matter-of-fact. Such highly institutionalized organizations may be called formal organization-like associations. Other voluntary associations have goals and programs that are much more radical and ideological, and are more at variance with what the participants believe to be the norms of the society; their members bring a relatively high degree of affect to their participation, and the organizational structure is likely to be informal and fluid. These less institutionalized organizations may be called social movement-like associations.

Early on, people simply appeared at GMHC, made themselves known, and donated their talents. In their frantic desire to help others and make sense of

AIDS, they created both administrative positions for themselves and service programs for PWAs and the community at large. While such sporadic productivity would do for a while, it would eventually impede development and undermine confidence, especially if dependability and predictability were lacking. Chambre (1991) believes that voluntary positions in AIDS organizations are often filled by people who found carepartnering others a way to channel their powerful emotional responses to the uncertainty and ambiguity of the epidemic, often their own fears about dying of AIDS, and later a way to mourn numerous losses of friends and family.

Since the mourning never ceases, what really sustains committed interest in GMHC is the circulation of volunteers, community members, and staff into and out of the position of a PWA. Virtually all volunteers and staff have some personal contact with PWAs, either in their private lives or in the main office, where many are employed. In this context, just keeping track of personnel is a relatively constant need, making recruitment by word of mouth (through the ranks) more likely (and beneficial) than professional recruitment for its own sake. In this sense, members of the community infold, forced to constantly take the role of the other in a determined way.

In terms of gay/AIDS organizations, this circulation is necessary because their effectiveness depends on their commitments, linkages, and accessibility. This dependency exists because community-based associations generally have an "intermediate" type of social organization, somewhere between "primary groups" on the one hand and firmly established and highly bureaucratized groups on the other. The general purpose of the voluntary association is believed to supplement, not supplant, already existing social institutions and programs. Gay/AIDS organizations are this type of organization because they are almost always funded locally, serve local clients, and are held together by informal social networks. Their primary group qualities define them.

In dozens of interviews from 1986 to 1989 with older and early GMHC volunteers, it was quickly noted that the power of the agency is in its volunteers and in the roles they perform and not in GMHC's formal operation, however efficient it now appears to be. The volunteers believe that GMHC will become ineffective and obtrusive in the future as its bureaucracy perpetuates itself and as the agency accepts more outside funding, loses local staff, and develops procedures that process PWAs as clients rather than as equals, that is, corporate owners and friends.

Nor do newer volunteers see GMHC's bureaucracy as benign. They grumble about what they see as a growing number of cumbersome service delivery requirements. Even in the 1986 survey, when asked what can be done to improve services that GMHC provides to PWAs and to indicate some not-so-gratifying experiences while volunteering, a substantial number of respondents complained that the agency's bureaucracy had to be "pared down" or "improved to facilitate interdepartmental communication." Not surprisingly, 27 percent of the volunteers agreed that some GMHC protocols were alienating to PWAs, 11 percent strongly agreed, and about 40 percent felt that some GMHC procedures interfered with effective volunteer work. They were referring to organizational concerns—officially sanctioned activities—not their own interpersonal and informal ties to PWAs.

There are also critics who would argue that GMHC was more efficient when it was more accessible, that is, when it was run informally, literally out of private homes and apartments, and when it was primarily concerned with the welfare of gay PWAs. Of course, the caseload was smaller then, and the needs of PWAs less varied and articulated. Everyone knew everyone else and these informal relations speeded service delivery. In 1986, 90 percent of the volunteers felt that it was to GMHC's credit that People with AIDS-related complex and recently diagnosed cases could still walk in for immediate support. With increasing numbers of PWAs, and with PWAs and carepartners being assigned to each other rather than "finding" one another, "drop-in" hours, to the chagrin of old-timers, have since changed to scheduled appointments.

More volunteer feedback was frequently stated as needed. Volunteers enjoyed "being on the front lines" and "having their opinions sought after." Few, if any, thought that the agency interfered with the carepartner-PWA relationship. Many volunteers requested that more standardized information and guidelines be made available for their use when advising PWAs. They also requested more staff, especially in financial and legal aid, "so that PWA requests for help would be facilitated." They wanted more crisis counseling and walk-in advisement and emergency services for PWAs.

It would be naive to think that such demands and concerns could be met by goodwill and sporadic administration. It is important to the community and GMHC's survival whether its "managers" can facilitate, rather than merely regulate, the work of the volunteers and whether bureaucracy and increased outside control make it more difficult for PWAs, especially gay PWAs, to negotiate for the services and personal attention they need and expect.

As will be argued in Chapter 12, GMHC's bureaucracy needs always to remain committed to a minimalist kind of administrative work to supply a context for creative, voluntary activity and to maintain continuity with the community.

PART THREE

The Significance of Gay/AIDS Volunteerism

11

GMHC and the Community Interest: Institutionalization and Successful Volunteerism

THERE IS ALWAYS THE POSSIBILITY that the iron law of oligarchy and goal displacement will emerge and dominate GMHC, making volunteers feel that they no longer have a say in shaping policy and in keeping the organization on course. There are several reasons why this development may take place, but there are conditions that will delay its occurrence. If GMHC becomes primarily an AIDS organization rather than a gay community initiative in regard to AIDS (because of increased outside funding and changing AIDS demographics), the attachment of gay volunteers to PWAs will deteriorate. In this context, PWAs will become clients.

In the traditional classificatory scheme of formal versus social movement associations, GMHC is actually expected to experience dissonance between PWAs, volunteers, and the community because of bureaucratization. "Its programs and spirit mark it as one sort of association," writes Kobasa (1990:288), "its structure, another." While GMHC's adventurous vigor on behalf of the community gives it its character and relevance, sociologists are wont to see its structure as more determinative and significant.

This struggle between institutional goals and client priorities, charismatic leadership and organizational needs, personal integrity and growth and procedural efficiency, and bureaucracy and creativity is described pessimistically by Max Weber as the eventual "routinization of charisma." While it parallels bureaucratization, this process is not synonymous with it. In terms of AIDS volunteerism, it refers to the ordering and expectations of the volunteer role, not necessarily the growth and institutionalization of the larger organization, even though both developments have an impact on one another.

165

Bureaucracy Versus Affectivity

For many sociologists, bureaucratization, the death of inventiveness, and the decline of connections are inevitable developments in formal organizations. For Max Weber the tension between interior and informal emotional identification with clients and the delivery of services to them, when subjectively determined by interactive individuals, is a secondary consideration of the needs-end rationality of the organization in question. Others, however, take exception, considering routinization neither fatal, determinative, nor even necessarily detrimental (Conger and Kanungo 1988). Ideally, as shown by Stark (1965), it can preserve the original charisma or creative energy, though not without difficulty.

In terms of volunteerism, burdening PWA care with organizational formulas will have serious implications for the community's ultimate empowerment. A decline in affective or identificational links would prepare the way for the agency to become an end in itself and to measure its relevance in terms of only the competent delivery of organizational objectives.

This consequence of formalization is important because weighing GMHC's success needs to shift from emphasis on organizational expectations (such as increased worker productivity) to the consequences of volunteerism on community integration and empowerment. In regard to AIDS, this shift means looking at GMHC's relationship (impact, commitment) to the community it is accountable to. This requires both defining the nature of good and effective volunteerism and identifying its source.

Concentrating on the issue of bureaucratic proliferation and domination, then, ignores the fact that administrative structures shield deeper phenomena that sociologists miss when looking at organizations in terms of only their official functions and internal operation. An emphasis on formal operations and programming ignores the phenomenon of empowerment, which is the significant question in both AIDS and gay volunteerism.

GMHC is unique because it exemplifies collective and concentrated altruism. It represents work undertaken against extraordinary odds totally by and for itself as a community. At GMHC, volunteerism came first and its organization later. Volunteers are the reason GMHC exists. By 1992, GMHC volunteers were contributing $2.5 million worth of formal services. It is the cathectic tie between the carepartners, however, that generates GMHC's popularity and success. As long as GMHC is gay sensitive, it will retain this character and the ability to restore self-esteem to PWAs. This quality is important because the needs of PWAs and the community at large are not just practical or rationally derived but go to the heart of collective continuity and personal identity.

According to Clark and Wilson (1961), the distinguishing feature of com-munity-identified initiatives is their solidarity incentives—the way they build community. And the best guarantor of community loyalty, notes Gamson (1991:49), is "a collective identity, that incorporates the idea of people as col-lective agents of their own destiny, and adopts a practice that encourages them to be active and collaborative." This is why, when one assesses GMHC's rele-vance and competence, it is more telling to look at community links, collective resources and commitments, volunteer incentives and opinions, and informal carepartner relations than administrative acumen.

Many volunteers, in fact, see GMHC as "the embodiment of the communi-ty." Nearly 88 percent of our sample felt "a sense of pride in being a member of GMHC." Over 83 percent claimed that volunteering at GMHC "has made them proud of gay people and the gay community in a new way." Apparently, volunteers identify with GMHC because it summarizes their concerns. It is not that altruism has limits, but that it is limited by empathy, affectivity, and community.

Given the vast majority of gay PWAs at GMHC, volunteers were "very con-cerned with the welfare of PWAs" and decried any delay in the delivery of ser-vices to them. Over 90 percent felt that the primary concern of GMHC staff should be meeting PWA needs. While 50 percent of the volunteers thought that GMHC's secondary concern should be their own needs, only 35 percent agreed that the organization was even generally responsive to them. Another 43 percent were indifferent to the question. Volunteers were not terribly con-cerned about bureaucracy and its needs (or even their own) and went about their business determinedly, if not independently, despite GMHC.

It seems that the more dedicated the volunteer, the more likely they were to find fault with the organization's administrative procedures. They found fault not because GMHC was ineffective or bureaucratized but because they had very high expectations, often knew their clients personally, wanted to get right down to the tasks at hand, and had no patience with or understanding of the simplest of procedures. Nearly 80 percent of the survey's respondents said that they felt free to agree or disagree with management over any issue.

The vast majority of volunteers indicated that their most gratifying experi-ence at GMHC was working directly with PWAs "through illness and dying." They savored discovering their skills and capacities to both share and grieve "with the community and the new friends made." As with AIDS volunteers generally, nearly 55 percent indicated that GMHC offered them an opportu-nity to discover their nurturing and empathetic skills. These respondents were from the early waves of volunteers from 1982 to 1986, when AIDS was emo-tionally charged, intimate, and personal and the agency (as an organization) was still evolving.

Unlike in organizational expectations, or in institutionalized charity, the effects of bearing witness to PWAs cannot be systemized, contained, or measured by bureaucracy. In AIDS agencies, administration should exist primarily to coordinate institutional activities, not prevent volunteers from tuning in to the unique struggles of each Person with AIDS in a way that comforts and secures them existentially beyond the delivery of ordinary services. Since the agency and the community are inherently collaborative, then so are the volunteers and the PWAs. They are irrevocably one another and each other. Community ties are those that bind and upon which AIDS organizations have to depend for relevancy and effectiveness.

In an article on the relationship of GMHC's growing diversity and gay identity, Jeffrey Braff, GMHC's short-term executive director (1989–1990), addresses the issue of whether the agency will remember its roots as the profile of People with AIDS changes. He writes:

> When I was interviewed for the position of Executive Director last fall, a number of questions that the Board of Directors asked me were about my gay identity and the gay identity of GMHC—How did I feel about that identity? Who did I see as GMHC's constituents?
>
> I told the Board then, and I tell anyone who asks me now, that one of the main reasons I was interested in working at GMHC was because the agency was founded **by** the gay community **for** the gay community—and that I was confident GMHC would **always** be there for the gay community. You ask about GMHC's name and will it be changed. The answer is no.
>
> GMHC serves, in many ways, all people with AIDS and works with all groups involved in the fight against AIDS. But our primary constituency is still the gay community. The statistics bear me out—gay and bisexual men make up 85% of our 2, 700 current clients, 80% of our legal services representation, and an estimated 45% of our Hotline callers. Gay men, lesbians, and those whom I call "gay positive" people, make up our staff, volunteers and donors. As I work with them, their dedication to our clients is inspiring. I agree that we cannot become complacent about reaching out to our brothers and sisters and letting them know we continue to be here for them. So let me take this opportunity to reiterate to you my personal and the organization's commitment to the gay community. It's always been up-front and always will be. **GMHC stands foursquare in the gay and lesbian community here in New York and will always work hard for unity in that community.** (Braff 1990:2)

GMHC as Gay Community

Since so much of what is being argued here is based on the assumption that what motivates altruism is community ties, it is necessary to determine whether GMHC and the gay community are contiguous with one another and how this relates to volunteerism as a form of humanitarianism. The 1986 survey, on which this study is based, included many questions measuring GMHC as the focus and locus of gay community during AIDS.

Although nearly all respondents were motivated by humanitarian concerns, most GMHC volunteers directed their attention to helping PWAs—a group they perceived of as primarily gay. In order to identify those volunteers who combined gay politics, humanism, and community identity in their volunteer-ism, I constructed a category called GMHCCOM (GMHC-Community) to see how many volunteers actually experienced GMHC as a reflection or exten-sion of gay communal life.

In order to be so categorized, respondents had to indicate either that they first came to volunteer at GMHC because they saw AIDS as *primarily* "a col-lective health problem for the gay community" (44 percent) *or* that they thought "gays should collectively identify with AIDS issues and/or People with AIDS because AIDS is often presented as a 'gay issue'" (39.1 percent). GMHCCOM respondents had to agree with these two fundamental options.

But to meet all the criteria for seeing AIDS, GMHC, and the gay commu-nity as intimately connected (GMHCCOM), respondents also had to have as a significant or very significant motive for volunteering that "they thought GMHC articulated community concern about AIDS effectively" *or* that they volunteered because their "friends were gay and they wanted to help them do something about AIDS." In the general survey, 37.4 percent said that the for-mer statement was significantly related and 27.7 percent said that it was very significantly related to their reasons for volunteering.

Most likely, helping friends was interpreted as assisting specific individuals. Yet 65 percent of the volunteers overall also indicated that they volunteered because "people in their community were getting very sick and needed help," members of the broader gay collectivity being considered friends. The com-munity in general or the community as friends is the context within which any altruism was exhibited for most volunteers who generally saw their efforts as humanitarian in principle though essentially directed toward gays.

In the survey, 11.5 percent indicated that helping their own friends was a significant reason for volunteering, but even fewer, 9.3 percent, indicated that this was a very significant reason. This finding is instructive only when com-bined with the fact that 84 percent were willing to help a PWA that they "did not know before." Gay consciousness, networks, and relations in AIDS are thus very broad. Nearly 42 percent of respondents indicated that it was very true for them that they realized that AIDS made them understand that "the survival of their people" was at stake. Twenty-eight percent said that this real-ization was somewhat true for them.

Interpreting these responses became clearer with the realization that gay politics and community life, like AIDS, have different meanings, however sim-ilar homosexuality might make individual gays to one another. It is probable that so many respondents were so identified with GMHC as the community, or AIDS as a gay issue, or the gay community as the extension or continuity of themselves, that they volunteered not because of specific friendships but because of practical personal and collective survival, their interests and that of the of the community becoming synonymous with one another.

This perspective, and the meaningfulness and usefulness of the category GMHCCOM, is buttressed by the fact that 63.6 percent of the respondents agreed and 23.9 percent strongly agreed with the statement that they felt a "sense of communal responsibility as far as AIDS was concerned and that GMHC best represented and articulated community needs." They joined an organized effort to fight AIDS because they felt helpless when they were alone. Forty-six percent agreed and 30 percent strongly agreed that "since AIDS was a collective problem, working alone for solutions would be less effective." Over 23 percent agreed and 18.1 percent strongly agreed that "GMHC should take a more public advocacy role on the rights of gay people generally."

Forty percent also agreed and nearly 14 percent strongly agreed that "AIDS was a civil rights issue in need of the communal response that GMHC offered." The remaining options were to agree (46.2 percent) or strongly agree (22.8 percent) that "before joining GMHC they realized that AIDS was an issue central to the survival of gay people" *or* agree (36.1 percent) or strongly agree (15.3 percent) that "AIDS issues cannot be separated from general gay rights issues." Given all these requirements, seventy-four, or 40.2 percent, of the volunteers surveyed felt very strongly about GMHC's role in preserving the community.

This relationship of GMHC to the community is both the starting point and the result of volunteering. The data tell us how much AIDS, gays, and GMHC overlap, summarizing the personal in a collective way. Calling the community to bear witness to itself distinguishes GMHC from all voluntary agencies and AIDS from all other illnesses. Indeed, 85 percent of the respondents indicated that it would upset them if GMHC "lost its sense of community."

By crippling friends and neighbors, HIV infection thus re-creates communal linkages and generates resistance among volunteers to any GMHC organizational agenda that is not collaboratively determined or collectively beneficial, that is, specifically helpful to gays. Together with what Poirier (1988) calls the "war on AIDS and gays," the environment of pending death keeps the community forever vigilant and committed to volunteerism and gay empowerment. The threat of AIDS helps contain defections from both the cause and any community AIDS organization dedicated to preserving the community. It is the ability to call GMHC to accountability that keeps it relevant. When challenged, it remains responsive and sensitive. Separating administrative concerns from community expectations would sound its death toll.

More practically, GMHC simply cannot afford to alienate both its funding and staffing source by treating PWAs indifferently. Gay funding, like volunteerism, is relatively specific. Government funding, however, can go only to AIDS agencies that do not discriminate in any way. If GMHC accepts outside funding, it means its services will not be delivered first and more directly to gay PWAs—the original intent of the founders. The agency was established with gay people in mind; though many are gay, today 43 percent of GMHC's clients are people of color.

Presently, GMHC has programs tailored to a variety of constituencies. Since government money is minimal at GMHC, it is somewhat paradoxical that gay men from the community, who have themselves given time and money to GMHC's effort, now have to wait up to two months to have their registration processed because staff and volunteers have spread themselves so thin through nonessential program proliferation.

This is a marked change from just seven years ago, when 75 percent of the respondents in our 1986 survey indicated that GMHC was very effective in its service for PWAs. In terms of GMHC's administrative policies, only 12 percent didn't then trust the decisionmaking skills of its leaders. Lately this confidence has been slowly deteriorating.

Yet to justify itself as "reasonable," efficient, powerful, and an important player in the AIDS industry, GMHC needs to be organized to gather and sustain both gay and public support. Given the pervasive beliefs about homosexuals as frivolous and incompetent "pansies" and the media's portrayal of gays as self-loathing, GMHC confirmed the gay community's credibility early on by establishing and reaching formal, organizational expectations. Because it identified with PWAs, the community of course assumed that it would continue to control the agency that was designed to serve it.

If volunteerism cannot be assessed in terms of only productivity and efficiency, GMHC needs to remain a gay community initiative for gay consciousness to be transformed in a way that facilitates empowerment. It is not that the needs of nongay PWAs are less urgent or that they should be ignored and abandoned. Rather, it is the fact that the agency began as the embodiment of gay community and that this is what motivates volunteers and defines the nature of the role that they perform—primarily healing homophobia. Undoubtedly, this goal and connection stand in opposition to both bureaucratization and the complete routinization of the volunteer role as experienced by the volunteers as representatives of the community.

Building Community or Organization

In the interlocking of community empowerment and AIDS volunteerism, it is necessary for gay volunteers to remain connected to their source—the PWA—

and for GMHC to remain faithful to its roots. Such linkages keep dedication constant. Volunteers need to remain unencumbered. For their commitments to be sustained, GMHC needs to prioritize gay needs. This will maintain the community's confidence. Given the data, gay volunteers work their best and give their all primarily to gay PWAs.

AIDS volunteerism cannot be successful if it is seen either as an indifferent private activity between individuals or as an impersonal, corporate, institutional endeavor serving only organizational ends. It cannot be useful if routinized so that the PWA does not come into his or her own autonomy. The volunteer role is not about patterns, procedures, or expectations, but about listening to the stories of the dying in a way that demands personal attention to their grief and isolation so that healing can commence. The agency needs to accommodate the PWA on his or her terms, not just routinely. The same is true of and for the volunteers.

To be successful, GMHC needs to retain what Helgesen (1990) calls an "interactive leadership style." This way volunteers will have ready access to staff, participate in effective programming, and be direct PWA advocates. Because PWAs are gay, GMHC has been able to have access to a bank of dedicated volunteers. When recruited, they are introduced into organizational operations and expectations. PWA needs, the nature of AIDS and HIV infection, and the experiences of PWAs are explained in depth. Volunteers learn enormous amounts of medical information and become exceptionally adroit at understanding New York's social welfare system. Consequently, PWAs learn to rely on volunteers and gain their trust as both their spokespersons and carepartners. Likewise, the agency offers support services for volunteers.

The great amount of encouragement presently given to PWA- and volunteer-initiated projects keeps volunteer morale high, and volunteers personally deliver many services beyond those assigned. In terms of their own daily needs, volunteers can meet regularly with one another, offer each other advice or assistance, and confer directly with supervisors and PWAs to resolve everyday problems.

When asked to suggest ways to improve volunteer morale and commitments, many survey respondents favored volunteer lounges, socials, and more "recognition for work well done." While consistently acknowledging the support they got from their "teams" and from their other buddies, they wanted more "moral support" from the staff and administration and more opportunity to interact and inform them of their own experiences. GMHC has been willing to regularly schedule support sessions for volunteers who need to talk about the "cumulative dying in their midst."

However, because the volunteer workload is so burdensome and so many individuals from the community give so much so consistently, GMHC rarely singles out individual volunteers for praise or recognition. Given the numbers of PWAs helped, the collective nature of the illness, the multitude of tasks that volunteers perform, and the democratic nature of GMHC's governance, this is not only impossible, but is also impractical. It would be divisive to single out some volunteers for special recognition when so many contribute so much.

Yet GMHC had to reward many of its dedicated volunteers with full-time staff positions, raising the question anew over whether volunteerism should be for "love or money" (Byrne and Caskey 1985). One survey participant wrote: "Frequently, it seems that our volunteer force is underused, yet we hire people for tasks such as typing, we pay messenger services ... etc." There are many reasons why this is so. If altruism has limits, so too do time and energy.

Because of the amount of labor involved in caring for PWAs, full-time volunteering by an entire agency staff or community is unlikely. There are many testimonies of early GMHC volunteers that indicate heroic efforts in carepartnering and expenditures of time, money, and energy. To survive, many volunteers simply needed to be compensated so that their own basic human needs for food and shelter could be met. Many volunteers actually felt guilty if they took a break or asked for some out-of-pocket reimbursement. Because they thought of themselves as primarily volunteers, they simply did everything for each other, on their own, all the time.

This dedication gave GMHC its glamour. The "star" quality attached to helping PWAs gives volunteerism a certain "expected glory" that not only fuels creativity and inventiveness but also makes being there a reward in itself. There is always the need to make dramatic public statements about AIDS, especially gay AIDS. This opportunity to be decisive and appreciated keeps confidence and expectations high and GMHC and its volunteers in the limelight.[1]

Since simultaneous empowerment is needed by both PWAs and volunteers, ideally they should be the primary determiners of GMHC's programs, how they are delivered, and the roles that volunteers should play. Given the social meaning of AIDS, PWAs cannot be healed in a fractured environment where they are used as instrumental objects of science, carepartner needs, or organizational objectives. To be known as people, PWAs need community and inclusion among their own.

Affectivity, Linkages, and Successful Volunteerism

There are now fewer indications that bureaucracy at GMHC will not outgrow itself and become an end itself. To stem unnecessary service and organizational proliferation, GMHC announced in October 1990 a temporary cutback in services and caseload growth. This gave administrators time to reflect on GMHC's goals and performance. After examining its options, however, GMHC's board adopted a strategic plan to manage short-term growth with the objective of maintaining quality care—not just for gays but for all its diversified clientele, that is, the "AIDS community."

While retarding growth a bit, this approach created a problem in identity and commitments. For many gays, it would have been wiser for GMHC to rediscover its gay roots and to become more specialized and focused rather than more democratic.

Limiting bureaucracy reduces organizational autonomy and keeps PWA needs primary. By maintaining face-to-face interactions, GMHC preserves the economics of PWA care and community support. Remarkably, writes Kobasa (1990:190), "the ratio of unpaid to paid staff hours at GMHC [is] ten times higher than the average ratio at other service agencies in the city, despite a doubling of paid staff in that year." In this way, GMHC can practice the politics of transformation by reminding itself that the needs of real people are paramount.

The carepartner experience tells us that caring for a Person with AIDS calls upon a range of physical, psychological, social, and spiritual interventions that cannot be easily predicted or managed, especially by outsiders. Ultimately, each PWA is an individual. A good volunteer understands what this person is going through as a gay person or as an AIDS sufferer. The encounter should reveal what particular area of life needs healing, not just attention. For gays, therefore, successful volunteerism means communalization—taking the role of the individual other as an extension of the collective self. This is how healing and nurturing become effective. And this is why GMHC needs to remain gay and not bureaucratically obsessed.

Although each individual case varies, the liaisons between carepartners and PWAs have a peculiar quality that is unique to gay AIDS. Even though it is in a secular, organizational context, volunteers are often brought into deep conversations with PWAs about sin, death, loss, resurrection, meaning, guilt, love, forgiveness. This is why it is impossible for volunteers to be formally prepared for all encounters with PWAs. GMHC cannot completely rationalize all volunteer functions because, like all roles, this activity keeps evolving as circumstances dictate, as the outside environment makes an impact on individuals, and as the importance or need for the delivery of certain services changes.

Working with AIDS patients affects individual and collective well-being and it is this link that both sustains and ties the experience of carepartnering together, giving it deep emotional and personal meaning. This not only makes it peculiarly effective but also defines GMHC's traditional character and usefulness. While GMHC volunteers have access to support groups, they learn what to do as much from listening to one another and reflecting on their experiences as they do from their supervisors.

AIDS care, I believe, is different from care for other infectious diseases because the issues are so political and so personal, the needs are so unique, the stakes are so high, and the time available is so short. As Larry Kramer insists, decisive action is important now because the community has nothing to lose: "We have already lost the war, soon we will all be gone." In this urgent context, however, the patient needs a friend and a healer, not only a surgeon, procedure, or demonstration. She or he needs peace of mind. Likewise, the carepartner needs to be fulfilled by bringing someone to wholeness at the trying moments that an AIDS diagnosis entails.

At the very least, a successful volunteer role in AIDS requires mutual respect so that the PWA and the carepartner can be restored to themselves and to their communities as sacred sources of identity and well-being. At gay service organizations, this is first done by accepting the sexuality and life-style of the PWA, the central focus and symbol of the community, and the reason why GMHC exists. Such a connection will contain "pure" managerial decisions and keep the foot soldier active in the decisionmaking process as it pertains to PWA care.

Roth (1973) empathetically describes this problem of "caring for the sick" as one between "professionalism and love." This conflict is rooted in an organizational ideology that assumes that calculated distance and emotional neutrality make for the effective delivery of services. Such an assumption fits patriarchal beliefs about where obligations and loyalties should lie and is utterly inappropriate in AIDS.

In successful AIDS volunteerism, the carepartner role needs to be played with what Carol Gilligan (1982) calls a "compassionate professionalism." For her, this role need not be affectively neutral to be effective. This is critical because empathy binds people together in a life-giving way. Gilligan draws her insights from the experiences of women who combine efficiency with emotional commitment to the caring tasks they generally perform.

In responding to the "routinization" of health care, especially when clients are categories of people that professionals do not like in general or as individuals, Roth (1973:175) says:

> It seems much more sensible to me that, instead of trying to eliminate affect from the care and treatment relationship, we harness positive affect to do the bulk of the task. The way to avoid job and career routinization is to put the caretaking tasks in the hands of those for whom the patient is always a special case, namely the people who love him.

The challenge in AIDS care for the GMHC volunteer, then, is one of overcoming indifference and emotional neutrality. To be an interested, responsible, and compassionate carepartner, volunteers have to identify with their charges. The wounded healer never allows a relationship to deteriorate into a power struggle or superior attitude of condescension when helping others. Rather, they stay "simpatico." Even though seeing the face of AIDS for the first time is terrifying (especially when becoming an AIDS sufferer oneself is a real possibility), this kind of feeling is necessary for one to "self-accept." Any conscientious gay person immediately understands this.

Carepartners of People with AIDS, whether they be family members, medical personnel, or volunteers, are not easily detached from their work. The needs of PWAs are so varied and personal that it is virtually impossible to be impersonally involved in carepartnering. In the model of transformation, there is nothing beneficial about a role or relationship that does not revolutionize, engage, or heal people.

In fact, when relationships are institutionalized, they often become detrimental to the effective delivery of services because they end up processing people rather than serving their needs. While its formal structure keeps GMHC functioning, the need for personal and responsive programming should retard the routinization of voluntary activity and keep GMHC aligned with the community that owns it. Informal networks keep the agency members "oiled," motivated, and responsive to crisis. GMHC's creativity is heightened because most staff are rotated from one position to another and often move themselves from a space of health to one of illness. Creating multiple perspectives from multiple vantage points keeps the agency tuned in.

While the volunteer role is becoming specialized within the agency's complex organizational structure, many staff members, if not all, also continue to be buddies or crisis intervention counselors. Keeping the administrative and volunteer roles from becoming too distinctive and separate, however, can be maintained only by promoting people already within the organization. Knowing one another and having diffuse relationships would guarantee that the "affective memories" and experiences of the community are carried over into the formal setting.

Gay volunteers are able to create and maintain an "autonomous jurisdiction" in the service of transformation. The activities of its "wounded healers," its volunteers, are based on compassion, commitment to the cause, and identification with PWAs rather than on mere organizational directives or fidelity to clients as such. Hence, GMHC remains adaptive and malleable, and the volunteer role transformative and politicizing.

The point here is that the life and spirit of the organization is greater than its bureaucratic integrity, public image, and specialized service objectives. GMHC is a community organization, in which participants are attached to one another outside of their shared space at the agency. Up to now, the volunteers and staff have been related to their clients at least socially, if not personally and politically. It is for these reasons that GMHC is not yet an ordinary or simply routinized social service agency and its volunteer role is not merely a rationalized one. AIDS volunteers are political innovators because their roles go beyond those typically prescribed by a social service organization.

GMHC and the Community Interest

As the AIDS crisis worsens and becomes more complex, it also appears less urgent, or so it seems to gays. The public has become desensitized through media overkill, and the disease, for many, remains minoritized or stigmatized. This leaves PWAs socially marginalized and politically isolated. As a result, HIV-positive people (no matter how activist they are) frequently withdraw from their own peer and support systems, increasing in turn their helplessness and, for many, their sense of failure as the disease progresses.

AIDS volunteers have to deal with despair among both PWAs and themselves as carepartners. People with AIDS often need immediate and personalized attention to regain a sense of composure and control. These moments of gloom are also very trying for the volunteer. To help the volunteers, the agency now offers weekly therapy and support groups. To help PWAs to live fully and for volunteers to grieve constructively (to regain their composure), GMHC's Volunteer Office developed and now regularly offers specialized grief and healing workshops. A similar service is offered to lovers and families of PWAs. It is in these encounters, at these breaking points, that lives become intertwined and transformed.

For many reasons, government and community social service agencies do not normally have to deal with emotions such as guilt, fear, self-acceptance, and stigma as intensely as GMHC volunteers do and as HIV infection requires. Nongay sympathy for past, present, and especially future PWAs remains minimal because the illness is often thought self-inflicted. British-born AIDS media critic Simon Watney (1987) claims that PWA needs are ignored because gay health problems are tangential, normally relegated to the fringes of sexually transmitted disease clinics.

In the AIDS crisis, unfortunately, gaining attention, support, money, and respect are but one set of issues. About the origin of AIDS as a social problem, Timothy Westmorland (1987:47–48), assistant counsel in the House of Representatives for the Subcommittee on Health and the Environment, writes, "We are losing the war against AIDS because of the Reagan administration, because of the politics of the budget, and because of the politics of sex." Part of the problem, he notes, is the AIDS bureaucracy operating out of Washington, the lack of a coherent and informed AIDS policy, and the competitiveness of the scientific enterprise: "The present administration is allowing us to lose it, and because, by and large, a good many of the press, the professionals in health care and in the health care industry, and the public are allowing the administration to allow us to lose."

In addition to the politics of the budget, Westmorland cites what he sees as the major problems in the politics of AIDS: the social status of PWAs and the fact that homosexuality is emphasized in AIDS transmission. Gay AIDS was ignored because it was thought to be collectively generated and self-inflicted. Gays were blameworthy because social boundaries and taboos had been broken during its transmission. Even after Margaret Heckler, the former U.S. secretary of health and human services, declared AIDS to be America's number one health issue, moneys allocated for AIDS research and PWA care remained unspent several years into the crisis.

When funds are available, no consensus exists as to where and how they should be allocated. While research funding efforts increased in 1986, money for PWA support services remain, even today, woefully inadequate and GMHC's resources have always been taxed to the limit by the growing demand for humane social services. Because of discrimination, a substantial amount of gay resources have had to be expended on legal and social matters rather than on direct care delivery.

To protect both gays and PWAs, GMHC has had to establish its own legal department to mount defenses on several fronts. In addition to assisting PWAs in writing binding wills, this division works closely with the Lambda Legal Defense and Education Fund, the National Lesbian and Gay Task Force, and the legal profession in general over issues of discrimination, entitlements, and rights. Lawyers, donating their time and energy, work to guarantee the civil and medical rights of PWAs and HIV-positive people.

GMHC's Legal Service staff are available free of charge for anyone with an AIDS or ARC diagnosis, whether registered with the organization or not. In 1990, 882 new clients were helped and over 2,000 legal matters resolved. Four attorneys work full time at GMHC, helped by a support staff of 350 volunteer attorneys who freely provide their services. Their numbers increase by about 25 percent a year. Since 1984, GMHC's legal services division has helped more than 4,000 men and women by providing crucial information and free legal services (Gay Men's Health Crisis 1990:10).

The legal issues surrounding AIDS and health care delivery never cease because they are often perceived as gay rights issues. In 1987, the Coalition for Public Health, a conservative public interest group, contended that intense pressure from "civil liberties" groups and homosexual activist groups has turned the nation's treatment of AIDS into a "political football rather than working to protect the public majority." Endorsing the plan of California member of Congress William Dannemeyer for mandatory testing and/or quarantining of all HIV-positive people, a fund-raising letter issued by the coalition states: "Clearly, 'gay activist politics' has no place in the AIDS crisis issue. For how can this deadly virus [*sic*] be controlled if we don't even know who has it."

GMHC maintains that since it was reacting to homophobic discrimination, the coalition distorted the facts to incite fear and panic: "The New Right people have made AIDS a political issue, not us." Fortunately, this politicization has both united the gay community behind GMHC and allowed heterosexual concern about gay and minority AIDS to surface, albeit disguised. GMHC became known throughout the United States because it was at the center of New York gay life both politically and socially.

If GMHC politicizes AIDS, it is because it assumes that gays are citizens, have rights, and should be helped overtly and directly, as though each individual were "everyman." This gay liberation stance justifies its existence and makes it possible to recruit highly motivated volunteers and exceptionally talented staff, fund-raise with relative ease, and capture both political attention and broad social recognition.

Just as GMHC's staff and volunteer core grew daily, so did the difficulty and intricacies of AIDS care management. There are still endless numbers of clients to help, programs to direct, and policies to be considered. GMHC, however, does not do everything for everyone. It never intended to. Just taking care of PWAs is a complex and heart-wrenching undertaking and there is only a limited amount of talent and time available. This requires the agency, the volunteers, and the community to prioritize needs and coordinate resources within an integrated ideological framework. If it did otherwise it would fail miserably.

It is shocking how gay AIDS is subsumed under the mantle of AIDS and PWA sympathy generally. Gays need to claim AIDS again. Democratization of the disease has done little for the community and only a little more for PWAs—not by acknowledging pluralism and community boundaries but by fusing us all into a false, unrecognizable, or faceless victim category. Even worse, all AIDS agencies in time will lose their autonomy unless they stay rooted to the communities that gave them birth. Ignoring the specific demographics of AIDS downplays the primary social fact that the disease is rooted in social structure.

12

GMHC as Organizational Success and Problem

THE CENTERS FOR DISEASE CONTROL declared AIDS an epidemic in October 1981. In May 1982, a handful of volunteers at GMHC were trained to field questions on its telephone hotline, which was busy immediately. When GMHC advertised for help five months later, 150 people responded. By 1982, there was a growing population of desperate clientele and an increasingly terrified community that needed home and health maintenance assistance in addition to trustworthy information. Requests for help forced GMHC to institutionalize two service requests—the "Buddy System" and the "Crisis Intervention Program"—their very names indicating both function and reality.

Fulfilling these needs fundamentally shifted the focus of GMHC away from direct political activity. Today, hundreds of newly recruited volunteers help out as buddies (direct care providers) and crisis counselors. While these two activities constitute GMHC's primary carepartnering effort for PWAs, they also serve to introduce the volunteer personally to the world of compounded human suffering. Working in tandem with PWA care are GMHC's other major programs in advocacy and prevention/education.

The development of Gay Men's Health Crisis, as what Morris (1984) calls a "movement halfway house," was influenced by two external social conditions: discrimination against gays and the need to generate concern about HIV fulmination among both gays and the larger public. Because the community lacked social legitimacy and respect, GMHC had to make both itself and the disease credible. It did this first by organizing in a professional manner. But it gained its stature primarily by questioning aloud the basis and grounding of early scientific inquiry into cause and prevention. By insisting on an informed scientific response, GMHC made both gays and the broader society take notice.

181

GMHC became so successful in articulating the language and crafting the terms of the AIDS debate that growing expectations created the phenomenon of what GMHC insiders euphemistically call "the religion of GMHC." People believed in the agency and treated it as a savior. At first, GMHC was asked to do everything and to do it well, which is what it did.

In itself, this is not remarkable. According to Gamson (1991:41), if a movement arises out of the fusion of individual and collective identities and receives widespread support from this fusion, it is not unusual for one particular organization "to embody the movement." This is what GMHC actually does, and in this way it is able to sustain its own role as "missionary."

To keep community morale high, GMHC had to establish an arena where volunteer competence could be expressed and community needs satisfied. Organizationally, this would be in planning and administration, but from the point of view of the PWA and community it would have to lie in efficient, but direct and personal, service delivery. Many gay-identified volunteers, who were recruited and then encouraged and rewarded for their inventiveness, became staff as their skills were discovered and their talents honed. In the process, volunteers felt appreciated and became bonded to the organization, which in reality they were creating from the ground up.

Determinedly taking care of urgent personal needs and threats to collective security simply makes the agency both more in demand and more appreciated by most everyone. Individual lives are being turned around, the community benefits, and the city is left off the hook by the gay community's magnanimity.

GMHC's reputation for dependability and know-how spread rapidly. In 1989 alone the agency appeared in over 300 articles and on 50 radio and TV programs. Such visibility also enhances credibility and helps GMHC build confidence in its management of AIDS and PWA care. Donated moneys and talent can then be allocated back to the community rather than to unnecessary bureaucratic proliferation.

GMHC's Stature and Success

Over the years, GMHC has received awards from many different quarters. Among the most notable places are the Office of the Mayor, the Veterans Administration, the Governor's Office, and the New York State Public Health Association. In appreciation of its commitment, GMHC received the 1988 Eleanor Roosevelt Community Service Award, the first of many similar recognitions. On May 22, 1990, the agency was awarded an honorary degree of Doctor of Humane Letters, *honoris causa,* by the New School of Social Research. The citation describes the agency as an "educational pioneer, public advocate, provider of comfort and hope."

In early 1990, while deputy executive director for policy, GMHC's present executive director Timothy Sweeney was named "Person of the Year" by the New York State Lesbian and Gay Lobby. On May 11, Leon Washington, GMHC food manager in recreation, was proclaimed the Veterans Administration Hospital's "Patient and Volunteer of the Year." GMHC received one of fifty-one citations, out of nearly 3,000 nominations, in the 1990 President's Volunteer Service Award Program for the tremendous work done by its volunteers. It was the only AIDS-related agency to be so honored twice.

Since social service agencies were not seeking PWAs (or, for that matter, drug-users or gays) as clients, it was necessary for the gay community to offer assistance to all the different publics affected by HIV. Here was one beleaguered population offering the gift of hope to the city at large yet garnering only minimal support in return, and only after AIDS had been heterosexualized. In a sense, GMHC is working against its own communal interest by "taking in everyone," but perhaps it is not working against its own organizational logic.

PWAs have always been shuttled around, often misled and mistreated by the city's medical and social service system. To facilitate direct action on emergency cases that get no institutional response, GMHC established an Office of Ombudsman, which is in daily contact with hospitals, physicians, public service officials, home care representatives, insurance offices, and others, trying to unblock PWA complaints about service. By 1990, the Office of the Ombudsman was helping to resolve over 1,500 health-related complaints—an increase of about one-third over previous years.

As reported in its 1988–1989 annual report, a typical day in the life of GMHC would find people at work lobbying for the landmark Americans with Disabilities Act (recently approved), assigning a buddy to a newly diagnosed PWA who lives alone and needs help with chores, mapping outreach strategies for people of color with community representatives, providing free legal representation for a mother with AIDS in court proceedings to arrange for her children's long-term care, explaining medical developments to one of many journalists, arranging both tdd (telecommunications for the deaf) hotline extension services and entitlements for an undocumented immigrant with AIDS, and so on.

As a human service agency, GMHC is expected to concentrate primarily on counseling and psychotherapy, emphasizing hotline services and psychologically oriented prevention programs. The exigencies of AIDS, however, forces it to do much more. GMHC now supplies a vast range of educational information, home care services, counseling, and planning expertise to a variety of community groups and city service organizations. By 1988, it was advising government agencies and informing the editorial content of many newspapers. GMHC frequently organized educational forums throughout the city and years ago warned of the dangers of unsafe sex and intravenous drug use. Capitalizing on gay community talent, it excelled in public relations.

By July 1982, GMHC had published and distributed 50,000 copies of a thirty-four-page newsletter, one of the first publications that explained comprehensively what was known to date about the disease. Six months later, 50,000 copies of a sixty-two–page newsletter were distributed nationwide. Later that year, 250,000 copies of a health recommendations brochure were distributed in New York City gay bars. GMHC's *Medical Answers About AIDS* has been circulated worldwide by the hundreds of thousands. It represents one of the most thorough guides on the subject printed to date. Everything at GMHC is done voluntarily by community members who donate their expertise.

By 1991, GMHC was regularly distributing over 1.7 million pieces of literature, making it the largest nongovernmental distributor of AIDS information and videos in the world. That same year, it gave away 1.4 million condoms. Education staff are continually developing new publications targeted to answer specific questions and address special populations. Two new publications are now directed at African-American readers and many others are done in Spanish for the Latino community.

GMHC also publishes *The Volunteer*. It keeps members, clients, volunteers, and donors informed of the latest changes in AIDS news, information, and GMHC policy/organization. Its circulation has doubled, reaching 110,000 readers by 1988. In trying to assist PWAs in gathering information on alternative drug therapies, GMHC also publishes *Treatment Issues*, which is mailed to 12,000 subscribers. It is a newsletter of experimental AIDS therapies and was edited by Barry Gingell, a medical doctor who recently died of AIDS. GMHC also has publications on a wide range of HIV-related issues.

In addition to offering bilingual informational films on AIDS, GMHC's education department produces a weekly cable television program called "Living with AIDS." A *Living with AIDS* guide, a booklet of resources in New York City, is now 184 pages long and is designed to provide PWAs and People with AIDS-related complex with a comprehensive list of AIDS programs and services. The guide also answers frequently asked questions about insurance, financial assistance, and legal matters that often arise for PWAs. Five thousand copies are distributed a year, often to other agencies devoted to chronic illness and health concerns.

The GMHC hotline, which now receives approximately 7,000 calls a month, now offers AIDS information services to the hearing impaired as well as providing increasing numbers of bilingual operators and available hours for Spanish speakers. The client services department publishes a resource guide, available upon request, for those who are HIV positive. On March 1, 1989,

GMHC cosponsored the first Pediatric AIDS Conference with the United Hospital Fund.

By funding, regulating, and reviewing research proposals and by supplying factual information about AIDS, GMHC gives much of its energy to creating a useful and rational scientific framework for understanding AIDS. Most of its time, however, is spent negotiating an adequate response from the public health delivery system and settling related civil rights and entitlement questions. In a system that rarely works well for any given population segment, GMHC too has to fight to get its share, even if at some other impoverished group's expense. GMHC also spends considerable time and resources trying to get the federal, state, and city welfare systems to respond more sensitively, efficiently, and responsibly.

In a short period of time, GMHC created a vast array of programs for virtually every constituency touched by the epidemic, including children. These programs help secure its centrality in AIDS service delivery. GMHC liberally lends its expertise, and often its money, to any groups that request its assistance—even though GMHC's funding remains private and gay community based throughout.

This generosity has now become a significant policy consideration, as it touches on the relationship of funding to ideological issues and organizational goals. Also, a more diversified AIDS industry began emerging in earnest after 1987, challenging, in effect, GMHC's primacy and ideological base. Extraordinary financial resources, however, continue to bolster and sustain its preeminence.

According to its 1989 yearly report, "financial independence has always been a tenet of GMHC's charter." Sustaining this autonomy, however, means cultivating gay community loyalty, even as PWAs and GMHC's staff and programming increasingly become less faithful to gays. In the beginning, everyone assumed that "AIDS was gay" and that most PWAs coming to GMHC would be gay as well. There was no other place for anyone with AIDS to find a home, and for a time this meant that gay people were primarily adrift and homeless.

Ten years later, this is no longer the picture. Today, AIDS appears in many populations, there are dozens of other AIDS agencies, gay AIDS resources are relatively depleted, outside funding is available, not all gays have died of AIDS, and volunteer altruism remains particularistic. Multiple AIDS services are now available, and AIDS care is centralized in a variety of organizations. For these reasons, a leap in commitments and connections to nongay PWAs is unnecessary. It is also unlikely that gays are willing to have the community totally subsumed under a democratic "AIDS community" identity. Yet GMHC as an organization remains committed to a universalistic ethos.

GMHC and Coalition Politics

More directly in line with its limited and public political agenda, GMHC is part of a coalition of sixteen AIDS advocacy and service organizations that, among other things, demanded that the manufacturer of AZT reduce the drug's price. While costing considerably less in Europe, AZT was approaching $10,000 a year here in 1987. In 1990, it cost between $5,000 and $7,000 a year, depending on quantity and frequency of use. A combination of ACT-UP strategies and AIDS Coalition pressure (including the threat of boycotts of Burroughs-Wellcome products) recently reduced the price by another 20 percent. With competition from DDI and DDC, the price is dropping even further. DDI comes in at about $2,500 a year.

On another front, a full-page ad placed by GMHC in the *Washington Post* on the day of a Senate Appropriations Committee hearing resulted in the committee approving a $30 million assistance plan to pay for AZT and other experimental drugs that GMHC wants offered in parallel track programs. In 1990, GMHC's Policy Department was also a central force in the passage of the Comprehensive AIDS Resources Emergency Act (CARE) that would provide "disaster relief" to American cities hit hardest by AIDS.

More recently, a dual press conference and a decision presented in an advertorial to join the boycott of the Sixth International Conference on AIDS was supported by GMHC. The intent was to denounce the immigration restriction that bars HIV carriers from entering the United States. A full-page ad, "Walls Will Not Protect Us from AIDS, But Knowledge Can," ran that day in the *New York Times, Washington Post,* and *International Tribune,* bringing international attention to the illogic of the federal ban.

GMHC has also played an important role in stimulating the development of several supportive and activist AIDS organizations at the national level. The oldest of these is the AIDS Action Council (AAC), a Washington-based lobbying group, and its subsidiary, NORA (National Organizations Responding to AIDS). The council represents 500 AIDS organizations nationwide and its lobbying efforts helped achieve a 30 percent increase in federal AIDS funding. Beginning in the late 1980s, GMHC granted AAC $275,000. This amount has been reduced annually since then.

On the state level, GMHC helped launch the New York AIDS Coalition (NYAC), based in Albany, which represents 200 state organizations. NYAC was able to secure a 15 percent increase in New York State AIDS funding. The New York Citizens AIDS Lobby (NYCAL), which has 3,500 members, is run out by GMHC's Policy Department and can flood, through its "phone tree," policymakers' offices with an immediate response to a piece of outstanding or urgent legislation. Twenty-six other AIDS agencies in the city formed the

Committee for AIDS Funding (CAF) under GMHC's leadership and worked to secure an additional $17.5 million in AIDS funding from New York City. Another $15.4 million was lobbied for and received in 1990.

The now disbanded National AIDS Network (NAN) was incorporated in February 1986 to network between AIDS organizations, provide them with training and technical assistance, and facilitate communications with national organizations including the American Red Cross and the American Medical Association. GMHC's first board president, Paul Popham, helped found NAN, and GMHC's former executive director, Richard Dunne, was its chairperson.

Perhaps it is because the field is so large and PWA needs are so diversified that GMHC has not been overly "territorial" about AIDS, although it might very well become so as resources change and the organization redefines its raison d'être. It has the money, power, and skill to dominate the field. It might even have the will, but if it does so by becoming the umbrella AIDS community, then only the organization will succeed, and only then at the expense of the gay community, which will lose its singular control of the issue and the agency if GMHC goes "public."

It might be wise for GMHC to continue spreading around its wealth and expertise and, in the future, to share the responsibility. With the funds generated at GMHC's 1989 AIDS-Walk New York, twenty-five different AIDS-related agencies shared $325,000 in grants and seed support. In 1990, $600,000 was distributed by GMHC to over fifty-two local AIDS service organizations.

GMHC presently shares custody for AIDS policy development by being a charter member of the New York AIDS Coalition, the Citizens Commission on AIDS, and the National Leadership Coalition. The latter organization is a broad-based group of corporations, churches, unions, and other institutions seeking to build a consensus around issues that all of its members can support, such as AIDS prevention education.

Some GMHC members also belong to the AIDS Resource Center (ARC), where the emphasis is on housing, home displacement, and living arrangements—services that GMHC has declined to offer. In fall 1987, a "Living with AIDS" fund began operations with the help and support of GMHC. Its objective is to provide moneys directly to PWAs to help with the high cost of AIDS care since GMHC itself provides only limited grants of up to $400, renewable only once. With GMHC support, over $120,000 was distributed in 1990 through the fund for emergency relief. $150,000 was again distributed in 1992.

Since resources are limited, however, it is unclear how cooperative all the AIDS-related organizations will remain over time. GMHC may actually be buying off discontent with its grants. There is some evidence indicating that agencies within a common field usually end up competing with each other for clients, staff, and funds. In June 1988, the *New York Native* ran a two-part story documenting fund-raising difficulties faced by smaller AIDS agencies in the shadow of GMHC and AmFAR, a national AIDS organization supported by actress Elizabeth Taylor and AIDS benefactor Dr. Mathilde Krim. Its tone suggested that jealousies and competition are developing within the AIDS industry. Generally, however, most AIDS or gay organizations claim, reports Whitlow (1988:44), to welcome the support and input of like-minded and committed agencies. To their benefit, they all have carved out different and specialized areas of concern.

Like all gay organizations, GMHC collects most of its funds from the "little guys," not from wealthy gays who may be reluctant to be identified as gay or supportive of a gay institution or, for that matter, a "homosexual illness."[1] Consequently, and despite community affluence (at least in terms of the gays infected early and mobilizing at GMHC), there has never been a lot of money to go around, mostly because a tradition of a broad gay philanthropy never existed. This makes GMHC's success even more amazing.

What might save AIDS agencies from either being co-opted by the state or becoming irrelevant to community concerns is that former GMHC staff are now scattered throughout the health care professions, still network with one another, and are still closely identified with GMHC and the community.[2] Furthermore, GMHC's membership currently so overlaps with other gay community organizations that a competitive and hostile institutional division within the community would cause so much dysfunction that it is unlikely to occur.

GMHC is now only one of many gay groups and AIDS-related organizations within New York and the country. Except for specific minority AIDS organizations, all draw their support from the same gay community. Since AIDS is communal in nature, every gay organization is affected. GMHC's funding, like AIDS, is virtually community contained and since gay money or expertise is behind virtually all AIDS organizations, the community collectively benefits by the redistribution of GMHC's wealth.

GMHC, Minority PWAs, and the AIDS Industry

As PWAs grew in number and type, they became increasingly misunderstood, their needs remaining unmet both at the city level and, because of their diversity and complexity, at GMHC, which at least made an effort to accommodate minority needs. The black and Latino communities, unable to embrace those with AIDS and support directly the gay community, as late as 1988 pushed their own disinherited into GMHC's care. This created a conflict of interests for GMHC, which was not expecting to service large numbers of minorities.

By 1987, the problem of minority AIDS at the agency became a significant social and programmatic issue. By then, 54 percent of the AIDS cases in New York City were found in black and Latino populations, putting minority and heterosexual women at a greater risk than gay men. According to Yolanda Serrano of the Association of Drug Abuse Prevention and Treatment, "the HIV virus [*sic*] is spreading like wildfire [within minority populations]" (Zwickler 1988c:7). As evidence she cites the 1988 finding that one in forty-three babies born in the Bronx is HIV positive. Undoubtedly this demographic shift and the growing maturity of minority AIDS agencies will have an impact on both how and whether GMHC remains a gay community initiative or becomes primarily an AIDS community organization.

GMHC responds as best as it can but cannot possibly handle even the 1990 estimate of over 200,000 people in New York City already infected with HIV as well as the 50,000 who have AIDS-related complex.[3] As of February 1992, 38,500 cases of full-blown AIDS had already been reported in New York. Even before then, "our caseload at GMHC," notes Tim Sweeney (then deputy director of policy), "has increased more than 100%, and in some cases, some of our caseloads have increased 900%" (Zwickler 1988c:6). Health officials estimate 35,000 new cases by 1995. The number of gays in this population will be large by any estimate, yet the community is literally shrinking in size and impoverishing itself by helping so many.

Since GMHC is overwhelmingly gay in terms of its interior logic, support, ambiance, and altruism, the minority question goes to the core of gay sensibilities, the nature and character of GMHC, gay communal boundaries and maintenance, and collective and shared identities. Because the increase in heterosexual cases has led to increased competition among AIDS agencies for scarce resources, GMHC's role as principal public advocate is being challenged. In one sense, this specialized competition helps maintain GMHC's institutional autonomy as a gay agency while it diminishes its scope, appeal, and power to control the field even though it takes care of nongay PWAs.

Moreover, as association with AIDS has become more fashionable, "outsiders" now can lay claim to the field. It is increasingly evident that the growing AIDS industry is free of gay control. Gay expertise is being minimized daily as other professionals and experts define the contours and content of the crisis. Were it not for GMHC's presence, AIDS news, seminars, conferences, and so on would be even more neutral or indifferent to gay concerns or inputs than they have already become.

It is a new form of marginalization to suggest that all gays know about AIDS and its transmission and that they don't need the money or more support. Actually, money is again being shifted to the bureaucratic and organizational systems of the class in power and away from the poor and disinherited as non–community-based AIDS agencies are established or as already existing institutions expand their hegemony over service delivery.

To be sure, minorities have begun to get involved in AIDS care, even though their potential to do more is not yet fully realized. In New York, a consortium of minority AIDS service agencies has been established and together with GMHC monitors the city's expenditures and appropriations for AIDS. Although they will never be financially autonomous, several minority AIDS organizations, like the Hispanic AIDS Forum and the Minority AIDS Task Force, have taken up political protest and carepartnering. Drug-users with AIDS also have an advocacy group. ACT-UP also frequently lobbies on their behalf.

Admittedly, minority AIDS agencies do not draw the broad support of their communities as easily as GMHC does. On the one hand, this is unfortunate since the gay community should not and cannot bear the brunt of care in this epidemic alone. On the other hand, if GMHC surrenders its share of public and philanthropic money to other groups vying for power, it will be able to maintain its historical character by having to depend on the gay community more.

In any case, GMHC (and the gay community) have neither the resources nor the wherewithal to become a citywide voluntary AIDS agency, even though this would sustain GMHC's preeminence by centralizing both PWA care and AIDS industry concerns. As a gay initiative, however, it would become dysfunctional if it created and managed programs for such a diversified clientele as prostitutes, drug-abusers, gay men, straight women, children with AIDS, and others, as great and legitimate as their needs may be.

GMHC Minority Programming

While GMHC has always had minority staff members, most of its early programs did not reach fully into the city's outer boroughs or attract minority interest. Educational efforts such as its prevention program—the "800 men project"—are gay dominated and essentially limited to popular gay neighborhoods in Manhattan. As is the case with all AIDS organizations, attempts to recruit more minority volunteers have proved, until recently, futile. Where some contacts have been established and where its efforts are not resisted, however, this situation is slowly changing, often for very practical reasons.

GMHC is presently building its future on its own democratization rather than on its special mission to the gay community. Paradoxically, the only way any voluntary agency can "really be on target, really understand the problems, and really come up with appropriate solutions," writes O'Connell (1976:114), "is through heavy involvement ... of the minority groups" it expects to serve. At GMHC, this could mean either gays or any Person with AIDS.

It seems that GMHC has opted for the latter. It now not only acknowledges but embraces the multiculturalism among its clients, staff, and programs. In September 1990 GMHC's board issued the following revision of its mission statement: "As a necessary and appropriate response to the diversity of clients and staff at GMHC, the Board has committed the agency to the realization of multiculturalism within GMHC and to the integration of multicultural principles and practices among all agency-sponsored programs."

GMHC's AIDS Prevention Department now pays increasing and special attention to African-American and Latino communities, making sure that general educational services are accessible.

> GMHC is a member of the Black Leadership Commission on AIDS and works closely with other existing organizations such as the Minority Task Force on AIDS, and the National Association of Black and White Men Together AIDS Prevention Project to help shape the ways information on AIDS is delivered. ... GMHC was asked to assist in the LUCES Committee's successful efforts to broadcast the AIDS educational film "Ojos Que No Ven" on National AIDS Awareness Day.

Other connected, but independent, AIDS services that GMHC both directly and indirectly supports include God's Love We Deliver. This agency brings quality home-cooked meals to homebound PWAs. Tuesday-night dinners for PWAs at St. Peter's Lutheran Church at the Citicorp Center were once organized solely by GMHC volunteer Peter Avitabile.

Multiculturalism and universalism, however, will take the agency beyond the confines of gay community interests, making the gay community, in effect, the "AIDS community." As such, GMHC would be an example of how a specialized community agency expanded its scope of interest to protect its preeminence rather than remain a local community initiative in competition with a larger industry it can no longer dominate. Or it could be a model of how an agency loses itself in a sea of bureaucratic irrelevance.

Ironically, part of the reason for GMHC being only one player in the field of AIDS service delivery is its own early policy of confining its resources to specific programs. Strained to the limit and restricted legally by its tax-exempt status, GMHC concentrates on carepartnering, advocacy, and education rather than on housing and direct and substantial financial aid. It thus fuels the AIDS industry by encouraging and supporting other agencies willing to supply a service or fill a gap that it could (or would) not fill itself.

One of the things GMHC cannot do is directly challenge the Federal Drug Administration's stand on experimental drug and treatment protocols—the very reason why the People with AIDS Coalition was formed. While lobbying for greater drug availability, this coalition also created a comfortable social environment for PWAs to meet and become organized into political entities. It is established in its own space with its own full-time staff and volunteer corps, many of whom are affiliated with GMHC.

The once trusted Community Research Initiative tried organizing and directing (with indirect GMHC support) alternative drug-testing programs for PWAs who wish to use experimental therapies. Many gays and GMHC partisans switched their allegiance and support to these two agencies and, of course, to ACT-UP.

Funding the Gay/AIDS Industry

Funding sources probably determine programming and policy development in minority voluntary organizations more than anything else. Community agencies are normally accountable to those they serve and those who support them. In the case of AIDS and GMHC, it is essentially gay people who are the funders and atypically (though now, slightly less frequently) the clients and care-partners as well. In itself, this resolves some problems while it creates others. As frequently happens in formal organizations, self-preservation can become an end in itself: The commitment to the original program or intent is no longer the end—just the maintenance of administrative power and positions and personal or private benefits.

In this situation, sincerity and dedication become measured by fidelity to organizational systems, making the volunteer experience orthodox and legitimate only when it is politically correct, that is, as defined within organizational boundaries. The corporate structure becomes the symbol of the organization rather than the volunteers, clients, or community; perpetuating it becomes the immediate goal. Increased funding, especially from outside sources, practically guarantees that this will happen.

While AIDS is not exclusively gay, GMHC most certainly is and what it is expected to be. This fact should guarantee a certain, if not demanding, community interest in GMHC's future. It also explains GMHC's considerable ability to successfully tap gay economic resources. For fiscal year 1987–1988, about 70 percent of GMHC's $6.9 million budget came directly from the community, only 26 percent of its income came from the government (8 percent from New York City, 13 percent the state of New York, and 5 percent from Washington, D.C.), and 3 percent from corporations. For all practical purposes, GMHC's 1988–1989 $12.5 million budget was, likewise, community derived. Less than 20 percent of these moneys came from government sources.

As of June 30, 1990, its revenue was $14.3 million, only 17 percent of which was derived from the city and state (none from the federal government). Nearly 80 percent represents contributions from individuals. Fund-raisers aside, in 1989–1990 the Development Department realized $8.3 million in net income from private contributions, a 21 percent increase over the preceding fiscal year. GMHC's yearly income and budget are now slightly over $20,000,000, with nearly 80 percent coming from private donors. Despite a shaky beginning, GMHC fund-raising abilities have become legendary.

On April 30, 1983, GMHC was able to host what was once considered "the biggest gay event of all time," filling the Ringling Bros. and Barnum and Bailey Circus at Madison Square Garden with 17,601 gay people and friends. That event grossed hundreds of thousands of dollars, as did a subsequent rodeo a year later, and put GMHC on its feet. With more corporate help, and minus a gay ambiance, in 1992 GMHC was again successful with a circus, this time as part of its ten-year anniversary celebration.

Of the many benefits held for GMHC, one of the most memorable is "The Best of the Best" at the Metropolitan Opera House on November 3, 1985. A full-house audience bought seats that cost $1,000 each to what the poster ad described as "a show of concern to benefit AIDS research and care" given by the theater and movie industry. Many Broadway theaters have also sponsored special fund-raising events for PWAs and GMHC in particular. A Sotheby art auction in February 1987 netted over $1 million for GMHC—up $500,000 from the year before. In 1988, the same event generated $1.75 million, of which $1.65 million (93.5 percent) was assigned directly for program funding.

GMHC's first "AIDS Walk" throughout Manhattan in 1987 brought in an additional $1 million that year. A year later, on May 15, another successful fund-raiser took place when over 15,000 "walkers" raised a record $2.5 million for the organization. Participants came from Broadway shows, local department stores, churches, and schools. Throughout the day 600 GMHC volunteers guided massive pedestrian traffic on the order of an Olympic game. It was one of GMHC's finest days, to be superseded only in 1989 when 16,000 walkers, backed by 123,000 sponsors, collected $3 million.

"AIDS Walk, NY 1990" broke even more records as the world's largest AIDS fund-raising event ever. The total amount raised was an astonishing $3,816,257—a 27 percent increase over projections. In this event, 25,000 walkers collected pledges from 200,000 sponsors. As reported in *The Volunteer* (July/August 1990), 550 teams, representing organizations as diverse as NYC Human Resources Administration (the largest team), Ralph Lauren, AT&T, and the Flight Attendants Union, displayed enthusiastic support for GMHC.

For GMHC, the event's volunteer effort was truly impressive. Nearly 1,400 people donated their time in the months before the event, running the phone bank, distributing information from tables that were set up, and putting up posters around the city. On the day itself, 1,000 volunteers handled registration, security, road crossings and checkpoints. "Their energy and enthusiasm," reports *The Volunteer*, "made a difference to all who walked." On May 19, 1991, 26,000 walkers raised an estimated $4,200,000. In addition to the 2,200 volunteers trained at GMHC in 1991, another 4,000 volunteers help out at these fund-raising events. A similar success took place in 1992 when $4.7 million was collected. Fifteen percent of the net proceeds was donated to other AIDS organizations, distributed largely through the New York City AIDS Fund.

On March 17, 1990, GMHC was the recipient of the proceeds of an Arista Records 15th Anniversary Concert to benefit GMHC and AIDS organizations nationwide. The sold-out event netted over $1,000,000 for GMHC. The October 1990 "Music for Life II" at Carnegie Hall, with chair Beverly Sills and artistic directors Leonard Bernstein and James Levine, was equally successful. In early 1991, GMHC presented "Dancing for Life II," with artistic director Jerome Robbins at Lincoln Center's New York State Theatre. On December 8, 1990, entertainers Nona Hendryx, Salt-N-Pepa, and Queen Latifah were among the live performers who helped GMHC rock the Javits Center. This first-ever "Dance-A-Thon" drew over 6,000 dance enthusiasts who helped raise over $1.25 million for the agency. In 1991, more than 8,000 dancers raised over $2 million at a party hosted by Deborah Harry, Eric Bogosian, and Cyndi Lauper.

After 1986, GMHC was able to draw upon the resources of larger philanthropic and charitable organizations such as the J. M. Kaplan Foundation and the Veatch Program of the Unitarian Universalist church. This support exists because of its organizational integrity and the efficiency and effectiveness of its own fund-raising department. Civil libertarian groups and those who fund progressive causes have little difficulty supporting GMHC projects since they normally fit their own agendas, especially since heterosexuals have appeared at risk. As in the entertainment industry, however, since 1983 many corporate and foundation donations to GMHC have come from insider pressures generated by informal gay social networks. In 1992, the Seagram's Company underwrote GMHC's expenses at the mammoth tenth anniversary "Circus for Life" celebration.

Among the largest corporate grants awarded was that from the Samuel and May Rudin Foundation for $150,000. Other notable grants were from the Ameringen Foundation for $100,000 and the Tisch Foundation for $10,000. In 1991, Bloomingdales's New York hosted a formal fund-raising evening, "Vive la France," for the dual benefit of GMHC and the Pasteur Institute in Paris. Twelve hundred guests raised $540,000. GMHC board members Judy Peabody and Jonathan Tisch chaired the event. The Tisch family gave GMHC a $250,000 challenge grant in 1992, the largest single gift in the agency's history.

The AT&T and American Express foundations are now major funding sources for GMHC's Library Project, through which hundreds of thousands of educational publications are distributed free of charge. The Ittleson Foundation made its first AIDS grant to GMHC for the computerization of client service records in 1989 and the Morgan Guaranty Trust made a substantial contribution to GMHC's Capital Campaign Fund. Considering that GMHC had no formal budget when it began, this is quite a development. Today, a five-person staff oversees complex accounting functions.

By June 1988, GMHC was spending just under $7 million on client services, education, public and medical information, advocacy, and policy development programs. This amount represents a 130 percent increase over the previous year. In the next fiscal year, GMHC spent $10 million, 90 percent of which went toward direct program services. By the end of its fiscal year (June 30, 1989), GMHC reported that it spent over $8 million for program services and related administrative efforts excluding fund-raising. Spending on client services programs increased 27.3 percent over the year before and spending for GMHC's public policy development and advocacy efforts increased 29.3 percent. Total spending on all direct program services increased over 15 percent from the previous year, whereas total spending on all supporting services, that is, management and fund-raising efforts, increased only 2.3 percent above the year before. In the 1987–1988 fiscal year, 73 percent of GMHC's expenses were paid with contributed dollars.

GMHC's fund-raising success, while telling us much about the democratization of AIDS, tells us equally as much about gay pride, gay priorities, and gay psychology and commitments. It also indicates the public's general appreciation and acceptance of GMHC as an AIDS service agency. The raising and allocation of funds at GMHC speaks well of gay people and GMHC's past relations with the community.

All these fund-raising events were successful and all these grants and awards were made because of GMHC's reputation, the nature of the cause involved, and the fact that AIDS has touched so many lives in society in general, the gay community, and the corporate world. The disease has devastated the art and fashion industry, among other professions. While the response of corporate America has been cautious, even in the fields where gay people abound, the generosity of individuals has been overwhelming.

GMHC Headquarters

In a move indicative of its stature and service commitments, GMHC opened its new headquarters in Chelsea (West 20th Street) in fall 1988, only blocks (yet seemingly miles away) from where it started. Over $5 million has been spent to acquire, renovate, and equip it. Previously scattered over five rented locations, all of GMHC's departments (with the exception of AIDS Professional Education and Communications) are now united in a six-story, handicapped-accessible, 37,000–square-foot space. GMHC still has to rent extra space, however, in two nearby buildings. The fund-raising, the purchase, and the renovation of the building, like all GMHC-related events, were coordinated almost entirely by volunteers.

Nearly everything the in-house staff needs, from computers, desks, and architectural repairs to office snacks and decorations, have been donated free or at cost, including the carpeting. One unique major expenditure was to complete recreation facilities, including a complete kitchen in which it is possible to prepare 600 meals a week to be served to participant PWAs.

With the new building, however, a different, if not exciting, new trend developed. Major corporations in the architectural and construction fields, not fearful of being identified with either an AIDS or gay cause, began making substantial donations in time, labor, goods, and services. According to construction adviser and architect Peter Stamberg, "it is hard for a manufacturer to turn down a charitable request from a major builder. But just as clearly, there is a sense of duty." Apparently, there is a real concern and commitment to the cause. GMHC board member Sam Watters notes, "Much of the architecture and design industry has been affected by AIDS. Every corporation we deal with has lost someone."

If moving to a single headquarters centralizes administration and service delivery, it also fuels bureaucracy. It was just about the same time as the move that GMHC began experimenting with an AIDS identity over its historical gay origins. The symbol of community, of *the* community, could no longer depend on a steady stream of gay volunteers, staff, or even clients—if for no other reason than death, fatigue, or changing and competitive interests and agendas (ACT-UP). The agency needs PWAs to survive. Yet in welcoming all PWAs, it retains one legacy and one type of legitimacy at the expense of an older, more politically significant, identity as a gay community mobilization.

Obviously, gay philanthropy is possible because the community identifies, supports, and depends on the agency and because the agency is credible in the eyes of both "outsiders" and old-time skeptics. Also, People with AIDS are everywhere, and in New York almost everyone knows someone who has died of the disease.

13

Homophobia, Bearing Witness, and Empowerment

THE PRESENT SITUATION OF GAY AIDS is akin to previous "medicalizations of homosexuality" wherein gays are defined as both biologically and psychologically sick. "Homosexuality as illness" is the renewed basis for social exclusion and is no less debilitating than overt violence. This idea often leads to self-denial and rejection, much like "homosexuality as sin" once did and, for many, still does. "Given the related systems of power and privilege," writes Irvine (1990:21), "theories and research concerning sexuality and gender are not simply academic but highly political in nature."

Because of AIDS, and the civil rights movement it generated, gay people again appear threatening to the nuclear family, the union of church and state, and the sexist underpinnings of capitalist economies. For the system, the disease surfaced at an opportune time. PWAs and homosexuals became the scapegoated explanations for institutional failures. Bolstered by medical or public health fears, a virulent and forever present gay bashing has dramatically increased.[1] Ignoring this phenomenon as a perverted crime of sexual harassment is a political strategy of direct intimidation designed to contain gay interests and power.

There is evidence that the largest group among people who are biased are those for whom homosexuals stand as a proxy for all that is evil. Gregory Herek (1984), a psychologist at the University of California who is researching homophobic social attitudes, sees the hatred of gay men and lesbians as a "litmus test" for being a moral person. Herek feels that such homophobia is often exhibited by those who adhere to orthodox religious beliefs claiming homosexuality is a sin.

Yale historian John Boswell believes that although by the early twentieth century the concept "homosexuality as sinful" was replaced in most people's minds with the scientific category "abnormal," this belief is not based as such

on empiricism or even the likelihood that most people even think of gay people as being a "category" with separate or unique needs and desires.

> The majority of people generally think of gay people as persons identical to them,
> who have chosen to do a bizarre and sinful thing that heterosexuals would never
> do. They could do it. But they never would. The fact that gay people in their view
> do choose to do this "awful" thing shows how "degenerate" they are: what "out-
> siders" they are. Since the heterosexual Christian majority would not choose to
> do it, they cannot imagine what motivates gay people to do so, and this removes
> people from the "normal" human realm. (Boswell 1987:24)

Whether justified by religion, medicine, or science, homophobia is a central
ingredient in sexist social arrangements. Institutionalized, it colors the fram-
ing of gay rights legislation, which, in turn, has an impact on the way PWAs are
perceived and treated. Because homophobia is often internalized, any gay mobilization concerning AIDS is truly astounding. Homophobia sets the agenda
in regard to AIDS. This is why and how it is political.

When GMHC was first founded, its primary concern was not carepartnering but monitoring and influencing scientific and attitudinal accuracy
in reports on both gays and AIDS. Through lobbying and networking, it was
able to exert appropriate pressure on the medical establishment to do needed
and responsible inquiry. Regulating AIDS research and therapeutic treatments is now all but out of GMHC's hands.

What GMHC continues to do with other groups is evaluate research inquiries into gay life, making sure that stereotypes are not at the base of medical
generalizations and policy proposals. It attends to the continuous political implications of how cause is defined and prevention regulated. Politicized gays
see these issues differently than the government does.

In the absence of interest and motivation, establishment science was decidedly nonaggressive in looking for a cure and a way to prevent infection. Virtually alone, GMHC successfully publicized the issue and changed this
situation. The agency has now switched attention away from identifying the
biological cause and scientific cure to prevention and safer-sex education.

The most dramatic and powerful medium for sustaining health, containing
AIDS, and helping PWAs remains the experience of community. Individual
identification with the history, values, and aesthetic of the larger collectivity in
all its diversity secures well-being. Voluntary service to others is the expression
of this pride because it manifests the joy of being both oneself and part of a
special people. Gamson writes,

> All social movements have the task of bridging individual and sociocultural levels.
> This is accomplished by enlarging the personal identities of a constituency to in-
> clude the relevant collective identities as part of their definition of self. The most
> powerful and enduring collective identities link solidary, movement, and organi-
> zational layers in the participants' sense of self. The movement layer is especially

critical because it is a necessary catalyst in fusing solidary and organizational identification in an integrated movement identity. (Gamson 1991:41)

Overt political activity regarding AIDS is born in the collective and shared
experiences of loss, fear, and pain. Personal experiences, when validated by a
collectivity, become political when raised to consciousness because trust is established.

AIDS and Self-Acceptance

Not all gays physically have AIDS. Not all PWAs are gay. Not all volunteers are
actively political. Not all PWAs are unhealed. And not everyone thinks of
AIDS as the only or even primary gay issue. But since AIDS is a collective illness with social boundaries, any sexually active gay person is at risk of loss both
healthwise and civilly. Thus all are called and need to bear witness. Conversely,
gay shame is evidenced in any unwillingness to respond to attacks on gay
rights, to offer support and solace to PWAs directly, and to accept AIDS as a
medical/scientific issue rather than a "divine curse" or moral question.

To change the moral coloring of the public and institutional response to
AIDS, unashamed public confrontations about AIDS, sexuality, drug use, and
gay life have emerged. Gay/AIDS spokespeople always appear particularly
centered and articulate. By being so forthright in their acceptance of their own
sexuality and those living with AIDS, they become validating signs of hope.

AIDS offers the primary opportunity for the community to identify and accept itself, to come out to itself and to the powers that be. In coming of age
this way, self-estrangement is ended. A healed gay consciousness empowers us
to bargain directly with American institutions over our own social identity and
location. By not being willing to again prove the legitimacy of gay life, the
community publicly celebrates its humanity, completeness, and autonomy by
taking on the cross of both protest and service.

As gay sexuality continues to be affirmed, validated, and made even more
purposeful, its energy becomes diffused into a wider range of activities and institutions. In the radical theology of Michael Valente (1970), sexuality placed
in the service of love is transformed. This is especially true for AIDS, where it is
automatically put into service and commitment to others. In effect, it transforms the community politically by changing interpersonal relations and expectations.

Since a substantial number of gays with HIV are products of the gay liberation movement, they are part and parcel of a living, though radically different
and still emerging, community. Ethnogenesis, begun in earnest in the 1970s,
is now clearly manifested in the growing institutional completeness of the
community. There is a recognizable gay culture and aesthetic as well as in-

creasingly positive recognition of their worth from many public sectors. There are social networks that link individuals and institutions to one another, making a crisis in one place a shared social and institutional problem.

It is the reality that the desire for both community and affection is now both publicly organized and possible that frightens both conservatives and liberals, moralists, and the sexually neutered. Of this emerging "queer" nation, theologian Kevin Gordon (1986:42) writes:

> The gay male community is more than a network of cruising areas. It is a dense network of groups and organizations, commercial and political activities, different personal beliefs and sexual styles. Nonetheless, what initially, and perhaps ultimately at some level, binds such persons together is the delicate tie of desire.

In terms of empowerment, AIDS turns a condition of marginality into the basis for community. This life in community makes living in peace with ourselves possible, especially since there is no easy way of differentiating who is actually sick and contagious or of determining who will be sick or well at any given moment. The gay mobilization in AIDS mirrors and encapsulates the totality of human needs and desires. It is the essence of communalization.

Conversely, AIDS hysteria is designed to oppress and destroy community. It goes far beyond the social and cultural annihilation of gays, the control of homosexual desire, or even the deinstitutionalization of gay community life. AIDS hysteria celebrates dominance over the individual by being rooted in the indivisible fusion of the sacred with the state. Though irrational, it is a calculated political strategy of containment.

For this reason, GMHC has to remain a community-based organization. It is the setting within which new relationships develop, attitudes are changed, and the experience of AIDS and being gay become redefined and understood. Not only do the agency and community legitimate each other (a necessary condition for the success of any movement or organization), but together they are able to draw their strength from a consensual and supportive population that supplies willing and informal recruitment networks. This is the reality and atmosphere in which AIDS volunteers operate and out of which their compassion, if not altruism, emerges.

In the 1986 survey, 43 percent of the volunteers indicated that they themselves had recruited others to volunteer. When asked to identify how they first came to volunteer, 18 percent said that they were introduced to GMHC through a friend. Thirty-three percent heard about GMHC (and the work it was doing) through the "gay media." Thirteen percent had lovers who had died of AIDS and "wanted to help others who were also sick with AIDS." A quarter of volunteers heard about GMHC through the mass media.

Like the illness, gay/AIDS volunteerism is particularly unique because it draws support primarily from an interactive network of politically identifiable people bearing witness to themselves in a way that transforms the nature and character of intragroup relations and intergroup politics. As in most social movements, AIDS volunteers are responding to a felt need. Volunteers believe change can occur and are willing to act on this belief.

In gay agencies, this change is accomplished more in the informal structure than through adherence to rationalized organizational objectives. While people become responsive when they feel empowered, GMHC support and success comes from those members of the gay community who "feel" for the PWA. Productive witnessing lies in the cathectic element that binds the community together to produce compassionate service.

Bearing Witness and Community Acceptance

Volunteerism in AIDS engenders awareness of the link between personal troubles and social (institutional) arrangements. This recognition of linkages, previously described as the "sociological imagination," is especially apparent, notes Sullivan (1990:19), "when death becomes less of an event and more of an environment." Even though the horror of AIDS leads some to believe that the private and public are two different worlds and survival means ignoring the issue, the political, nevertheless, always remains personal. They interact through a complex dialectic, pulling together thought and action to create for an individual a unique relationship to the world, out of which empowerment is born. Bravmann writes:

> It is never easy to participate in a world that does not even know we exist unless we tell them, a world that remains silent about us unless we speak up, renders us invisible unless we show our faces, and then avoids us, taunts us, and denies us once we present ourselves: often, participation becomes impossible. ... If we abandon the search for a non-existent private world, we will be able to act not in spite of but rather because of our perpetual public existence. (1987:20)

For the privatization of both AIDS and gay life to be rejected, a journey inward to the depths of the soul and the center of consciousness is required. For gays, being surrounded by stigma, suffering, and death goes to the core precisely because AIDS touches on questions of meaning, sexuality, faith, and identity. "And the stigma associated with homosexuality," writes Fowlkes (1990:646), "has contributed to the stigma of AIDS, the disease associated with homosexuality."

As an existential dilemma, the nightmare of AIDS challenges all our human assumptions about who we are, the overall purpose of our lives—even the goodness of god and society. The volunteer confronts these issues head on, daily overcoming despair to find meaning. Toby Johnson notes,

Perhaps unwittingly, a major consequence of the AIDS tragedy in gay culture has been the awakening of what might be called spiritual concerns. For many gay people, AIDS has brought a premature acquaintance with death and a consciousness of serving the sick and needy. Such awareness of the fragility and transitoriness of life has long been considered [necessary] for spiritual development. Spiritual here does not mean religious. It means seeing oneself and one's life in a larger context in which it makes sense to ask personally transcending and otherwise meaningless questions such as "What is life for?" "What's the meaning of all this?" and "Why do we die?" (1988:77)

AIDS volunteerism sets the ground for resolving these questions by turning bearing witness to "the poorest of the poor" into the fusion of the personal and collective interest, the source not only of identity and meaning but of power. By putting the individual and the community in opposition to the moralizing state, bearing witness in AIDS becomes subversive political activity. It shifts the seat of authentication from institutions to living and feeling individuals united in a common life and journey.[2] This is what volunteerism in AIDS accomplishes.

The older social order of institutional primacy over individuals is especially oppressive and vicious when it is legitimated by a "pornographic" theological distinction between homosexuality and the human desire for expressing it (Hunt 1987). In this patriarchal theology, being homosexual is considered morally neutral while homosexual activity is considered sinful. This is an anti-human and violence-producing theology since it separates feelings from action and being. Ironically, this dehumanizing theology often supports unforgiving compassion to the very victims of its own loathing. Through its "mercy," stateside theology actually perpetuates social injustice by leaving gays socially abandoned and homophobia unchallenged. In reality, its own image of, and foundation in, a loving god are undermined.

"Homosexuality as sin" authenticates "homosexuality as illness." Politically, it reinforces the social control of individual conscience by assuming the holiness and sinlessness of those who have social and reproductive power. In turn, the lack of social and/or religious legitimacy permits hostility and increases psychic fragmentation and cognitive dissonance. Socially and psychologically, it separates gays from one another and from society. As a result, the journey of the self toward both wholeness and "holiness" remains hampered and left incomplete.

Cleavages of the soul in this peculiar gay predicament are resolved by the construction of a different and shared meaningful world, free of the expectations and brokenness of the old. It is this process of collective "world building" that allows individuals to experience themselves as valid. Gay volunteerism brings the community together in a way that redefines and re-creates meaningfulness. "To achieve justice, groups that are oppressed or dominated must become subjects in history, not merely objects," notes Gamson (1991:37). He encourages people "to take a role in creating their own world, individually and collectively."

Destroying the hateful images of the self through self-acceptance is also the death of a specific consciousness, way of life, and gestalt. In the older social order, condemned individuals became negatively politicized, withdrawing in fear to private, safe places, thus leaving the majority in control, a collective gay life discounted, and the community of brothers and sisters abandoned. Internalized guilt, a reflection of social rejection, is isolating. Self-doubt especially restricts the development of mental and social wellness and a meaningful life.

This is why the religious or cultural stigma is such an important explanatory factor in AIDS volunteerism and why a theological language is peppered throughout this sociological report. Reclaiming the sacred or the self is central to the resolution of AIDS because, when expressed in connections to a person, the volunteer is brought back to his or her sacred sources and thus empowered.

Volunteerism frees gays from "emanation," that is, living within what Halpern (1987) calls "the confines of the old myths." The true self becomes complete by being brought into contact with the undifferentiated inner source of being (the sacred). This source is now manifested as a connected, inner "god of transformation" who invites us to journey to wholeness through self-acceptance, now defined as linkages with the other—the Person with AIDS as an extension of the self.

Volunteering in AIDS, then, is a process of differentiation of the self from oppressive "others." It is liberating because through it, human beings can shape their ego consciousness in relationship to its personal and transpersonal unconscious source that I have identified as the sacred within. As shared affectivity and relationship, the sacred becomes social in the most basic sociological sense. The community, as a result, becomes self-actualized and authenticated because it becomes shared and interactive through voluntary witnessing.

Reclaiming the Sacred and Empowerment

Considered sinful "others" and social outsiders, gays are often blamed for "causing AIDS." If this is believed, this blame further depoliticizes the community by encouraging its dissolution and legitimating its oppression. Discovering the community as the source of sacredness and political activity is unlikely under these circumstances. In this context, the church-state union has jurisdiction over gay life. Stateside religions do this by domesticating the sacred, that is, reducing it to institutionalized practices that support the social order and work against pride for gays, equality for women, and the social inclusion of minorities.

We, the abandoned people in need of service, have allowed social organizations to co-opt the sacred, taking it out of our hands, out of ourselves. Disguised as a patriarchal god, we have allowed the sacred to be used against us. In the best Durkheimian sense, the anomie or *dérèglement* resulting from marginalization and isolation from the sacred is social and political immobility and self-hate.

For a stigmatized minority to accept this social arrangement is to live within the politics of incoherence. This patriarchal social order causes the isolation and competitiveness that pits gays against "straights," the majority against the minority, PWAs against the healthy, the self against the community, and god against the individual. The solution is to fuse the individual and collective interest so that both are legitimated. It is in this context that volunteerism becomes political activity. For gays, volunteerism frees the community from outside control and sets it on the path of autonomy. Guilt ends and linkages and political action are fostered when individuals realize that their personal experiences are in line with what is confirmed as real by the community.

The act of volunteering is one of self-affirmation for both the individual and the community. Becoming healed like this, writes Abalos (1986:119) is such a sin "against the orthodoxy of the fathers" that it increases reactionary oppression. That is why this healing can be sustained only by individuals living in and within community. To do otherwise is to invite uncertainty and to remain politically inept. Political action comes from the space of self-acceptance and dignity on the collective level.

Unconquered guilt relates to AIDS in several ways. In addition to fostering disassociation from illness as a political issue, it makes death more fearful and the care of PWAs less likely. All these conditions indicate incoherence—the breaking of connections between the self and community—and are dysfunctional for both individual *and* collective survival. Guilt reflects an incomplete religious journey, leaving us all violated and self-loathing. Many gays living in such homophobic environments feel uncomfortable for being either sexual or living in community as a gay people, occasionally abandoning them both for the closet. In practice, the effect is neuterization and depoliticization and increased suspicion between HIV negatives and positives. By connecting the community to the PWA in a common journey of hopeful self-discovery, AIDS volunteerism allows us to reclaim each other as sacred sources.

The sacred has to be rescued from the tribalism of institutionalized religion. It must be redefined as a living source that sees us as gays, and through our suffering, as its own. And this is done in, and through, community. Indeed, the AIDS volunteer is political precisely when she or he lives in community, wherein each person is seen as a unique face of the sacred. This implies that the sacred is not finished and that as an undifferentiated source needs our participation to continuously create the cosmos. Therefore, god needs to hear from us the nature of our suffering as gays so that the sacred can respond to us not in the old finger-pointing manner of the orthodox patriarchal God, but as the loving god of transformation and equality.

As through volunteerism, we must celebrate ourselves as the responsible determiners of our own truth (identity). This way justice will be achieved on our terms. The existential crisis caused by AIDS is tempered only by our willingness and ability to take charge of the situation. Bearing witness allows the volunteer and the PWA to participate as equals in the mystery of self-discovery and self-acceptance, ending the suspicion about our lives. Carepartnering is important because it restores purpose. This is why reclaiming ourselves as sacred is political and threatening to social structure.

Outsiders already, gays are set further in opposition to the body politic by AIDS. Exclusion affects integration and solidarity with the community in the most basic sociological sense since the legitimacy of one's being is fundamentally undermined. This separation from the "source of mystery" often leads to instrumental social and sexual relations, which only exacerbate AIDS and increase self-rejection. Instrumental sexual activity, itself a response to the "immorality" and illegitimacy of male bonding, is central to AIDS fulmination and would be less likely to occur if gay relationships were institutionalized. Shilts puts it this way:

> For all the acceptance gays had gained, homosexuality still was not accepted as equal. ... A prevailing morality that viewed homosexuals as promiscuous hedonists incapable of deep, sustaining relationships ensured that it would be impossible for homosexuals to legitimize whatever relationships they could forge. Prejudice has a way of fostering the very object of its hate. (1987:206)

Illegitimacy and exclusion, however, give us an opportunity to take a new turn in the spiral of our own story. Accepting the reality of AIDS in our individual and collective lives makes us actors in our own history. By identifying with ourselves, with PWAs, we challenge the cosmology of the whole Western cultural tradition of white, heterosexist, male privilege. Rediscovering the sacred by giving witness in a fraternal way recreates our identity in a defiant way. Incredibly, we are subject to increased social abuse in the midst of a profound "death threat."

Transformation: What GMHC Volunteers Do and Achieve

Many of GMHC's organizational functions and the roles it assigns volunteers are determined by its internal development and its relationship to outside institutions and constituencies. To get funding and community support, it defines its mission and function in secular, pragmatic, and universal terms. In a sense, it is a "value-free" organization (ironically, a secularist political posture in itself) that emphasizes responding to the physical and psychosocial needs of PWAs, as if these were the total universe of human desires.

On a practical level, this definition of its mission is functional. It is in the common interest to establish rapport around basic needs rather than disruptive philosophical questions about values, beliefs, and the meaning of illness, dying, death, or even AIDS.

On the formal level, GMHC is a place for gay men to meet for practical, instrumental reasons. The services delivered are objectively recognized as good, important, and worthy, and the willingness to dispense them unencumbered by ideological and relational problems attracts recruits. One of GMHC's major strengths is that it can deliver expert, professional assistance nonjudgmentally. Informally, of course, GMHC is an emotional homecoming.

For these reasons, it is very difficult to assess what exactly GMHC volunteers do or even what they should do. We know only what they are supposed to do, in the official sense of what practical tasks they are assigned. As a group, they do all these things. But they also give of themselves emotionally, thus becoming dramatically transformed.

Even though volunteer roles are defined by the organization to accommodate the changing demands and needs of the PWAs, the relationship of the carepartner to the PWA remains transformative by its very nature. Bureaucrats, sociologists, and theologians will define and interpret the volunteer's work differently. And the volunteers themselves will have their own goals as they note and react to the individual terror and isolation of each PWA.

Obviously, GMHC administrators will define expectations differently than the hands-on volunteer. The volunteers, who may at any given moment be going through some heartbreaking emergency that they were not instructed about in any training guide, will delimit reality, priorities, and needs their own way. A volunteer may be involved in a faith crisis or a suicide intervention, hardly anything the agency can prepare them for. She or he may be the only link between a PWA and the face of humanity. Volunteers are people who help hold it all together for both the PWA and community. What they do, and what they are supposed to do, then, is a question of definition, which will vary by perspective and vantage point if not by the various personal and subjective ideologies of the volunteers themselves.

Because of the interface of gays with AIDS, it is necessary to define volunteers as anyone involved in AIDS from the point of helping and offering support. On the one hand, GMHC volunteers are members of the organization and are subject to whatever expectations and regulations are imposed on them. On the other, they must do whatever their instincts, insightfulness, and commitments tell them. In this way, volunteers remain connected to both the organization and the community. They are links in a chain of relations within and between GMHC (the gay community) and the outside world.

In a very real sense, the entire gay community in New York is involved in GMHC through the composition and connections of its volunteer corps. There are official GMHC volunteers, from which the data in this book have been collected, and unofficial volunteers who simply connect with GMHC when necessary and who perform many of the same deeds. In terms of carepartnering, trained and registered GMHC volunteers' official responsibilities are to deliver very basic services. They shop, clean house, and take the mail in and the dog out. They also plan programs for PWA recreation and bring people to parties, shows, and their homes when necessary and requested.

More informally, volunteers serve as role models and community guides. They watch friends struggle with their deterioration, sharing their joy if they rebound, suffering with them if they don't. Volunteers spend hours of time forming or attending support groups for families, lovers, friends, and themselves. They are almost always on call, always listening to the stories of those living with AIDS and those dying. Others hang out at the office, stuffing envelopes, answering phones, guiding the sick, filling out their medical forms, and sharing advice. Others join in protest demonstrations whenever they can. They are thus conduits of information and initiators of social change.

Volunteers take PWAs out on walks and to the theater, often having to shield them from the glares of the public. Some go with PWAs to church or temple. Often they listen to their confessions. Some become intermediaries between patient, family, friends, lovers, and doctors. Many volunteers formulate and distribute AIDS literature, work on the hotline, and counsel and support people just diagnosed. Other volunteers prefer to specialize in instrumental tasks at GMHC, reserving their personal energies and commitments for friends who become sick.

All volunteers bring a sense of peace and security into the lives of PWAs. Volunteers also get their hearts tried, their souls wrenched, their faith shaken, and their hands dirty. Often, they become the eyes and ears of PWAs and help hide their degradation. They bathe the fragile and carry them to bed, helping them live with dignity.

But mostly they prepare people to die in peace. They do this by helping PWAs cope with the mental, social, and medical trauma of the present. They listen, guide, advise, share, and help people to survive a day longer. Volunteers encourage PWAs to forgive, to connect to themselves, and to avoid surrendering to the cascading worlds around them. Volunteers do what each individual case requires, oftentimes going beyond the established or expected protocol. Much of what they do, and who they do it for, is by chance rather than by plan or assignment.

No one knows exactly how volunteers connect with PWAs, what they share or talk about in private, why one buddy or PWA is favored over another, or what they really mean to each other and do for one another. Their intimacy is often spontaneous, taking place at bizarre moments and in strange circumstances. Sometimes they are mismatched and miss the point completely. Volunteerism in AIDS leads to unpredictable situations and predicaments. Volunteers are people who respond creatively.

What do volunteers do, then, that makes their response so timely, sacred, different, and political? The answer is found, I believe, in what occurs on the individual level, within and between people even though this exchange is often left unarticulated and underreported. I am referring to the primary drama of self-discovery and personal renewal in the face of untold suffering and horror. It can be described only as an exercise in becoming centered, an experience in transformation for those who have come to know the human face of AIDS.

It is simply an astounding human experience to be involved in the life of anyone living with AIDS. The only way to describe it is to call it, as Whelan (1989) does, a "privilege." That PWAs are willing to share such a personal and critical event as having AIDS with strangers becomes for many volunteers the primary experience of a lifetime. The things volunteers give and do are also given or done to them in return.

To lose a friend or someone entrusted to your care is tragedy enough. To be surrounded by such pain, dying, and death on a massive scale is simply overwhelming, and this compounded loneliness is the living environment now for gay people everywhere. People are dying. Most are gay. To say that gay people are dying is to make a true political observation, and it is this fact, which cannot be ignored, that turns this general health issue into a gay men's health problem. Hence the corporate title Gay Men's Health Crisis summarizes a politic and places the problem in a proper structural context. GMHC's name and high public profile have kept the issue identified with the gay community. To translate both a medical condition and a community of people into a corporate identity is to both identify the problem and set the tone of debate over what to do, how to do it, and who will do it.

It is thus significant that the chosen vocation of nearly all volunteers is to be involved with two or three PWAs at one time. The volunteer must learn on the spot, therefore, how to be present, how to cope and draw on the collective resources and wisdom of the community. A good or successful rapport, however, or a positive resolution to a problem, does not necessarily occur between all PWAs and their particular buddies. Volunteers also learn to accept disappointments.

If GMHC volunteers do more than they set out to do—more than what is required by the political economy of the agency—it is because the exigencies of AIDS require that they do so. And much of what is done is born of necessity, without benefit of formal preparation. Largely beyond the scope or conscious intent of GMHC, volunteers are forced to learn about dying and death, funerals, homophobia, guilt, and fear—all at the same time. They learn a lot about how to manipulate the health care system, how to get efficient social service delivery. On a much deeper level, volunteers learn to forgive and to accept the work they have to do.

Whatever the case, connections are established when volunteers and PWAs realize that they can talk and listen to one another. It is within the context of these relationships that the self is freed from isolation and the particular loneliness and emptiness that AIDS engenders ends. It is these ties that heal and become the basis for self-acceptance and political activity. It is these ties that surpass in importance those ties with families and other social institutions. Unlike the hospital social worker, the volunteer is a representative of the community, a fellow traveler, connecting on the level of experience and feeling.

14

Gay/AIDS Volunteerism as Political Innovation

BECAUSE IT EMBODIED long-cherished American values about self-help, individualism, and autonomous problem solving, GMHC generated the first communalization of AIDS—the antidote to both religious bigotry and homophobia. Whenever individuals living in community bear witness to one another, they validate their own existence and enter the political arena with a sense of entitlement. Gallo (1989:131) writes, "The Kingdom of God will be constructed not through the charity of the elites, but through the efforts of the organized poor."

Carepartnering with a PWA constitutes this philanthropic "life of the spirit." Antidoting existential despair, AIDS volunteerism is about breaking relations to the self and connections to others, to institutions, and to social systems so that new visions can be created and new alliances formed. When individuals face suffering and loss, they find that it is only in community that justice is sustained and moral courage persuades. Transformation politics of this kind is not about anger or hatred toward individuals or bureaucracies. It is about receiving respect—acknowledgment that we too are real people.

Bearing witness in AIDS epitomizes this transformation, and a community celebrating itself this way not only challenges the present social order but also threatens its sustaining religious imagery. To shift legitimacy from institutionalized forms offering approval to authenticating individuals is subversive political activity. In this sacred humanism, the person is celebrated rather than the power derived from adhering to a domesticated God, as desired by the state and established religion.

Years before any American religions formally responded to AIDS, thousands of volunteers were already giving witness to PWAs, "washing their feet," as it were. These volunteers were seeking neither permission nor acceptance; they just did what had to be done. In a time of uncertainty, volunteers simply ministered to human needs on their own.

211

In celebrating the gift of their gay lives, AIDS volunteers are political innovators who bring the community to the truth about itself at a critical autobiographical moment that takes people out of themselves, out of their own closets, and leads them to their own creativity as persons. And nothing challenges the spirit or transforms the individual more than the face of someone with AIDS.

Bearing witness allows us to turn inward and to realize that the oppressive links between our own lives as gay people and that of the society around us can be broken and changed for the better by our connections to ourselves. In AIDS carepartnering, we are helped as much as those we serve to transform our self-concepts and politics in positive ways.

If gay social movements of the past were characterized by collective political behavior and external alignments, the present effort is concerned with subjective, internal, and personal changes—a metamorphosis in both behavior and relationships. AIDS volunteerism is qualitatively different from previous gay social movements because it immediately dismisses inertia, egocentricity, homophobia, isolationism, and political neutrality.

Most gay organizations are instrumental in nature. They are held together by rationalized procedures and by shared objective goals. GMHC, however, cannot afford to be "affectively neutral." Its purpose is to ensure our survival through passionate service and support by creating community. In addition to supplying creature comforts, gay AIDS agencies create a new balance of power, offer a new vision for the community, and furnish a new way of reaching it.

Beyond Stonewall: GMHC and the New Gay Politics

For heirs of and participants in the Stonewall riots of 1969, the contemporary gay response to AIDS is quite instructive, if for no other reason than its broadness. If Stonewall prepared the way, "coming out" now means putting the liberated self in service to others. In this post-Stonewall age, collective consciousness and individual well-being are united, and political agendas now revolve around internal and interpersonal issues, not only politically correct group or class relations.

The volunteer is fundamentally a political innovator because she or he steps out of the ordinary boundaries of relationships, doing what other outside specialists (doctors, social workers, priests) are supposed to do, but doing them in a way that empowers. AIDS volunteers define reality from within a shared experience with those suffering, both accepting their lives and celebrating them. This way the community itself declares its own wholeness and ritualizes its pride in the ceremony of coming out in service to the PWA and to the gay community.

That some gay politicos and critics of gay/AIDS volunteerism do not acknowledge the link between this activity and empowerment is a function of the conventional definitions that they share of the sacred, politics, volunteerism, and the process of social change. GMHC itself frequently defends, to no avail, its policies and positions within the same social-order models used by its detractors.

In his reports on AIDS, Larry Kramer (1987a), a former GMHC patron, wonders aloud about what he sees as gay apathy and indifference toward AIDS. Fearing that the war against AIDS has already been lost, Kramer calls gays to active aggression. The revenge advocated by Kramer, however, belongs to the politics of incoherence because it leaves unresolved questions of equality and justice. Instead of celebrating the rather large and dramatic gay response, he recoils at both government indifference and at GMHC's "incapacity" or unwillingness to be confrontationally political.

Kramer sees no political dimension or usefulness to volunteerism, preferring, instead, a direct public advocacy role focusing on funding, replacement of incompetent personnel in various health agencies, suspension of scientific drug treatment procedures, and the return of all social service activities on behalf of PWAs to public agencies and the state, away from GMHC.

Despite his ideological and ahistorical beliefs, however, Kramer's assessments about government indifference and the future consequences for gays for being "apolitical" are generally quite accurate and deserve attention since he, more than anyone else, turned AIDS into a public rather than private issue, thus saving thousands of lives. Kramer wants a "Manhattan Project" approach to AIDS and skillfully decries the ineptitude of government bureaucracies to resolve AIDS issues adequately, attentively, and compassionately. He is right to a point, at least in established political paradigms. But it is in this way that the strategies and objectives proper to healing are distinct from those of the politics of power.

Kramer recognizes the virulence of homophobia and attributes institutional disinterest in AIDS to its presence. He fails, however, to accept the contingencies that most gays live under because of its pervasiveness. Unfortunately, Kramer misses the point by not addressing the issue of how homophobia within the gay community is healed. While he acknowledges that it retards integration into the community, he continues to underestimate how AIDS would have undermined politicization were it not for GMHC and volunteerism. Oddly, it was Kramer's powerful 1983 article "1,112 and Counting" in *The New York Native* that made this point the most.

By supplying political behavior with a new grounding and determination, volunteerism was the first expression of this collective solidarity and consciousness. Kramer simply assumes that all gays are "out" in public as an act of defiance. For him, protesting AIDS is natural and automatic. Many of us, however, fear the economic repercussions (that is, regarding employment) of being so publicly gay or out of the closet as he is.

Kramer (1989) argues for justice in AIDS by presenting the experience of Jews in the Nazi holocaust as a reference point for gays. While tragic in its own right, AIDS is different because of the incapacitating effects of both self-rejection and institutional indifference. If Jews died because of intent, gays are dying from neglect.

Though moving, Kramer does not directly argue his case from the experiences and suffering of gays either under nazism or capitalism but does so by inference and comparison. He sees gays as the Jews of Germany and writes primarily of "their horror," rather than our own, which he presents only analogously. Understanding the situation of the European Jews, he believes, will produce outrage and moral sensitivity to the plight of PWAs and gays, something that did not happen even for the Jews (Wyman 1986).

Gays have a moral and ethical right to life, just like the Jews of Europe did, not because we are in need but because we are a legitimate people with legitimate human claims. Not recognizing the special gift of gayness is to allow us to perish. Homophobia robs us all of this opportunity and is as much an illness as anti-Semitism is.

The starting point of our defense should be our sacredness, not our similarity to the experience and situation of European Jews, which failed to create, except in a few covert instances, the response that gay organizations like GMHC, ACT-UP, and Queer Nation now encapsulate. If it were futile to believe that anti-Semitism existed in the 1940s, hardly anyone in America thinks that institutionalized and internalized homophobia does not exist. Many think it should exist as state policy. This is why we always have to be so vigilant.

Self-hate is a real problem, but to suggest that its solution is a "gay zionism," as Kramer does, is another. For him, another "slaughter of the innocents" can be prevented through the establishment of gay "elitism"—a position indicative of the politics of incoherence. From the perspective of healing, this is rejected as inherently dehumanizing because it emphasizes exclusivity rather than inclusiveness. Kramer responds to hate with hate and anger. Despite disclaimers, he operates within a traditionally patriarchal political paradigm. AIDS suggests that radical institutional and personal transformation is necessary so that no group or person will be seen as a dispensable "other." Kramer wants to rob Peter to pay Paul.

Kramer is not interested in either gay self-acceptance or authentication as a primary and basic saving strategy. Therefore his anger, however understandable, is left unresolved and misdirected. He neither accepts nor grasps the language of transformation or radical social change. To suggest that the fate of Jews in Europe would have been different had they been more militant rather than vigilant is to miss the point that hate and violence kill the soul and sicken the spirit.

In the long run, fighting hate with hate does not resolve anything. Victory here means that power and oppression are simply switched from one group to another. In contrast, fighting hate with self-pride accomplishes quite a lot: It sets a moral tone, and it empowers. It also turns potential victims into people. This politic does not rule out self-defense since institutions do violence to people, collectively and individually, and people need to protect themselves at all costs. Only now protest is directed outward onto institutions and ideas as the sources of oppression, not at hate-filled individuals. The moral cement that holds protest together is pride and dignity and the resultant willingness to cooperate no longer with social or individual evil. Without institutional changes, misanthropes will simply reproduce themselves.

Insisting, as Kramer does, on articulating issues within a customary political agenda, deploying a strategy of change that is confrontational within already established boundaries and procedures, gives legitimacy to existing jurisdictions and images of sacredness. As an idea and strategy, it is rooted in the time and space of the 1960s. Much of the politics of AIDS today reflects narrow assumptions about both its causes and cures, its meaning as an illness, the process of social change, and the origin of individual responsibility.

Ironically, even though it is considered to be less political than ACT-UP, GMHC actually is able to break and re-create linkages in two areas: relationships and self-acceptance—themselves the radical sources of all political activity. Traditionalists, like Kramer, assume that political activity begins on the public level rather than with the individual who becomes self-accepting through integration with the community. These same social-order strategists are also forced to focus on AIDS as purely a scientific/medical issue rather than as a psychosocial and political dilemma because this is the only agenda their ideology can sustain.

The primary issue is what needs to be done now until a cure is found. How the community will survive and exist, how gays as a people self-define, and what the content of the gay inheritance left to the next generation will consist of are equally significant questions. The basis of survival and continuity (the central question), while needing legislative support, must be grounded in something more deeply meaningful than science, medicine, and biological survival. Being alive, of course, and having some political power are essential and fundamental to existence, but alone they lack purpose, meaning, and context.

Unfortunately, commonplace political activities and vocabularies of analysis reinforce secular or simplistic understandings of the source and nature of both power and sacredness; indeed, they are often put together. In this way, they actually reaffirm the legitimacy of oppressive and orthodox institutional arrangements, beliefs, and their subsequent authority over human behavior. As such, these strategies are not nearly as radical as those that require that we, like everyone else, struggle daily with our own authenticity and integrity as a people.

Communalization (Healing) as Political Innovation

Being outsiders allows gays to locate the sacred in places other than society and in unusual ways. Discovering the alternative "god of transformation" carries profound political and social implications for us. In stateside religion we are left without humanity. Fortunately, in being denied the god without, the sacred within becomes less foreign, more reachable and knowable.

While an insider God is called upon to legitimate discrimination, such patriarchy disenfranchises all of us. Intrapsychically, interpersonally, and socially, many of us become doomed to a life of incoherence when established religion uses the language of sin, guilt, and punishment to describe our lives and contain our behavior, making bonding together virtually impossible. Subsequently, the fear of exposure and the rejection of connections to similar others becomes crippling.

It is from this position of marginality and fear that volunteerism has created a radical and authentic religious experience in opposition to societal religion. Gay/AIDS volunteerism takes us back to basics, back to the self in a binding, accepting way. Approval and integration into mainstream religion, then, is not the issue since inclusion would only reaffirm the validity of patriarchal religion and culture over us and separate us from ourselves. Of necessity, this religion is anti-gay, anti-sexual, and anti-women, and therefore anti-human.

Surrendering control over one's personhood to such a foreign and unauthentic entity would be self-destructive. By moving the locus of the sacred from a domesticated God to the center of our underlying creative being, communalization prevents this potential alienation. For the life of the spirit to both nourish and be nourished, we must be in continuous opposition to hostile and indifferent institutional religious forms. This way the self can remain sacred, creative, relevant, and political.

As an autonomous act, AIDS volunteerism is political because it is born in linkages. It is sacred because it cements the self to others. The affirmation necessary to be political is manifested when an individual and community give recognition to one another. This entails a conscious choice of rejecting the drama of exclusion inherent in patriarchal religion and substituting it with mutuality, in which each person is a face of the sacred. This process is fundamental to healing because being healed means freedom from self-rejection, as does bearing witness.

For gays, volunteerism heals because it accentuates the dignity of everyone. Gay humanity and the valuableness of PWAs are accepted as a given. Hence the community points to inclusiveness, whereas the conventional religious meaning of holiness is exclusionistic because becoming whole is available only to those who return to patriarchal orthodoxy, the "true faith." Healing denies the validity of the "reified God" in societal religion and the manner and settings in which "He" is "worshipped."

Gay volunteerism in AIDS heals by affecting the way relationships between people are structured and presented. It is a political experience with the radical task of shaping an environment wherein people can publicly celebrate their sexual identity. This transformation begins after the self acknowledges its right to claim sacredness for itself and those it is connected to. This new pride, integrity, and dignity lead to kinship and political activity on behalf of the self as a member of a life-giving community. Being healed is dramatic and radical because it occurs outside the traditional channels of religious legitimation.

Healing for gays neutralizes religion's control of both the sacred and the secular, rendering ineffective its claims to relevancy, truth, and the power to define. Self-acceptance challenges religion's power over individual behavior because authenticated people are connected to themselves and seek reconciliation with the world for its and their own sake. The strategies and goals of healing are therefore distinct from those of the politics of power. In the model of healing, the sacred and institutional religion are not synonymous. In fact, they are at odds.

Ultimately, the sacred, as *the* mystery in our depths, cannot be made safe or domesticated, as claimed by so many religious organizations. It can't be used to divide and destroy people. This is why integration with the community is the most basic solution to the problem of both bigotry and "brokenness." Integration restores us to wholeness and allows us to control our own lives by bringing home the sacred, by reinterpreting basic religious ideas so that their original transforming message empowers once again. Healing leaves people free to discover and/or create the mystery of the sacred in their own lives and in that of others.

It is not that support from organized religion for either gay rights or increased AIDS funding would not be helpful or even useful on the political level. Rather, it is the hypocrisy of such support, too little coming too late, after all too much damage has been done to the gay psyche and spirit, that is unfortunate. It is the attitude of "hate the sin, love the sinner" that turns gay people into abstractions and indicates that organized religion considers gay sexuality an aberration. For this reason alone it should be condemned and shunned.

Where sexuality is concerned, to separate the spirit from the body, the emotional from the relational, and feelings from the mind is to destroy the individual, leaving only guilt and shame in its place. Gay sexuality is one expression of humanity's sexuality; it is part and parcel of how we are in the world and of how we choose to define and accept ourselves as living and different embodiments of the sacred. Our gayness is our gift to ourselves and the world, and communalization helps us to recognize and act on this awareness.

Unlike the politics of power, self-acceptance creates a much different way of life because it directly confronts and altogether rejects the social order and legitimating power of societal religion. Healing is a political strategy because it restores individuals to themselves, to their own bodies, to their own sexuality, and to the community. It confirms our experience of the world. An AIDS volunteer allows his or her political potential to emerge and be expressed in a way that integrates and binds us to one another.

When we gay and lesbian people give witness to ourselves in AIDS, we stand in the presence of others and personally and politically reject not only individuals who sermonize against us but also the whole social and political structure that gives others the right to be so exclusive. Because of AIDS, we can no longer participate in patriarchal, tribal religion, which is, by definition, exclusive, as we create and celebrate a ceremony of mutuality and community. Because of healing, a sacred, autonomous (yet obviously connected) self is now in opposition to the social order. By definition, the structure and affairs of society, religion, and government are challenged.

It is at the point of healing, at the point of giving witness, therefore, that the sacred, the political, and the personal are joined. Our autonomy allows us to forge a new history; it dawns on us that one man nurturing another man or woman is finally, in the words of South African playwright Athol Fugard, "the central arena of history."

Self-Acceptance (Communalization) as Radical Political Paradigm

As a political strategy, healing is much more radical than the established politics of power, the standard psychological or sociological approaches to change that leave human relations sacrificed. Healing assumes equality and forgiveness by destroying customary notions of illegitimacy and any guilt or sin rooted in being different. Healing adds a dimension of legitimacy that affirms worthiness in the simple act of being. It also speaks of freedom from shame, freedom from self-denial, and the fear of being known, and, most important, freedom from crippling self-hatred and projected or protracted anger.

Anger and revenge are part of the politics of incoherence and defamation and have to be consciously rejected and brought into the politics of healing so that energy can flow outward in the service of personal and social transformation. Competition and revenge leave unresolved questions of equity, forgiveness, and justice. If these are left unaddressed, the old order is simply re-created to the advantage or disadvantage of some other displaced group. In typical "power-conflict" models of intergroup relations, having power is the source of pride and self-authentication. In the paradigm of healing, empowerment is the capacity to create and re-create a social order based on respect for the individual.

Dennis Altman's 1986 work on AIDS and gay power relates the illegitimacy of gays to political impotency and the lack of "legal recognition." In the model of transformation, these conditions exist because the old social order requires the disembodiment, and hence disenfranchisement, of some groups and ultimately the alienation of all groups from one another. Unlike shunted-aside minorities, gays and women are normally cast out because they cannot justify their uniqueness within pornographic theological and social systems. Patriarchal religions exercise control over sacred imagery and society, making God knowable only through conformity to rules and regulations rather than through relations.

When gays are unable to witness PWAs or show sexual responsibility, they indicate self-rejection and a conservative social-order understanding of god, religion, and the source of the authentification. Yet all around us, among our friends, there are new images of god and new faces of the sacred at work that AIDS has generated and that accepting the communalization of AIDS sustains.

What makes gay liberation threatening is its new basis in witnessing: The community legitimates itself by creating and claiming personhood, through which it takes on both religious and political meanings. For the oppressed, there can be no real or complete healing within the law and none between the self and the law. Transformation takes place outside officially established social patterns and cannot or need not be constrained by them. Nor can typical political vocabularies be useful here since they rely on the language of power and control, hierarchy and exclusion, that are proper to traditional political paradigms and not to healing.

People must claim freedom when being political. This is how they capacitate themselves to destroy inadequate linkages and then to create and nourish fundamentally new and better relationships. Institutions consist of the linkages by which people bind together in a social union. All of us are capable of taking these institutionalized ways of relating into our own hands to break and re-create time and time again.

Thus healing goes beyond the normal political processes and leads to a transformation of consciousness and behavior in the way that relationships are established. It results in the ability to nurture and mend—to be feminine. Healing is the development of the expressive, the capacity to be intimate, and the incorporation of the affective into the personality—all traits that gay men have often been hated for allegedly having. Conversely, when these traits were missing, gay men were accused of being macho, impersonal, manipulative, and selfish.

Becoming healed has been misunderstood and undervalued as a political strategy because it begins with the individual in relation to his or her own self as linked with others rather than to public institutions and control of the political processes. In this way it also contradicts prevailing psychological wisdom. By leading to the ideologically unpopular or heretical diminishing of the ego, it ends the isolated self-sufficiency assumed so central to maintaining both American society and individual mental health. Gay volunteerism threatens establishment psychology by requiring connections, forgiveness, and political action. Psychotherapy, in contrast, too often creates and emphasizes egocentricity and autonomy, as if the individuation of ego is the solution to all personal problems.

For me, it is the mutuality of AIDS that makes healing both so appropriate for gay men and so threatening to society. Surrendering the will to vulnerability and mutuality ends hatred. It ends passivity. From these links with others, a new political order emerges. To thus nurture and reorder society, cultivating and celebrating the anima of men is required.

This idea is not easy to accept because sexism demands that heterosexual men be "honchos" and gay men be "gender failures." Thus many of us have often tried to embrace masculinity in the extreme, although it is generally destructive of holistic relationships. This was done to avoid the stigma of being depicted and assessed as effeminate. This point is central to our whole argument about the uniqueness of the gay GMHC volunteer who is doing "essentially women's work" without having been socialized to do so.

What is profoundly ironic about gay/AIDS volunteerism is its ability to help men accept themselves by nurturing the feminine through care-partnering one another. This is why the new gay empowerment is so feared and often resisted. It is this power to connect intimately with others in a way that reorders relationships among (and hence between) the sexes that established religion abhors. In AIDS, this connecting also lessens the collective psychosocial terror of imminent and pervasive death and dying from a stigmatized illness and life-style.

When gays learn to nurture one another, to love, accept, and express the affective in themselves and affirm it for others, the very meaning of what gay is and the daily relations of gays to one another are irrevocably altered. To the dismay of conservative religious organizations, once one is healed, nothing is more apparent than the passionately loving and sensual nature of both god and the "inner self." And it is this passionate god that calls us to love ourselves. The "tribal God" of law, rules, and punishment is displaced by the god of love and equity. Religious institutions and a heterosexist society cannot allow this rediscovery of a god with an infinite number of manifestations because it would profoundly challenge the privileged male relationship to power over women, gays, and minorities.

Healing and Social Change

Contemporary politics regarding AIDS, then, is essentially the politics of power and assimilation, fought on the terms of the oppressor for the sake of acceptance into a system already distorted by its own elitism and arbitrariness. As society begins to respond to AIDS, all that America's bankrupt health care system can do is shift its limited resources from one needy group to another. And history has shown that incremental change rarely leads to fundamental social transformation.

A positive response to AIDS cannot be made at the expense of some other group in need. This incapacity to deliver equitable services to a wide range of disadvantaged groups reveals the utter futility of the politics of power. In the paradigm of healing, to be political is not just public activity on behalf of a cause for the sake of accommodation. There are radical ways of being gay and political that have more to do with relationships and culture than with civics alone.

Michel Foucault (1982:36) has argued that it is not only "a matter of integrating this strange little practice of making love with someone of the same sex into pre-existing cultures: it's a matter of constructing cultural forms." Culture building requires connections, and healing is a new social form because it links people to one another and thus their own sacredness. It is its own ethic and becomes the starting point of cultural development and social change.

Even the traditional strategies used daily by American interest groups, while available and useful in the short run (for example, to increase government research funding), will not be fully successful for AIDS because they do not require a change of heart, a reconciliation, or a rehumanization like that created by healing. To date, the official response to AIDS mirrors institutionalized social attitudes, prejudices, and arrangements, especially as they relate to ideology, the location of responsibility, and the specialization of labor.

There is no new social order, no new humanitarianism, and no collective or common good envisioned in the old strategies. One group merely replaces another in the power struggle for so-called limited resources. The "new politics" suggested here is essentially different because it doesn't operate out of the paradigm of anger and revenge. It goes much further. Together with the desire for justice, it uses linkages and compassion as its impetus. Justice is required in the resolution of AIDS because gays are people and citizens. The politics of national interest needs to reflect this fact.

According to Abalos (1986:141), a Chicano architect of the new politics: "The real work and real political participation is to recreate ourselves as species-being and the world according to our newly discovered selves. Political work means forging fundamentally new and better relationships to self, others, problems, and our sacred sources." For him, the issue is "to discover individuals who share a common consciousness in regard to a particular kind of work" so that people can participate in a constant process of breaking and remaking relations for the sake of real advancement and change. Volunteering in AIDS supplies the opportunity and setting for this to happen because of what it does for the PWA and the community as a function of bearing witness. Social change begins here as the self is discovered as holy. Fortunato (1983) refers to this as the "healing journey of gays." He recognizes the need for us to "grieve" over the experience of being exiled by so many American institutions and to overcome our isolation—not by becoming included in these institutions but by being free of them with joy.

Likewise, political scientist Manfred Halpern (1987) believes that both self and communal identification coming from psychic well-being are factors necessary for change or positive healing. In his view of relationships, individuals or groups move from a situation of emanation (being an extension of someone else) to one of incoherence (breaking a relationship) and then move beyond power interactions to the experience of transformation, the creation of fundamentally new and better relationships.

For Halpern, recognizing oneself as a "source of mystery" leads to self-affirmation and subsequent negotiation and bargaining from a position of strength rooted in one's sacred sources and in one's own community. The claiming of one's own dignity, as part of the undifferentiated sacredness of being, for the self and by the self, means that respect is no longer a privilege bestowed but is something deserved or required by virtue of one's humanity. The issue becomes one of rights, not legitimacy or proven worthiness. It can now be proclaimed by gays that discrimination, abuse, neglect, and rejection will no longer be tolerated, nor will the system that creates and maintains it.

In terms of AIDS, this healing means that we, as a special people, will never again have unsafe sex, sustain instrumental relations, recede or hide from sight, cease to celebrate an authentic existence, or live in and with fear. Healing, then, defines a psychology, sociology, and theology of gay liberation. It is the wellspring for, and consequence of, authentic volunteering in AIDS because it ends powerlessness by saving a life and a people.

Healing: Beyond GMHC and Volunteerism

For many thousands of gay men, AIDS is the source, the generator of this rebirth of self-acceptance as expressed in nurturing. "The daily living of our lives," says Bravmann, "causes—forces—us more directly to address the nature of our public and private selves, more accurately to apprehend the meaning of our actions." He also acknowledges the relation of this self-awareness to political activity and writes: "We have demonstrated to ourselves and the world that, even as a community fraught with differences, disagreements, and inequalities, we can take hold of the world as we experience it and convert this knowledge into powerful emotional, cultural, and political activity" (Bravmann 1987:20).

Given the reality of AIDS, gay volunteerism in AIDS is the manifestation of this politicization. It is essentially the politics of transformation because it is life-giving and necessary to gay people's survival and for AIDS to be contained.

That even the threat of both personal and communal annihilation does not move more or all gays to action is rather astonishing. For Larry Kramer, it is terribly depressing and disappointing for many reasons. Despite GMHC's success, he sees bearing witness as a denigration of GMHC's original purpose and a response, he feels, that doesn't really matter. Kramer has publicly disengaged himself completely from what he calls "GMHC's Red Cross role." He favors instead the political activity of ACT-UP, another activist group he founded, which has also both disappointed him and distanced itself from him.

Perhaps the answer to his quandary as to why there are not more gays involved in the gay/AIDS movement can be found in the conditions that healing transforms. A paradigm like healing, which stresses political activity as another face (function) of self-adjudication, offers a better explanation for lack of involvement than Kramer's emphasis on laziness, indifference, and ignorance.

As political innovators, GMHC volunteers represent a radical shift away from not only the structural and functional confines of organized religion and health care delivery but all corporate systems that end up simply processing people. Considering that Americans prefer to privatize affections and the responsibility for health and welfare, "coming out" in public to volunteer is a real change, a real challenge and threat that Kramer underestimates. Social arrangements, after all, are fundamentally political in nature and need full citizen participation to be fair.

Institutionalized discrimination, lack of community, lack of pride, and private adjustments to discrimination have made it impossible for us to inform the decisionmaking process, making volunteerism the contemporary way to express our interests and articulate our concerns and express our humanity.

Without healing, gays and other citizens can privatize AIDS. We can individually avoid it, we can protect ourselves, by going back into the closet, moving to other cities, and trying to survive on our own. Healing in the context of AIDS, however, is integration with the community and its collective life and begins with the awesome awareness of being in an ongoing and accepting relationship with a profoundly loving sacred source, often called the "undifferentiated other," the ground of our being or, more mystically, "the cloud of unknowing." It thus empowers and restores emotional health.

Healing forces public or political action to take place in justice, with compassion and affection, and without the crippling fear of self-exposure. This context is important for the gay community and the gay liberation movement precisely because of the role of "moral" ideas in the civil oppression of gays.

AIDS has created a crisis not only for gays but for mainstream churches and moral entrepreneurs precisely because it is a disease of the most hated, the most broken, and the most disinherited. In this country, we have the condemnatory morality of the Judeo-Christian tradition coexisting with the living experience of crucified gays and drug-users who bear, increasingly with women and children, the brunt and burden of AIDS. For all practical purposes, AIDS is the physical manifestation of homophobia and minority social rejection.

If ever there was a base for a liberation theology in the United States, it is the experience of gays and AIDS patients. Gays, prostitutes, and drug-users are among the most broken of the broken (precisely because of religion's proscriptions) while being in need of the preferential treatment of the poor demanded in liberation theology. This point must be stressed since one cannot heal any of the segregation and distancing caused by AIDS without challenging organized religion's preference for the privileged and the institutionally appropriate theology that sustains its power in society. Indeed, the best of liberation theology accentuates a preference for the poor, including the poor of heart, which gays and people with AIDS most certainly are.

It is the transforming god within us that inspires us to step forward with urgency because the minority and gay poor are dying before their time. With this in mind, healing can be seen as the challenge of restoration to oneself and of gay people to one another and to the wider community in the face of despair from mounting and unnecessary deaths.

Healing has to happen to ensure survival as a people. For persons with AIDS, the GMHC volunteer, and for carepartners in general, the experience of volunteering is one that is life-giving and supportive, since healing brings the gifts of inner peace, self-acceptance, and hope to those in need—the carepartner and the PWA.

Quite bluntly, the sadistic "God of authority," law, and punishment is clearly rejected here. "He" is being replaced by a living and more just face of the sacred, a god of equality, love, and justice. We do not have to be reconciled to a legalistic God/judge. A loving god will seek our humanity and respond to us in our suffering. Just as women have taught god about their lives and have reclaimed "her face" as their own, so too do we teach god of our suffering and re-create the face of the sacred as a compassionate being.

Our whole Western tradition tells us that god entered human history precisely to struggle with us as co-creators of the world. It is the domestication of the sacred in organized religion that has interfered with this awareness and process. Our god stays fast, is supportive of our needs, and leads us to renewal and change. To be authentically sacred is to be actively involved in the world, to change it, and to remake it with mercy and love.

Epilogue: Toward the Future

IT IS NOT EASY to write a book about a complex and constantly changing topic. New information is announced daily and old theories about the origin, cause, transmission, or control of AIDS fall by the wayside. It is necessary to stay current not only with the policy proposals of an ever-evolving "AIDS industry" but also with the changing needs and politics of the gay community. They intersect so frequently and so intensely that they exist as one.

Interpretations of how GMHC and nonprofit-sector ideology interface remain dependent on assumptions, contexts, and vantage points. In AIDS, this is evident in the way that problems develop and are resolved, often redefining organizational mandates in the process. Take, for example, the complex issues of minority AIDS, women and AIDS, and the participation of both these constituencies in GMHC. Just as the agency was becoming more democratic, minority AIDS organizations became more adept at manipulating the medical and federal bureaucracies to their own interests. As a result, GMHC may ultimately end up serving fewer minority PWAs at the same time, ironically, that multiculturalism has become a commitment there and gay infection rates have begun decreasing.

In terms of survival, GMHC has adapted to the changing meaning of AIDS and to policy developments originating in the larger societal and institutional arena affecting its own public. Likewise, the AIDS generation I knew and the volunteers I worked with are fast disappearing from the scene, only to be replaced by younger, less idealistic, and more pragmatic recruits. On a personal note, not only are all my friends dying, but so are the early founders and staff of GMHC. A few survivors are moving into other challenging positions in the AIDS employment sector or in private business.

A generational shift at GMHC means that memories are shorter. Those "inheriting" GMHC did not come of age in the 1960s and seem less willing to accept stigma; these attributes will affect the character of the agency, how AIDS becomes defined politically, and how volunteerism is practiced. For the previous generation, AIDS was known intimately—as a social context.

By the end of 1990, GMHC had just about outgrown itself and began to retrench. Likewise, its high-tech ambiance, created by its reliance on state-of-the-art communications systems (answering machines, videos, beepers), and its complex division of labor made the timing of my study even more appropriate, as a breed of volunteers and style of administration were fast disappearing. Access to information became difficult at about the time my research was coming to an end.

It is not that personnel were less responsive; rather, it was because news, personalities, priorities, if not people themselves, were changing, and at very rapid rates. It even became difficult to determine when and how to end this study. With the first decade of GMHC and AIDS coming to an end, I simply decided to stop writing with the appointment of GMHC's current director, Tim Sweeney, and new board president, Jeff Soref. By 1992, they became the last of a struggling generation trying to keep one foot on the future and the other on the heartbeat of GMHC's cathectic past.

The outcome of this dialectic is difficult to predict. The fact that change is a constant, however, becomes part of the process of understanding GMHC, AIDS, volunteerism, and the political process as it pertains to gay empowerment.

In the beginning, carepartnering was personal, determined, and charged. By 1990, there were fewer new male volunteers, and they were considerably younger (in their twenties as opposed to their late thirties) and further distanced from the experience of peer group and generational loss. For the most part, new volunteers know about and practice safer sex. Generally, these recruits are very willing to be vocal about being gay or even having AIDS. They are part of a larger and broader activist generation of gay men and women (the generation that followed those who began GMHC and that, hopefully, will survive AIDS). For many of them, AIDS has become routinized. Much like GMHC, it is part of everyday life.

Carepartnering in AIDS is now for survivors; it is less a vocation to bear witness and more of an obligation to put in appropriate time. Preliminary data collected over 1990, 1991, and 1992 in conversations with numerous new volunteers indicate that they are involved in AIDS because they simply want to do their share. This is but one of the many causes they are involved in, while for a whole generation of gay men, AIDS was the only thing to be concerned about if one wanted to live.

AIDS is accepted now as an interrelated and multifaceted illness. By 1991, the obvious political complexity of the disease made it impossible to understand GMHC outside the political economy of the 1990s. Without intending to, the entire gay AIDS service industry reflected the federal government's encouragement and rediscovery of community altruism.

In addition to being affected by ideological pressures, GMHC continues to metamorphose concomitantly with changing government priorities and the demographics of both AIDS and its volunteers. Also, it is increasingly being shaped and defined by sources outside of traditionally afflicted populations.

When I began this study, the story of GMHC and volunteerism was unique. The agency was a sole voice, and PWAs were mostly gay and white. Now there are hundreds of AIDS service organizations nationwide and dozens of gay/AIDS activist groups locally. ACT-UP, for example, has been able to capture the spotlight, greatly broadening the scope of both AIDS and gay concerns. "Queer Nation" has become as controversial and topical as both its predecessors for its unabashed claiming of queer pride, power, and politics. For many younger gays, it is again better to be "queer," that is, different, than to be "gay." This attitude is an incredible development and challenge to GMHC.

At the very least, embracing "queerness" as a substitute gay identity and political stand indicates the evolution of gay consciousness beyond GMHC's traditional (and proper) image and its respectable social behavior. Suddenly, "queers," not the gays of the 1970s, are "doing the streets," if not irreverently then with iconoclastic aggression and pride. Many of these activists are interested in AIDS because it is a gay issue and not necessarily because it is a personal health crisis or real fear (assuming safer-sex is practiced), as it is with so many other and older GMHC members and supporters. They are young but want to be identified with the community and its problems in a broader sense. In many ways, they are the Stonewall generation all over again, only this time they are anti-gay establishment as well. Queer Nation applies the spirit of GMHC and the street smarts of ACT-UP to the issue of gay bashing. In this way collective survival is tied to self-defense.

Meanwhile GMHC became a corporate entity with specific and often narrow bureaucratic concerns. In many ways, this development leaves the field open to other gay or AIDS organizations with other specialized agendas. GMHC now joins many other organizations in institutionalizing delivery of specific services to PWAs, if not facilitating their integration with other gay or city agencies. In addition to working with community groups like God's Love We Deliver, the AIDS Resource Center, and the American Foundation for AIDS Research, it has increased its collaboration with other health-related organizations such as the Lighthouse, the Red Cross, and the American Cancer Society. This collaboration is necessary because there are, for example, blind People with AIDS who need GMHC's advice and gay People with AIDS who have become blind and need the Lighthouse. These linkages, while productive, also produce, fuel, and integrate an AIDS industry establishment, making innovative, grass-roots planning more difficult and even less acceptable.

If GMHC joined the politics of homophobia with the politics of scientific research and health care delivery to secure a distinctive place in history, then it now has to surrender some of its control and monopoly of the agenda on AIDS to other gay political groups. For example, ACT-UP, going beyond GMHC, works directly and aggressively with the issues of treatment protocols and the availability of drug therapies. Queer Nation concentrates on civil defense, self-esteem, and the right to be different.

GMHC's specialty rests in calling the broader society to see gays the same way that the community experiences and responds to People with AIDS, that is, as suffering and in isolation, as members of the human family, and as extensions of the self and ourselves. In the words of GMHC's executive director, Tim Sweeney, "We have to make people *feel this crisis.*" We are all entitled to be heard and have our mutual needs addressed.

Because of GMHC, sex education in America can no longer be discreet or shameful. Not only are millions of gay men across the country practicing safer sex, but teenagers in New York are learning about condoms because of GMHC. "Research priorities will never be the same," notes Tim Sweeney at GMHC's tenth anniversary address (July 15, 1991), "the way that clinical trials are designed, how placebos are used, what informed consent really means, etc." GMHC's message, aimed at the pharmaceutical industry, is now echoed by women with breast cancer and people with Alzheimer's.

Access to health care is forever altered. GMHC services (particularly its hotline and crisis intervention programs), designed by the same people they serve, are being copied all over the world. In New York, GMHC made Blue Cross give PWAs open enrollment. GMHC is credited with making Medicaid pick up private insurance premiums.

GMHC has also altered the meaning of gay community. It has brought the community together as a family in service to itself, whether it is through direct care, the GMHC-sponsored proxy bill that lets gays and PWAs choose who makes their health care decisions, or the Brachi decision, which lets gay men keep their lovers' apartments after death occurs.

As long as AIDS affects gays and as long as GMHC stays identified with the gay community, there will be spirited volunteers whose sense of urgency and crisis makes their commitment to serve a vocation rather than a duty. And they will flock to GMHC because of the urgency of the work that it does. GMHC's health and relevance is based on the covenant it has made with the gay community and its PWAs. A change here forebodes a different, albeit ill, future.

GMHC's historic identity, autonomy, and mission are jeopardized in ways other than by shifts in who funds it or who its clients and volunteers are. Since it is an established, mediating agency, powerful institutional leaders will probably continue to reward only those organized groups willing to cooperate with them, thereby setting each AIDS constituency up against the others.

From about 1985 to 1988, for example, the government generally funded those agencies that corresponded to its own model of what and how an epidemic is caused, defined, and controlled. Co-opting escalates when funding shifts to powerful and insistently ideological government sources. The allocation of federal money could result in government control of service delivery, much like when the debate about AIDS education and prevention became skewed by political considerations to emphasize heterosexual transmission.

Likewise, augmented income (regardless of source) also encourages growth, hence more bureaucracy and the need for more space, not to mention volunteers, staff, clients, and services. Increased professionalism will eventually dominate operations at the expense of common sense. The formal institutional worlds of health care delivery, funding and regulatory agencies, and so on outside of GMHC are not going to respond to demands, tears, or organizational ineptitude. If it were organizationally wise for GMHC to become a formalized entity to get the attention and support of the mainstream political and social establishment, the question remains as to how to sustain volunteer enthusiasm, affectivity, compassion, equality, accessibility, and other qualities in this evolving administrative and professionalized context.

Although these organizational concerns are continually being addressed at GMHC, as the organization grows and administration becomes more specialized, managers will undoubtedly become distanced from their staffs, the volunteers, and even the PWAs. Using the informal structure to resolve problems is already becoming less possible for gay clients and volunteers and, for that matter, everyone else. In 1993, 230 paid employees are doing more specialized jobs. As such, they will become increasingly unknown to one another even though they are now working in a single facility.

Depending on who one speaks to at the agency, a different picture of GMHC's operation emerges. As demonstrated, volunteers are generally pleased with the organization but have some reservations about specific agency practices. Occasional letters to GMHC's newsletter, *The Volunteer,* and to local gay community newspapers complain that the organization is not doing enough and is not working fast enough or that it should give more money to sick and/or impoverished PWAs. Many volunteers suggest that changes of this type, if adopted, would violate long-standing policy, however, and they frequently indicate ignorance of the organization's purpose, history, and mission.

For many community-oriented volunteers, GMHC is getting too big, too impersonal, and too ineffective in terms of swiftly solving the many personal problems that PWAs have. There are so many different constituencies represented among PWAs that their needs have become increasingly varied and not always reflective of gay or even AIDS issues. Most likely, the community assumes that the money it donates is being spent primarily on gay concerns and on gay PWAs, who are expected to have easy and primary access to GMHC services.

People in the gay community or with AIDS, however, are not neutral about GMHC. Too many depend on it and feel that they have a right to influence its operation. And they do, by virtue of being either a community member, a donor of goods and services, a contributor, a PWA, or a volunteer. For many, the board of directors is too conservative; for others, the volunteers are too demanding. The PWAs may seem less influential, while at other times their needs and requests are immediately addressed.

Of course, there are other problems and a growing, if novel, list of complaints such as long staff lunches, mechanical answering machines, waiting lists, fewer drop-ins, more formalities, and assistants to assistants. Internally, there are resentments over budgetary allocations, and certain departments (financial aid and advisement) seem never to have an adequate staff. Actually, how much paid staff GMHC really needs is a constant concern and hard to gauge.

The agency is also caught up in the dilemma of where and how to recruit its clients, volunteers, and staff and how to assign them. The appointment of Jeff Soref (an insider) as GMHC's new board president is an interesting case in point. Like so many other volunteers, Soref first considered volunteering in 1981 at the request of Nathan Fain, a GMHC founder. After a close friend died of AIDS, Soref, a gay man, said to himself, "This is my fight." For him, "Not being part of the fight was unthinkable." In addition to his volunteer work, he helped raise money for GMHC's new building and his efforts helped lay the groundwork for the AIDS Action Council.

Internal growth, professionalism, and affective and effective volunteer experiences are central to both GMHC's identity and its problems. Should volunteers come from the community and be PWAs? Should they work their way up the organizational ladder or should staff be hired only because of their expertise and competence? How volunteers are assigned, of course, should be a function of their skills and interests. Now, however, there are other sociological considerations—like race, sex, age, and sexual orientation—that need to be considered. Likewise, the criteria for advancement are debatable. The characteristics of dedication, loyalty, creativity, and ideology are all possible considerations.

What needs to be maintained is the dialectic between staff, volunteers, PWAs, and the larger gay community. At GMHC, whether gay volunteers will continue to carepartner minority and heterosexual drug-users remains to be seen. Another question is whether the staff should reflect the client load, the gay community, or the preferences of outside funding sources. The way these questions are addressed will have an impact on GMHC's identity, its goals and mission, and the way, even reason, it delivers services. For GMHC to at least maintain loyalty and a commitment to communalization, it should insist on a carepartnering experience for all its staff so that they can be at least affectively related to their work.

In one sense, GMHC keeps adjusting to the times, the issues, and the ever-changing settings in which AIDS pulls the community and puts the organization. The growing heterosexualization of AIDS and GMHC, for example, is a novel development and, depending on one's vision of the agency, is either good and bad.

In 1990–1992, some training sessions consisted of nearly 40 percent women. In terms of GMHC's history and identity, this blessing is also problematic. How and why this change has occurred is an important question in itself. Has it happened because gays are tired and AIDS has claimed as many gay lives as it will? Or is it because women now have an opportunity to act out traditional roles by caring for their gay friends? Perhaps more women now volunteer because it has become their issue as well. At the very least, this demographic change means different motives for volunteering that will impact on the experiences, objectives, roles, and outcomes of carepartnering. What this development implies for the agency itself is a totally different question altogether.

Morale remains high because of the exigencies of AIDS, which require high commitment and concentration on the immediate task of delivering some relief to a PWA. Volunteer enthusiasm is sustained through attachments and respect. If these characteristics remain an administrative theme, this enthusiasm will be difficult to dampen. Volunteers' input and spirit, if kept constant, will stand in opposition to bureaucratic ordering and allow them to continue the work of healing. It is with a sense of gratitude and high expectations, therefore, that volunteers come to GMHC to serve and make peace with AIDS and themselves and by so doing unintentionally write a new chapter of gay history.

For some, however, this "seizing the moment" is becoming increasingly unlikely. In her recent book *Inventing AIDS*, Cindy Patton (1990:18–21) decries the evolution of the AIDS industry from community political activism to co-opted formal organizations. Like Kramer, she prefers and recommends a return to the early activism of the gay/AIDS movement and fails to note the political dimension of volunteerism or see it as significant. Yet they both leave unanswered the question of how homophobia is to be healed (for political activism to commence) and how a large-scale effort to assist PWAs can be done effectively without efficient organization.

In Patton's understanding of politics, volunteerism, and altruism, the possibility of being empowered is lost simply because AIDS service agencies are now organized and compete for government funding. Hence the effort is splintered and any association with AIDS is for instrumental or organizational gain only, not community welfare. While she is correct in noting that since different organizational divisions (client services, education, prevention) can now link themselves directly to government funding sources, further increasing their narrowly focused autonomy even within AIDS agencies themselves, the ability for an AIDS organization to control its staff and its future remains potent only if funding is community generated.

For Patton, AIDS service organizations and their justifying ideologies are now not only de-gayed but defined by managers with limited interests. Bureaucracy, for Patton, means surrendering control of the field by the community, which would be true, of course, if the community lost its interest in the agency or the agency changed its focus and identity. However, gays and People with AIDS have always enthusiastically turned to GMHC for support and help. Bureaucracy aside, it remains a home and safe haven.

GMHC is caught between its democratic ideals and the fact that nongays, especially privileged white heterosexual males, have been indifferent, if not hostile, to either the question of gay rights (as a civil issue) or the needs of PWAs as a unique class of medically indigent citizens. Now that there is money to be made in AIDS, heterosexual professionals, Patton (1990:21) correctly notes, "are now collecting the salaries in areas of AIDS research, public administration, and journalism, *as the experts,* the neutral professionals who are above politics and frequently have no contact with people in the communities most harshly affected by AIDS."

As AIDS continues to become de-gayed and more evenly distributed throughout risk populations, GMHC will have to struggle to maintain its own autonomy, character, and integrity. The irony is that GMHC is a "temporary" organization in a shifting, long-term, crisis situation. How it will effectively manage itself when its own gay staff and volunteer corps are themselves falling victim to the very disease they are trying to contain is a constant dilemma. In such circumstances, how is commitment sustained and continuity of services ensured when the in-house staff and volunteers themselves get personally and directly caught up in the drama?

On one hand, this conundrum guarantees high dedication and determination. On the other, a decline in service and community confidence is likely, especially if sick staff are eventually let go. Can good procedures sustain GMHC in the absence of committed individuals and community input? Can following protocol alone maintain service and sustain ideals? I think not: A sense of community is also necessary.

This research addressed some of these concerns while articulating the significance of GMHC and volunteerism to the history of the gay rights movement. By concentrating on the experience of carepartnering PWAs (rather than on GMHC as such), I learned that only those who lived in community and became connected to one another, or who were at least willing to acknowledge their wholeness by accepting themselves through the PWA, embraced the community in its fullness and remained steadfast.

Notes

Preface

1. The sociology of religion typically distinguishes between "church-type" religious organizations, which identify and support the state and national culture, and "sects," which normally stand in opposition to the sanctification of secular social systems and norms. In terms of this book, this distinction explains little since virtually all Western religions historically are politically and institutionally homophobic. "Stateside" is used as a general category to include any type of religious organization that supports the social order, especially the sexual status quo between men and women. Durkheimian sociologists would find this definition acceptable since they would consider religious and social ideologies to be one and the same. I am using "stateside" more precisely to mean any religion that unquestionably supports nationalistic American institutions and values especially as they pertain to sex roles, sexuality, marriage, and family life.

Chapter 1

1. Likewise, organizations such as the AIDS Project in Los Angeles, NO AIDS in New Orleans, AIDS Atlanta, the AIDS Arms Network in Dallas, and the Kaposi Sarcoma Education and Research Foundation in San Francisco fulfilled similar functions and supplied comparable services. How some of these community-based initiatives developed and how these organizations were established are detailed in Shilts (1987) and Perrow and Guillen (1990) and are themselves worthwhile, if not intriguing, stories.

2. This changed somewhat in fall 1985 with the publication of my article on morals and medicine in the *Journal of Religion and Health*. The autumn 1988 issue of *Social Research* is dedicated to AIDS. In the public policy and literary fields are contributions by Fee and Fox (1988), Altman (1986), and Bayer (1989a). In 1988, Douglas Crimp edited a volume of readings examining the social construction of AIDS as a disease problem. Among recent works in sociology are Patton (1990) and Perrow and Guillen (1990). In spring and summer 1989, *Daedalus* published a series entitled "Living With AIDS," and *The Millbank Quarterly* (1990, Vol. 68) examined AIDS as a disease of society.

3. Fortunately, this project was partially funded by Seton Hall University, my employer, and GMHC, which absorbed the expense of questionnaire reproduction and

distribution. The moneys offered by the university's Summer Research Grant program in 1986 allowed me to spend three months preparing the research instrument. With another university grant in 1988, I was able to spend that summer interpreting the data and preparing the manuscript for publication. Both GMHC and Seton Hall have been more than generous in their support, giving me the liberty to come and go at will in undertaking and completing this study. In no way whatsoever did they interfere with my work or try to bias it.

Chapter 2

1. In fact, GMHC at first thought that religion or religious ideas in any shape or form were not a concern of gays, and later it thought of them as something that would be divisive in AIDS care delivery. Given the character of the prevalent church-state religion, this is a valid observation and position. Questions of faith, belief, holiness, and meaning, however, are of a different nature, especially for the PWA.

2. Generally, the less centralized a religion the more likely it is to be supportive of gays and women. Many Quaker and Unitarian communities, for example, have befriended minorities and actively minister to gays and PWAs and support women's rights, as do the gay-identified Metropolitan Community Church and Congregation Beth Simchat Torah. The same is true of the Episcopal Diocese of New York and Newark, New Jersey, which further denounce patriarchy in their support of women's ordination.

3. This is not to say that some gays do not seek a home in patriarchal religion. After being expelled by the Jesuits, their longtime supporters, for example, Dignity, New York, a gay Catholic group, regularly protested their status to Cardinal O'Connor, who had engineered their expulsion. It is baffling to think why individuals would want to be part of an organization that publicly defiles and detests them. These assimilationist goals do not stem from the space of healing and stand in total opposition to what gay empowerment and the claiming of the sacred mean.

4. However, Catholic bishop Anthony Bosco of Greensburgh, Pennsylvania, is quoted as saying, in a daring act of independence, that he found it difficult to understand "how anyone who values life as a gift of God would fail to see that the life of the homosexual or the drug-abuser is as sacred in God's eyes as is the life of the unborn fetus." While true, one has to wonder how and why gays and drug-users were used in the same breath, especially in the context of illness. Both Catholics and Lutherans continuously punish and condemn their own gay clergy, forbidding ordination to out-of-the-closet seminarians (Gross 1990:B6). Their commitment to drug-users is less than honorable.

5. In a basic New Testament sense, volunteers and PWAs confess their humanity to each other and receive "communion" from one another. One other new voluntary group that buys food for home-bound PWAs is actually called "God's Love We Deliver."

Chapter 3

1. New York once planned to offer abortions to poor women who are HIV positive. There are varying proposals to quarantine gays and other undesirables and there is re-

sistance to implement needle-exchange programs. Note also the less-than-vigorous interest in reducing the iatrogenic transmission of AIDS in Africa.

2. Jim Levin (1988:14) of the Gay Independent Democrats (of New York City) noted that before AIDS he often had trouble getting support because "many people were afraid to belong to any organization with the word 'gay' in its title." The presence of AIDS, never mind GMHC, would only confound this problem.

3. The simmering issue of when and how HIV was discovered, and by whom, has been continually resurrected and is important because it has resulted in considerable time being lost in finding a cure. The cause was not quickly made known because of competition between American and French researchers. Hence finding a cure was delayed (the *New York Times*, Saturday, October 6, 1990, p. A1).

Chapter 4

1. The speculation about the causes of African AIDS is frequently both racist and sexist. Not only is homosexual behavior vehemently denied, but the virus is presented as acting differently by race and nationality. Although epidemiological patterns may vary, the fact that equal numbers of women and men have AIDS does not mean that African AIDS is heterosexually transmitted from women to men. It probably means that infected men have given it to women. Men (and women) may have gotten infected through needle sharing, homosexual or bisexual activity, or unsanitary medical practices. But to suggest that African women gave HIV "back" to men through their numerous syphilitic sores and untreated genital ulcerations, though possible cofactors, is clearly demeaning. Effective HIV transmission from women to men, while possible, has yet to be clearly demonstrated in a significant number of cases, especially in the United States.

2. Regardless of the count, given the length of time between infection and illness and the ability of affluent gay men to hide their diagnoses, it is virtually impossible to trust any estimate of which group is sick or infected the most or who has died of AIDS. Any random reading of *New York Times* obituaries would prove that dozens of single men dying in their thirties from pneumonia and lymphomas and survived by their mothers are gay men. I personally know a half dozen people who died mysteriously and unexpectedly, including three Catholic priests who died of AIDS. In any case, the issue is not which group has suffered the most. All have lost tremendously.

3. During the 1992 International AIDS Conference in Amsterdam, California medical scientists announced that numerous cases of an AIDS-like disease have been found among people without HIV infection. Whether this virus is new, a variant of HIV, or a necessary cofactor in AIDS fulmination has yet to be determined. That HIV might not be the only biological cause of AIDS has profound medical, scientific, and social implications.

Chapter 5

1. State and religious charity can be at odds with one another as they search for and offer services to specific interest groups and populations. The state generally prefers

that religious organizations be charitable, but there are populations, like gays, who would be excluded by them and who would thus require state support and intervention. In effect, the state helps "leftovers"—people who cannot or will not be offered charity from religious organizations in a nonreformist way without condemnation. The issue addressed here is the attempt by religious organizations to limit the largesse of the state toward PWAs and the fear of the state to contradict religious beliefs.

2. The only consolation is that geneticist Dr. Frank Lilly, on openly gay GMHC board member, was appointed to the commission, though reluctantly, in 1987. Still, Reagan's agency literally did nothing for a year except be dissolved and then have new members be reappointed, thereby beginning anew another cycle of indifference and insufferable waiting.

3. Fortunately, however, and after long gay protest, the recommendation of its former chair, Admiral J. D. Watkins, that one of the best deterrents to AIDS fulmination would be antidiscriminatory legislation led to the recent passage of the Americans with Disabilities Act. This act will relieve PWAs and other handicapped individuals of gross discrimination in limited areas of concern.

4. In the evolution of civil rights protests, violent responses occur when legal and social pressures fail to stem violence against the minority. Because they have virtually nothing to lose, it would not be surprising if gays, especially gay PWAs, simply utilize retaliatory violence in self-defense against gay bashers and homophobic institutions. It is remarkable that such violence has not occurred yet; it indicates considerable restraint on the part of the gay community. A violent response would not only cancel a stereotype about "pansies" but put the city on warning that it will again burn, as it did for blacks.

5. This is no idle speculation. Beginning years ago with Michael Maye, the fire commissioner who physically attacked members of the Gay Activist Alliance, in more cases than would be expected, the attackers are Irish Catholics. In Park Slope (an Irish Catholic neighborhood in Brooklyn, until recently under the control of homophobic council member Thomas Cuite) and Jersey City, anti-lesbian and anti-gay violence is clearly seen as "an Irish thing," much like their problems with sex generally. *Daily News* columnist Jimmy Breslin hails from Park Slope (as I do), and despite his support for the gay and lesbian contingent from Ireland who asked to march in the 1991 and 1992 St. Patrick's Day parades, his homophobic remarks about AIDS and gays are typical of the area. Much the same is true of Park Slope writer and columnist Peter Hammil.

Chapter 6

1. The Centers for Disease Control withheld its pledged support for twenty-five AIDS educational programs designed to use videos illustrating safer-sex techniques because they described safer homosexual sex. Explicit heterosexual visuals had been used for decades throughout the country, but now the federal government did not want to appear as supporting illegal activities.

2. This is a very sensitive issue, impossible to clarify from all the conflicting data. Although AZT is toxic, the government, after having received input from Burroughs-Wellcome, officially insisted that it clearly lengthens the life span of those who are HIV

postive. This report has recently been called into question. Other experimental drugs such as DDI and DDC are believed to be equally effective but are unproven in classic clinical trials and are not easily accessed. They too have negative side effects, as do drugs that are now used to control PCP, a primary killer of AIDS patients. Since it is impossible to know the starting time of an infection or why only some patients respond to medications, it is difficult to determine the whys and hows of longevity. Many AIDS patients also self-medicate, a practice that in any case contaminates scientific accuracy.

3. Likewise, touting the benefits of "clean drug works" and the use of condoms as AIDS preventives, though helpful, actually misses the point about oppressive social arrangements that can literally drive people to drugs or other forms of dysfunctional behavior.

Chapter 7

1. GMHC has publicly acknowledged this fact. Two longtime and outstanding volunteers, Judith Peabody and Joan Tisch, acted as co-chairs together with their husbands for GMHC's tenth anniversary celebration, "Circus for Life," at Madison Square Garden in 1992. As written in the program journal, "Their endorsement of the event encouraged numerous corporations and individiuals to join the battle against this devastating disease."

2. The phenomenon of increased women's participation in AIDS volunteerism is not restricted to New York. In both San Francisco and Los Angeles, more and more women are being trained as volunteers. Many of these women are being siphoned off from other activities and agencies. This may be adding to the shortage of volunteers generally.

3. GMHC also feeds itself well. Its parties and fund-raising affairs are generally considered impeccable in their taste, if not their extravagance. And these events do not have an impact on GMHC's budget: They often serve as fund-raisers, and attendees bring their own fare. GMHC's famous Moveable Feast is community generated, and all the food is donated by volunteers. This year it took an entire city block in front of the office to handle the overflow gathering of volunteers, staff, board members, benefactors, and PWAs. For whatever reason, minority participation was minimal.

4. While the vast majority of AIDS volunteers in the United States are gay males, for the country on the whole these ratios vary somewhat (Krieger and Appleman 1986; Omoto and Snyder 1990; Appleby and Sosnowitz 1987; Shilts 1987; and Kübler-Ross 1987). GMHC's 1989 annual report indicates that males now constitute 78 percent of the volunteer corps. Virtually no male volunteers, however, are heterosexually identified. Newer volunteers are also somewhat younger.

5. This view, popularized by Banfield (1970:250), misses the long history of the "moral sensitivity approach to charity" and so cannot distinguish between motivations and consequences. Banfield is indifferent to charitable acts based on an element of gemeinschaft, or community, "in which good is done because the donor wishes to maximize the needy's well being" and is rewarded for doing such. According to Banfield, because doing good is personally beneficial in this case, such behavior is neither charitable nor altruistic.

6. This is not to say that minority members and women are not engaged in remarkable acts of charity for PWAs specifically. If anything, given class and gender distances between PWAs and the general and minority populations, minority volunteerism, formal or otherwise, is true and extraordinary altruism.

Chapter 8

1. This earlier view of gay community organizational mobilization is also challenged by Winkle (1991) in his review of the gay community's response to AIDS in Chicago as compared to other at-risk populations.

2. It is possible that those who were unaware were also unconcerned. But they may also have been extremely and subjectively militant, saying, in effect, that it could not happen because they wouldn't allow it to.

3. I believe this is because many respondents defined being gay in terms of sexual activity rather than community ties and simply preferred to change their behavior to save themselves and preserve older gay sexual mores. However, by changing their own behavior and protecting themselves, they were in fact protecting the common good.

Chapter 9

1. The Gay Men's Health Crisis, Inc., was the premier gay organization of the United States, only recently challenged in popularity and importance by activist groups like ACT-UP and, more closely at home, the growing AIDS industry. However, GMHC remains the largest fund-raising organization and easily sustains wide community support and national preeminence. By contrast, the Howard Brown Memorial Clinic in Chicago, the largest AIDS social service agency in the Midwest, served only 600 PWAs in 1989. At that time, GMHC was registering about 150 new clients each month.

2. The now well-known and highly political and popular AIDS Coalition to Unleash Power (ACT-UP) did not exist in 1986. It was born out of the absence of a strong and traditional gay activist response to AIDS in the political arena, especially by GMHC. Co-founded by Larry Kramer, an original founder of GMHC, it drew many GMHC members as well as many who became disenchanted with GMHC's agenda and what they saw as political hesitancy. Kramer has since gone on to attack ACT-UP as well as all other gay and AIDS organizations in the country and city (Kramer 1990b).

3. Actually, the *Native* at that time was relatively ubiquitous, as were dozens of other publications, which means that gays had access to communal news rather readily and independently of institutional affiliations.

Chapter 11

1. In 1991 GMHC declared an anniversary "call to action" ("ten years, ten days, ten deeds") to reinvigorate and demonstrate interest in AIDS. It consisted of massive education efforts, street theater, political action, prayer, thanksgiving, commemoration

services, and special programs targeted at women and minorities. It was designed to precede and coincide with World AIDS Day on December 1, 1991.

Chapter 12

1. This is not to say that individual gays have not been extraordinarily generous, for they certainly have. Wills and estates have named GMHC as beneficiary, and the agency receives many substantial gifts and donations from community members who wish to remain anonymous.

2. Former GMHC executive director Mel Rosen headed the New York State AIDS Institute until 1987, Rodger McFarlane directs Broadway Cares, and GMHC's former director for policy David Hansell has recently been appointed to New York State's AIDS Advisory Council by Assembly Speaker Mel Miller. Early GMHC board member and PWA Robert Cecchi was also appointed to the council, where he served until 1988, by Governor Mario Cuomo. Until his recent resignation, the council advised state health commissioner David Axelrod on AIDS issues and policy.

3. These numbers are actually reduced by half because of projections made from extrapolated San Francisco data in July. They are inappropriate demographic approximations for New York because they misconstrue and misrepresent the amount of drug use both in the city and among gays (Lambert 1988c,d).

Chapter 13

1. Mr. Matt Foreman, executive director of New York City's Gay and Lesbian Anti-Violence Project, reports that violence directed against people believed to be homosexual rose 65 percent in the city last year, but the New York City Police Department found a 113 percent increase, from 47 incidents to 102 (*New York Times*, May 27, 1991:L21,L24).

2. In contrast, stateside religions normally function to separate their adherents from themselves as they experience the world, thus making them servants of "false Gods" (Abalos 1986). When they legitimate social indifference to basic civil rights and human needs by not identifying homophobic social institutions, these religions become divisive, reinforcing the status quo by their lack of charity and concern. Their corporate theologies are used to punish outsiders, separating them further from the human community. In the context of AIDS, condemnation and lack of recognition increase personal anxiety about identity and/or having anything to do with gays, AIDS, or PWAs as special embodiments of the sacred.

Bibliography

Abalos, David. 1986. *Latinos in the United States: The Sacred and Political*. Notre Dame, Ind.: University of Notre Dame Press.

———. 1978. "Strategies of Transformation in the Health Delivery System," *Nursing Forum*. Vol. 17:3, pp. 284–316.

Adam, Barry. 1987. *The Rise of a Gay and Lesbian Movement*. Boston: G. K. Hall.

Adams, David. 1987. "Ronald Reagan's 'Revival': Voluntarism as a Theme in Reagan's Civil Religion," *Sociological Analysis*. Vol. 48:1 (Spring), pp. 17–29.

———. 1986. "The Imperative to Volunteer: A Theme in American Civil Religion." Paper presented at the annual meeting of the Association for the Sociology of Religion, New York, August.

Adler, Patricia, and Peter Adler. 1987. *Membership Roles in Field Research*. Newbury Park, Calif.: Sage.

Allen, Kerry. 1983. "Status Report: Volunteering in America, 1982–83," *Voluntary Action Leadership*. Winter, pp. 22–25.

Altman, Dennis. 1986. *AIDS in the Mind of America*. New York: Doubleday.

———. 1982a. *The Homosexualization of America*. Boston: Beacon.

———. 1982b. "Sex: The New Front Line for Gay Politics," *Socialist Review*. Vol. 12:5 (September 10), pp. 75–84.

Altman, Lawrence. 1992. "Researchers Report Much Grimmer AIDS Outlook," *New York Times*. June 4, pp. A1, B10.

———. 1990. "Antibodies Seem to Protect Fetus from AIDS," *New York Times*. May 1, p. C2.

———. 1988a. "Outlook on AIDS Termed Bleak," *New York Times*. June 13, p. A13.

———. 1988b. "What's in a Name? Often Confusion," *New York Times*. July 12, p. C3.

———. 1981. "Rare Cancer Seen in 41 Homosexuals," *New York Times*. July 3, p. A20.

Appleby, George A., and Barbara G. Sosnowitz. 1987. "From Social Movement to Social Organization: Voluntary AIDS Projects in Connecticut." Paper presented at the Convention of the Society for the Study of Social Problems, Chicago, August.

Arno, Peter. 1988. "The Future of Voluntarism and the AIDS Epidemic." Pp. 56–70 in *The AIDS Patient: An Action Agenda*. Edited by David E. Rogers and Eli Ginzberg. Boulder: Westview Press.

_____. 1987. "The Contributions and Limitations of Voluntarism." pp. 188–192 in *AIDS: Public Policy Dimensions*. Edited by John Griggs. New York: United Hospital Fund.

_____. 1986a. "AIDS: A Balancing Act of Resources," *Business and Health*. December, pp. 20–24.

_____. 1986b. "The Nonprofit Sector's Response to the AIDS Epidemic: Community-Based Services in San Francisco," *American Journal of Public Health*. Vol. 76:11 (November), pp. 1325–1330.

Atwater, Lynn, and Howard Robboy. 1972. "The Sociology of Doing Good." Paper presented at the convention of the Society for the Study of Social Problems, New York, August.

Babchuk, Nicholas, and Alan Booth. 1969. "Voluntary Association Membership: A Longitudinal Analysis," *American Sociological Review*. Vol. 34, pp. 31–45.

Babchuk, Nicholas, and John N. Edwards. 1965. "Voluntary Associations and the Integration Hypothesis," *Sociological Inquiry*. Vol. 35 (Spring), pp. 149–162.

Babchuk, Nicholas, and C. Wayne Gordon. 1962. *The Voluntary Association in the Slum*. Lincoln: University of Nebraska Press.

Babchuk, Nicholas, Ruth Marsey, and C. Wayne Gordon. 1960. "Men and Women in Community Agencies: A Note on Power and Prestige," *American Sociological Review*. Vol. 25 (June), pp. 339–403.

Babchuk, Nicholas, and Ralph Thompson. 1962. "The Voluntary Association of Negroes," *American Sociological Review*. Vol. 27:5, pp. 647–655.

Badcock, Christopher. 1986. *The Problem of Altruism*. New York: Blackwell.

Banfield, Edward C. 1970. *The Unheavenly City*. Boston: Little Brown & Co.

Barringer, Felicity. 1992. "Figures Show Fall in Giving by Rich Even as Ranks of Millionaires Grow," *New York Times*. National report, p. L16.

Bayer, Ronald. 1989a. "AIDS, Privacy, and Responsibility" (Part 2), *Daedalus*. Vol. 118:3 (Summer), pp. 79–100.

_____. 1989b. *Private Acts, Social Consequences: AIDS and the Politics of Public Health*. New York: Free Press, Macmillan.

Bell, Alan, and Martin Weinberg. 1978. *Homosexuality: A Study of Diversity Among Men*. New York: Simon and Schuster.

Bellah, Robert. 1985. *Habits of the Heart*. Berkeley: University of California Press.

Berger, Peter. 1967. *The Sacred Canopy: Elements of a Sociological Theory of Religion*. Garden City, N.Y.: Doubleday.

Berube, Alan. 1988. "Caught in the Storm," *Outlook: National Gay and Lesbian Quarterly*. Fall, pp. 9–19.

Blau, Peter M., and Richard W. Scott. 1962. *Formal Organizations: A Comparative Approach*. San Francisco: Chandler.

Bordowitz, Gregg. 1988. "Picture a Coalition." pp. 183–196 in *AIDS: Cultural Analysis, Cultural Activism*. Edited by Douglas Crimp. Cambridge: MIT Press.

Boswell, John. 1987. "The Gift of Difference." Paper presented at a seminar of the Consultation, Union Theological Seminary, New York, March 20.

Braff, Jeffrey. 1990. "Diversity and Gay Identity," *Volunteer*. Vol. 7:3 (May/June), p. 2.

Brandt, Allan. 1988. "AIDS and Metaphor: Toward the Social Meaning of Epidemic Disease," *Social Research*. Vol. 55:3 (Autumn), pp. 413–435.

Bravmann, Scott. 1988. "Assessing the March on Washington: Progress Within the Lesbian and Gay Movement," *Sociologists Lesbian and Gay Newsletter*. No. 55 (Spring), pp. 3–8.

———. 1987. "Heart in a Havenless World: The Politics of Building a Gay and Lesbian Community," *Christopher Street*. Vol. 10:9, no. 117, pp. 16–20.

Brodsky, Joel I. 1985. "Accept Us as We Are: Stigma, Inequality and the Homophile Voluntary Association." Master's thesis, University of Nebraska.

Byrne, Richard A., and Faye Caskey. 1985. "For Love or Money?" *Journal of Extension*. Fall, pp. 4–7.

Byron, Peg. 1991. "HIV: The National Scandal," *Ms*. Vol. 1:4 (January-February), pp. 24–29.

———. 1983. "AIDS and the Gay Men's Health Crisis of New York," *Rodeo Journal*. New York: GMHC.

Cahill, Kevin. 1983. *The AIDS Epidemic*. New York: St. Martin's Press.

Callen, Michael. 1988. "If HIV Doesn't Cause AIDS, What Might?" *PWA Coalition Newsletter*. No. 31 (February), pp. 36–40.

Chambers, Clarke A. 1985. "The Historical Role of the Voluntary Sector in Human Service Delivery in Urban America." pp. 3–29 in *Social Planning and Human Service Delivery in the Voluntary Sector*. Edited by Gary A. Tobin. Westport, Conn.: Greenwood Press.

Chambre, Susan M. 1991. "Volunteers as Witnesses: The Mobilization of AIDS Volunteers in New York City, 1981–1988," *Social Science Review*. December, pp. 531–547.

———. 1989. "Responding to Uncertainty by Bearing Witness: Volunteering as Collective Behavior in the AIDS Epidemic, 1981–1988." Occasional Paper, Center for the Study of Philanthropy, CUNY, N.Y.

———. 1988. "Volunteers and AIDS: Organizations' Responses to a Public Health Emergency." Research proposal for the Center of Business and Government, Washington, D.C.

Chapin, F. Stuart, and John E. Tsouderos. 1956. "The Formalization Process in Voluntary Associations," *Social Forces*. May, pp. 342–344.

Christ, Carol P., and Judith Plaskow. 1979. *Womanspirit Rising*. New York: Harper and Row.

Clark, Peter B., and James Q. Wilson. 1961. "Incentive Systems: A Theory of Organizations," *Administrative Science Quarterly*. Vol. 6 (September), pp. 129–166.

Collins, Alice H., and Diane L. Pancoast. 1976. *Natural Helping Networks: A Strategy for Prevention*. Washington, D.C.: National Association of Social Workers.

Conger, Jay A., and Rabindra N. Kanungo. 1988. *Charismatic Leadership: The Elusive Factor in Organizational Effectiveness*. San Francisco: Jossey-Bass.

Crimp, Douglas (editor). 1988. *AIDS: Cultural Analysis, Cultural Activism*. Boston: MIT Press.

Daniels, Arlene Kaplan. 1985. "Good Times and Good Works: The Place of Sociability in the Work of Women Volunteers," *Social Problems*. Vol. 32:4 (April), pp. 363–374.

Davis, King E. 1984. "An Alternative Theoretical Perspective on Race and Voluntary Participation." pp. 147–163 in *Voluntarism and Social Work Practice*. Edited by F. Schwartz. New York: University Press.

D'Emilio, John. 1983. *Sexual Politics, Sexual Communities*. Chicago: University of Chicago Press.

Denneny, Michael. 1990. "A Quilt of Many Colors: AIDS Writing and the Creation of Culture," *Christopher Street*. Vol. 12:9, pp. 15–21.

D'Eramo, James. 1988. "Ticketed for Negligence," *Christopher Street*. Vol. 11:2, pp. 14–26.

———. 1984. "Allan L. Goldstein, M.D.: AIDS Prevention Therapy," *New York Native*. No. 98, p. 19.

Des Pres, Terrence. 1976. *The Survivor: An Anatomy of Life in the Death Camps*. New York: Oxford University Press.

Drake, St. Claire, and Horace R. Clayton. 1945. *Black Metropolis*. New York: Harcourt Brace.

Dugger, Celia. 1992. "H.I.V. Incidence Rises Among Black Mothers," *New York Times*. Metro, May 1, p. B3.

Eckholm, Erik, and John Tierney. 1990. "AIDS in Africa: A Killer Rages On" (Part 1 of 4), *New York Times*. September 16, pp. 1, 14.

Farber, Celia. 1992. "Fatal Distraction," *Spin*. Vol. 8:3, pp. 39–45, 84, 90–91.

Fee, Elizabeth, and Daniel Fox (editors). 1988. *AIDS: The Burden of History*. Berkeley: University of California Press.

Fettner, Ann Guidici, and William Check. 1984. *The Truth About AIDS*. New York: Holt, Rinehart and Winston.

Flynn, J. P., and G. E. Webb. 1975. "Women's Incentives for Community Participation in Policy Issues," *Journal of Voluntary Action Research*. Vol. 4:3–4, pp. 137–145.

Fortunato, John E. 1987. *AIDS: The Spiritual Dilemma*. San Francisco: Harper and Row.

———. 1983. *Embracing the Exile*. New York: Seabury Press.

Foucault, Michel. 1982. "The Social Triumph of the Sexual Will: A Conversation," an interview by Gilles Barbadette (translated by Brendon Lemon), *Christopher Street*. No. 64, pp. 36–41.

Fowlkes, Martha. 1990. "The Social Regulation of Grief," *Sociological Forum*. Vol. 5:4 (December), pp. 635–652.

Fox, Daniel M. 1988. "AIDS and the American Health Polity: The History and Prospects of a Crisis in Authority." Pp. 316–343 in *AIDS: The Burden of History*. Edited by Daniel Fox and Elizabeth Fee. Berkeley: University of California Press.

Fox, Daniel M., Patricia Day, and Rudolf Klein. 1989. "The Power of Professionalism: AIDS in Britain, Sweden, and the United States," *Daedalus*. Vol. 118:2 (Spring), pp. 93–113.

Fox, Daniel, and Emily H. Thomas. 1987. "AIDS Cost Analysis and Social Policy," *Law, Medicine, and Health Care*. Vol. 15:4 (Winter), pp. 186–211.

Fox, Renee C., Linda H. Aiken, and Carla M. Messikomer. 1990. "The Culture of Caring: AIDS and the Nursing Profession," *Millbank Quarterly*. Vol. 68: Supplement 2, pp. 226–256.

Fumento, Michael. 1989. *The Myth of Heterosexual AIDS.* New York: Basic Books.

Gallo, Jeanne. 1989. "Basic Ecclesial Communities: A New Form of Christian Organizational Response to the World Today." Ph.D. dissertation, Boston University.

Gamson, Josh. 1989. "Silence, Death and the Invisible Enemy: AIDS Activism and Social Movement 'Newness,'" *Social Problems.* Vol. 36:4 (October), pp. 351–368.

Gamson, William. 1991. "Commitment and Agency in Social Movements," *Sociological Forum.* Vol. 6:1, pp. 27–50.

Gay Men's Health Crisis. 1990. Gay Men's Health Crisis, Inc., Annual Report. New York: GMHC.

———. 1989. Gay Men's Health Crisis, Inc., Annual Report. New York: GMHC.

———. 1987. Gay Men's Health Crisis, Inc., Annual Report. New York: GMHC.

Gilligan, Carol. 1982. *In a Different Voice: Psychological Theory and Women's Development.* Cambridge: Harvard University Press.

Gilman, Sander L. 1988. "AIDS and Syphilis: The Iconography of Disease." Pp. 87–108 in *AIDS: Cultural Analysis, Cultural Activism.* Edited by Douglas Crimp. Cambridge: MIT Press.

Goldstein, Richard. 1987. "AIDS and Race: The Hidden Epidemic," *Village Voice.* March 10, pp. 1, 23–27, 30.

Gordon, Kevin. 1989. "The Sexual Bankruptcy of the Christian Tradition: A Perspective of Radical Suspicion and of Fundamental Trust." Pp. 169–213 in *AIDS Issues: Confronting the Challenge.* Edited by David G. Hallman. New York: Pilgrim Press.

———. 1988. "Can There Be Faith and Theology After AIDS?" Paper presented in James Memorial Chapel, Union Theological Seminary, New York, April 16.

———. 1986. *Homosexuality and Social Justice.* San Francisco: Consultation.

Gordon, C. Wayne, and Nicholas Babchuk. 1966. "A Typology of Voluntary Associations." Pp. 24–28 in *The Government of Associations.* Edited by William A. Glaser and David Sills. Totowa, N.J.: Bedminister Press.

Greeley, Andrew. 1974. *Ethnicity in the United States.* New York: Wiley.

Greenberg, David. 1988. *The Construction of Homosexuality.* Chicago: University of Chicago Press.

Griggs, John (editor). 1989. *Simple Acts of Kindness: Volunteering in the Age of AIDS.* New York: United Hospital Fund.

———. 1987. *AIDS: Public Policy Dimensions.* New York: United Hospital Fund.

Gross, Jane. 1990. "Lutherans Punish 2 Churches for Gay Ordinations," *New York Times.* July 19, p. B6.

Guggenbuhl-Craig, Adolf. 1971. *Power in the Helping Professions.* Dallas: Spring Publications.

Guterbock, Thomas, and Bruce London. 1983. "Race, Political Orientation, and Participation: An Empirical Test of Four Competing Theories," *American Sociological Review.* Vol. 48:4, pp. 439–453.

Haeuser, Adrienne A., and Florence S. Schwartz. 1984. "Developing Social Work Skills for Work with Volunteers." Pp. 23–34 in *Voluntarism and Social Work Practice.* Edited by F. Schwartz. New York: University Press.

Halpern, Manfred. 1987. "Choosing Between Ways of Life and Death and Between Forms of Democracy: An Archetypal Analysis," *Alternatives.* January, pp. 5–34.

———. 1969. "A Redefinition of the Revolutionary Situation," *Journal of International Affairs.* Vol. 23:1, pp. 54–75.

Hammil, Pete. 1986. "Doing Good," *New York Magazine.* October 13, pp. 35–39.

Hammonds, Evelynn. 1987. "Race, Sex, AIDS: The Construction of Other," *Radical America.* Vol. 20:6, pp. 28–36.

Handlin, Oscar. 1954. *The American People in the Twentieth Century.* Cambridge: Harvard University Press.

Handlin, Oscar, and Mary Handlin. 1961. *The Dimensions of Liberty.* Cambridge: Belknap Press of Harvard University Press.

Harrington, Mark. 1990. "The Roads Not Taken," *Outweek.* No. 68 (October 17), pp. 28–29.

Heise, Lori. 1988. "AIDS: New Threat to the Third World," *Worldwatch.* Vol. 1:1, pp. 19–27.

Helgesen, Sally. 1990. *Female Advantage: Women's Ways of Leadership.* New York: Doubleday.

Herek, Gregory M. 1984. "Beyond 'Homophobia': A Social Psychological Perspective on Attitudes Toward Lesbians and Gay Men," *Journal of Homosexuality.* Vol. 10:1, pp. 1–21.

Hilts, Philip J. 1991. "Panel Faults Leaders on AIDS Epidemic," *New York Times.* September 26, p. A24.

———. 1990a. "AIDS Advocates Are Angry at U.S. but Its Research Chief Wins Respect," *New York Times.* September 4, p. A14.

———. 1990b. "Bush in First Address on AIDS, Backs a Bill to Protect Victims," *New York Times.* March 30, pp. A1, A18.

———. 1990c. "Evidence Is Said to Increase on Microbe's Role in AIDS," *New York Times.* June 22, p. A18.

———. 1990d. "House Approves $4 Billion in Relief for AIDS," *New York Times.* June 14, p. B9.

———. 1990e. "Panel Issues Broad Attack on U.S. Response to AIDS," *New York Times.* August 22, p. B4.

———. 1990f. "Poorer Countries Are Hit Hardest by Spread of AIDS, U.N. Reports," *New York Times.* June 13, p. A8.

———. 1990g. "Senate Approves a Major Cut in AIDS Related Relief for Cities," *New York Times.* October 11, p. D23.

———. 1990h. "Spread of AIDS by Heterosexuals Remains Slow," *New York Times.* May 1, pp. C1, C12.

———. 1990i. "$2.9 Billion Bill for AIDS Relief Gains in Senate," *New York Times.* May 16, pp. A1, A24.

———. 1989a. "AIDS Panel Finds U.S. Failure in Providing Care," *New York Times.* National section, December 7, p. A26.

———. 1989b. "AIDS Treatment Costs Put at $5 Billion a Year," *New York Times.* National section, September 15, p. 18.

Hodgkinson, Virginia A., and Murray S. Weitzman. 1988. *Giving and Volunteering in the United States: Finding from a National Survey.* Washington, D.C.: Independent Sector.

Hoffman, Martin. 1968. *The Gay World: Male Homosexuality and the Social Creation of Evil.* New York: Basic Books.

Holleran, Andrew. 1990. "The Incredible Shrinking City," *Christopher Street.* Vol. 12:8, pp. 5–7.

———. 1988. *Ground Zero.* New York: New American Library.

———. 1987a. "Reading and Writing: AIDS Is Not the Only Thing Spread by a Virus," *Christopher Street.* Vol. 10:7, pp. 5–7.

———. 1987b. "Trust," *Christopher Street.* Vol. 10:9, pp. 4–8.

Howard, Jane. 1984. "The Warrior," *Esquire.* Vol. 102:6 (December), pp. 270–276.

Humphreys, Laud. 1972. *Out of the Closets: The Sociology of Gay Liberation.* Englewood Cliffs, N.J.: Prentice-Hall.

Hunt, Mary E. 1987. "Theological Pornography: From Corporate to Communal Ethics." Paper presented at a seminar of the Consultation, Union Theological Seminary, New York.

Irvine, Janice. 1990. *Disorders of Desire: Sex and Gender in American Sexology.* Philadelphia: Temple University Press.

Johnson, George. 1988. "Dr. Krim's Crusade," *New York Times Magazine.* February 14, pp. 30–34, 109.

Johnson, Stephen. 1987. "Factors Related to the Intolerance of AIDS Victims," *Journal for the Scientific Study of Religion.* Vol. 26:1 (March), pp. 106–111.

Johnson, Toby. 1988. "Celibacy—the Case for: Monks, Mystics and Men's Communities," *Outlook.* Summer, pp. 75–79.

Kateb, George. 1988. "I.V. Moral Dilemmas: An Introduction," *Social Research.* Vol. 55:3 (Autumn), pp. 455–460.

Katoff, L., and R. Dunne. 1988. "Supporting People with AIDS: The Gay Men's Health Crisis Model," *Journal of Palliative Care.* Vol. 4, pp. 88–95.

Kayal, Philip. 1987. "Doing Good, Doing 'Dirty Work': The AIDS Volunteer." Paper presented at the annual convention of the Eastern Sociological Society, Boston, May.

———. 1986a. "'Healing' Maladaptive Sexual Behavior." Paper presented at the Society for the Study of Social Problems. New York, August 27.

———. 1986b. "The Religious Factor in AIDS." Paper presented at the Society for the Scientific Study of Religion, Washington, D.C., November 14.

———. 1985. "Morals, Medicine and the AIDS Epidemic," *Journal of Religion and Health.* Vol. 24:3 (Fall), pp. 218–238.

Kayal, Philip, and L. San Giovanni. 1984. "Objectivity in the Sociology of Sexuality: Sexism and Homophobia," *Free Inquiry into Creative Sociology.* Vol. 12:2 (November), pp. 161–166.

Kobasa, Suzanne C. Ouelette. 1990. "AIDS and Volunteer Associations: Perspectives on Social and Individual Change," *Millbank Quarterly.* Vol. 68: Supplement 2, pp. 280–294.

———. 1987. "Stress and Resilience in AIDS Volunteers." Unpublished NIMH grant application. New York: Research Foundation of CUNY.

Kolata, Gina. 1991. "Federal Study Questions Ability of AZT to Delay AIDS Symptoms," *New York Times.* February 15, pp. A1, A22.

———. 1990a. "AIDS Advocates Find Private Funds Declining," *New York Times.* August 7, p. A16.

_____. 1990b. "News of AIDS Therapy Gain Delayed 5 Months by Agency," *New York Times.* November 14, p. A1.

_____. 1988a. "AIDS Virus Found to Hide in Cells Eluding Detection by Normal Tests," *New York Times.* June 5, pp. 1, 28.

_____. 1988b. "Recent Setbacks Stirring Doubts About Search for AIDS Virus," *New York Times.* February 16, pp. A1, C13.

Kramer, Larry. 1990a. "A Manhattan Project for AIDS," *New York Times.* July 16, p. A15.

_____. 1990b. "Second-Rated to Death," *Outweek.* No. 69 (October 24), pp. 48–50.

_____. 1989. *Report from the Holocaust.* New York: St. Martin's Press.

_____. 1987a. "Dear Richard," *New York Native.* No. 197 (January 26), pp. 1, 12–15.

_____. 1987b. "Taking Responsibility for Our Lives," *New York Native.* No. 219 (June 29), pp. 37–40, 66.

_____. 1987c. "Whose Constitution Is It Anyway," *New York Native.* No. 234 (October 12), p. 16.

_____. 1983. "1,112 and Counting," *New York Native.* March 14. p. 1.

Kramer, Ralph. 1987. "Voluntary Agencies and the Personal Social Services." Pp. 240–257 in *The Nonprofit Sector.* Edited by Walter W. Powell. New Haven: Yale University Press.

_____. 1981. *Voluntary Associations and the Welfare State.* Berkeley: University of California Press.

Krieger, Nancy, and Rose Appleman. 1986. *The Politics of AIDS.* Oakland, Calif.: Frontline Press.

Kruijer, Gerald. 1987. *Development Through Liberation.* Atlantic Highlands, N.J.: Humanities Press.

Kübler-Ross, Elisabeth. 1987. *AIDS: The Ultimate Challenge.* New York: Macmillan.

Kuropat, Rosemary. 1989. "Response to Darrel Yates Rist," *Christopher Street.* Vol. 11:11, pp. 17–18.

Lambert, Bruce. 1990a. "AIDS Groups Feel the Fiscal Crisis," *New York Times.* Metropolitan section, May 6, p. 38.

_____. 1990b. "AIDS in Black Women Seen as Leading Killer," *New York Times.* July 11, p. B3.

_____. 1990c. "Panel Says Government Is Not Leading AIDS Fight," *New York Times.* April 25, pp. A1, A17.

_____. 1990d. "10 Years Later, Hepatitis Study Still Yields Critical Data on AIDS," *New York Times.* July 17, p. C3.

_____. 1990e. "2 Urban AIDS Trouble Spots Found," *New York Times.* May 3, p. B10.

_____. 1989. "In Spite of Crisis, New York Lacks Basic Services for AIDS Patients," *New York Times.* January 2, pp. A1, B2.

_____. 1989a. "AIDS Panel to Organize After Delay of 7 Months," *New York Times.* July 31, p. A9.

_____. 1989b. "Black Clergy Set to Preach About AIDS," *New York Times.* June 10, p. L29.

_____. 1989c. "In Shift, Gay Men's Health Group Endorses Testing for AIDS Virus," *New York Times.* August 16, pp. A1, B6.

_____. 1988a. "AIDS Estimate Refined for N.Y.," *New York Times.* August 11, pp. B1, B5.

_____. 1988b. "AIDS Survey Shows Course of Infection," *New York Times.* July 5, pp. B1, B4.

_____. 1988c. "The Cool Reaction to New York's 'Good News' on AIDS," *New York Times.* July 21, pp. B1–B2.

_____. 1988d. "Halving of Estimate on AIDS Is Raising Doubts in New York," *New York Times.* July 20, pp. 1, B4.

_____. 1988e. "New York City Cuts Its Estimates in Half for AIDS Infection," *New York Times.* July 19, pp. 1, B5.

_____. 1988f. "N.Y. Called Unprepared on AIDS," *New York Times.* July 14, p. B1.

_____. 1988g. "Official Split on Inquiring About AIDS," *New York Times.* August 1, pp. B1–B2.

_____. 1988h. "Puzzling Questions Are Raised on Statistics on AIDS Epidemic," *New York Times.* July 23, p. B4.

_____. 1988i. "U.S. Confronting AIDS with a Sense of Realism," *New York Times.* February 17, pp. A1, B10.

Leigh, Carol. 1988. "Further Violations of Our Rights." pp. 177–182 in *AIDS: Cultural Analysis, Cultural Activism.* Edited by Douglas Crimp. Cambridge: MIT Press.

Lerner, M. J. 1971. "Observer's Evaluation of a Victim: Justice, Guilt, and Veridical Perception," *Journal of Personality and Social Psychology.* Vol. 20, pp. 127–135.

Lessor, Roberta. 1987. "AIDS and Social Science: The Case for Verstehen Research Methodology." Paper presented at the annual convention of the Society for the Study of Social Problems, August, Chicago.

Levin, James. 1988. "New York's First Gay Political Club," *New York Native.* No. 278 (August 15), p. 14.

le Vine, Barbara Grande. 1990. "A Board Member Speaks: First Time Volunteer," *Volunteer.* Vol. 7:3, p. 5.

Levine, Carol. 1991. "The Citizens Commission on AIDS: A Private-Sector Response to an Epidemic," *Nonprofit and Voluntary Sector Quarterly.* Vol. 20:3, pp. 329–349.

_____. 1989. "Introduction." Pp. 13–18 in *Simple Acts of Kindness.* Edited by John Griggs. New York: United Hospital Fund.

Levine, Martin. 1982. "Fearing Fear Itself." Pp. 14–17 in *Acquired Immune Deficiency (Syndrome)*–GMHC Newsletter. Edited by GMHC. New York: GMHC.

_____. 1979a. "Gay Ghetto." Pp. 182–204 in *Gay Men: The Sociology of Male Homosexuality.* Edited by Martin Levine. New York: Harper.

_____. 1979b. *Gay Men: The Sociology of Male Homosexuality.* New York: Harper.

Linebarger, Charles. 1987. "California Republicans Label Safe-Sex Literature Obscene," *New York Native.* No. 238 (November 9), p. 11.

London, P. 1970. "The Rescuers: Motivational Hypothesis About Christians Who Saved Jews from the Nazis." Pp. 241–250 in *Altruism and Helping Behavior: Social*

Psychological Studies of Antecedents and Consequences. Edited by J. Macaulay and L. Berkowitz. New York: Academic Press.

McNeill, John. 1976. *The Church and the Homosexual.* Kansas City: Sheed, Andrews and McMeel.

Mann, Jonathan, Daniel Tarantola, and Thomas Netter. 1992. *AIDS in the World, 1992: A Global Report.* Cambridge: Harvard University Press.

Margolis, H. 1982. *Selfishness, Altruism, and Rationality.* Cambridge: Cambridge University Press.

Marin, Barbara A., and Gerardo Marin, editors. 1990a. "Effects of Acculturation on Knowledge of AIDS and HIV Among Hispanics," *Hispanic Journal of Behavioral Sciences.* Vol. 12:2 (May), pp. 110–121.

_____. 1990b. "Hispanics and AIDS: Special Issue," *Hispanic Journal of Behavioral Sciences.* Vol. 12:2 (May), pp. 107–109.

Marotta, Toby. 1981. *The Politics of Homosexuality.* Boston: Houghton-Mifflin.

Masters, William H., and Virginia Johnson. 1988. *Crisis: Heterosexual Behavior in the Age of AIDS.* New York: Grove-Weidenfeld.

Miller, Harland. 1982. "Altruism, Volunteers and Sociology." Pp. 45–54 in *Volunteerism in the Eighties.* Edited by John D. Harman. New York: University Press of America.

Minnis, Myra S. 1951. "The Relationship of Women's Organizations to the Social Structure of a City." Ph.D. dissertation, Yale University.

Morris, Aldon D. 1984. *Origins of the Civil Rights Movement.* New York: Free Press.

Murray, Stephen O. 1988. "AIDS, Gay Men, and (Invisible) Sociology." Paper presented at the annual convention of the American Sociological Association, Atlanta, August 24.

_____. 1987. "A Note on Haitian Tolerance of Homosexuality." Pp. 92–100 in *Male Homosexuality in Central and South America.* Edited by Stephen O. Murray. New York: Gai Saber Monographs no. 5.

Navarre, Max. 1988. "Fighting the Victim Label." Pp. 143–146 in *AIDS: Cultural Analysis/Cultural Activism.* Edited by Douglas Crimp. Cambridge: MIT Press.

Navarro, Mireya. 1991a. "AIDS Definition Is Widened to Include Blood Cell Count," *New York Times.* National, August 8, p. D21.

_____. 1991b. "AIDS Takes Emotional Toll on Those Trying to Help," *New York Times.* Metropolitan news, February 12, pp. B1, B3.

_____. 1989. "AIDS and Hispanic People: A Threat Ignored," *New York Times.* December 29, pp. A1, B4.

Naylor, H. H. 1985. "Beyond Managing Volunteers," *Journal of Voluntary Action Research.* Vol. 14:2–3, pp. 25–30.

_____. 1967. *Volunteers Today.* New York: Associated Press.

Nichols, Tom. 1988. "Taking the Initiative," *New York Native.* No. 283 (September 19), p. 14.

O'Connell, Brian. 1976. *Effective Leadership in Voluntary Organizations.* New York: Association Press.

Odendahl, Teresa. 1990. *Charity Begins at Home: Generosity and Self Interest Among the Philanthropic Elite.* New York: Basic Books.

Oliner, S. P., and P. M. Oliner. 1988. *The Altruistic Personality: Rescuers of Jews in Nazi Europe.* New York: Free Press.

Omoto, Allen M., and Mark Snyder. 1990. "Basic Research in Action: Volunteerism and Society's Response to AIDS," *Personality and Social Psychology Bulletin.* Vol. 16:1, pp. 152–165.

Osborn, June. 1990. "Dispelling Myths About the AIDS Epidemic," *Proceedings: AIDS Prevention and Services Workshop.* Princeton, N.J.: Robert Wood Johnson Foundation.

———. 1989. "Public Health and the Politics of AIDS Prevention," *Daedalus.* Special Issue: *Living with AIDS.* Parts 1–2: Vol. 118:3 (Spring), pp. 123–144.

Palmer, J. L., and I. V. Sawhill (editors). 1984. *The Reagan Record.* Cambridge, Mass.: Ballinger Press.

Patton, Cindy. 1990. *Inventing AIDS.* New York: Routledge, Chapman and Hall.

———. 1985. *Sex and Germs: The Politics of AIDS.* Boston: South End Press.

Perlmutter, Felice Davidson. 1984. "The Professionalization of Volunteer Administration." Pp. 117–128 in *Voluntarism and Social Work Practice.* Edited by F. Schwartz. New York: University Press.

Perrow, Charles, and Mauro F. Guillen. 1990. *The AIDS Disaster: The Failure of Organizations in New York and the Nation.* New Haven: Yale University Press.

Petit, Sarah. 1989. "Bearing Witness," *Outweek.* No. 25 (December 10), pp. 43–45.

Phillips, Michael. 1984. "Motivation and Expectation in Successful Volunteerism." Pp. 139–146 in *Voluntarism and Social Work Practice.* Edited by F. Schwartz. New York: University Press.

Phillips, Sarah Rengel. 1991. "The Hegemony of Heterosexuality: A Study of Introductory Texts," *Teaching Sociology.* Vol. 19 (October), pp. 454–463.

Pifer, Alan. 1987. "Philanthropy, Voluntarism, and Changing Times," *Daedalus.* Vol. 116:1 (Winter), pp. 119–132.

Piliavin, Jane, and Hong-Wen Charng. 1990. "Altruism: A Review of Recent Theory and Research," *Annual Review of Sociology.* Vol. 16, pp. 27–65.

Plummer, Ken. 1975. *Sexual Stigma: An Interactionist Account.* London: Routledge and Kegan Paul.

Poirier, Richard. 1988. "AIDS and Traditions of Homophobia," *Social Resarch.* Vol. 55:3 (Autumn), pp. 461–476.

Ports, Suki. 1988. "Needed (for Women and Children)." Pp. 169–176 in *Cultural Analysis and Cultural Activism.* Edited by Douglas Crimp. Cambridge: MIT Press.

Rabinowitz, Dorothy. 1990. "The Secret Sharer," *New York Magazine.* Vol. 23:8 (February 26), pp. 102–114.

Ranke-Heinemann, Uta. 1991. *Eunuchs for the Kingdom of God: Women, Sexuality and the Catholic Church.* New York: Doubleday.

Rasky, Susan. 1990. "How the Politics Shifted on AIDS Funds," *New York Times.* May 20, p. A22.

Register, Cheri. 1987. *Living with Chronic Illness.* New York: Free Press.

Reisman, David. 1954. *Individualism Reconsidered and Other Essays.* Glencoe, Ill.: Free Press.

Richards, Catherine. 1958. "A Study of Class Differences in Women's Participation." Ph.D. dissertation, School of Applied Social Sciences, Case Western Reserve University.

Rose, Arnold. 1967. *The Power Structure: Political Process in American Society*. New York: Oxford University Press.

————. 1954. *Theory and Method in the Social Sciences*. Minneapolis: University of Minnesota Press.

Rosenhan, D. L. 1970. "The Natural Socialization of Altruistic Autonomy." Pp. 251–268 in *Altruism and Helping Behavior*. Edited by J. Macaulay and L. Berkowitz. New York: Academic Press.

Ross, Aileen D. 1958. "Control and Leadership in Women's Groups: An Analysis of Philanthropic Money Raising Activity," *Social Forces*. Vol. 37 (December), pp. 124–131.

Roth, Julius A. 1973. "Care of the Sick: Professionalism vs. Love," *Science, Medicine and Man*. Vol. 1, pp. 173–180.

Sagarin, Edward. 1966. *Structure and Ideology in an Association of Deviants*. New York: Arno.

Sallach, David L., Nicholas Babchuk, and Alan Booth. 1972. "Social Involvement and Political Activity: Another View," *Social Science Quarterly*. Vol. 52:4, pp. 879–892.

Salsberg, Sheldon. 1971. "Membership and Participation in Formal Voluntary Associations by Urban Male Homosexuals." Ph.D. dissertation, New York University.

Schwartz, Florence S. 1984a. *Voluntarism and Social Work Practice*. New York: University Press.

————. 1984b. "Voluntarism, Volunteers and Social Work Practice." pp. 41–50 in *Voluntarism and Social Work Practice*. Edited by Florence Schwartz. New York: University Press.

————. 1982. "The Rights of Volunteers." Pp. 70–74 in *Volunteerism in the Eighties*. Edited by John D. Harman. New York: University Press of America.

Shilts, Randy. 1987. *And the Band Played On*. New York: St. Martin's Press.

Sikov, Ed. 1988. "Media Watch: The Truth According to Cosmos," *New York Native*. No. 249 (January 25), p. 15.

Silin, Jonathan. 1987. "Dangerous Knowledge," *Christopher Street*. Vol. 10:5, pp. 34–41.

Sills, David. 1968. "Voluntary Associations: Sociological Aspects." Pp. 357–378 in *International Encyclopedia of the Social Sciences*. Vol. 16. Edited by David Sills. New York: Macmillan.

————. 1959. "Voluntary Associations: Instruments and Objects of Change," *Human Organization*. Vol. 18 (Spring), pp. 17–21.

Singer, Merrill, Z. Castillo, L. Davison, and C. Flores. 1990. "Owning AIDS: Latino Organizations and the AIDS Epidemic," *Hispanic Journal of Behavioral Sciences*. Vol. 12:2 (May), pp. 196–211.

Smith, Constance, and Anne Freedman. 1972. *Voluntary Associations: Perspectives on the Literature*. Cambridge: Harvard University Press.

Smith, David Horton. 1985. "Volunteerism: Attracting Volunteers and Staffing Shrinking Programs." Pp. 225–252 i> *Social Planning and Human Service Delivery in the Volunteer Sector*. Edited by A. Tobin. Westport, Conn.: Greenwood Press.

————. 1982. "Altruism, Volunteers & Volunteerism." Pp. 23–44 in *Volunteerism in the Eighties*. Edited by John D. Harman. New York: University Press of America.

————. 1975. "Voluntary Action and Voluntary Groups," *Annual Review of Sociology.* Vol. 1, pp. 247–251.

————. 1966a. "The Importance of Formal Voluntary Organizations for Society," *Sociology and Social Research.* Vol. 50:4, pp. 483–494.

————. 1966b. "A Psychological Model of Individual Participation in Formal Voluntary Organizations: Applications to Some Chilean Data," *American Journal of Sociology.* Vol. 72 (November), pp. 249–266.

Smith, David, and Jon Van Til (editors). 1983. *International Perspectives on Voluntary Action Research.* Washington, D.C.: University Press of America.

Snyder, Mark, and Allen M. Omoto. 1991. "Who Helps and Why? The Psychology of AIDS Volunteerism." Pp. 219–239 in *Helping and Being Helped: Naturalistic Studies.* Edited by S. Spacapan and S. Oskamp. Newbury Park, Calif.: Sage.

Solomon, Nancy. 1992. "Should Lesbians Practice Safe-Sex? Does Anyone Know?" *Outlook.* No. 16 (Spring), pp. 46–52.

Sontag, Susan. 1988. *AIDS and Its Metaphors.* New York: Farrar, Straus and Giroux.

Sorokin, Pitirim. 1950. *Altruistic Love.* Boston: Beacon Press.

Stark, Werner. 1965. "The Routinization of Charisma: A Consideration of Catholicism," *Sociological Analysis.* Vol. 26:4 (Winter), pp. 203–212.

Steinfels, Peter. 1988a. "Catholic Bishops Vote to Retain Controversial Statement on AIDS," *New York Times.* June 28, pp. A1, A16.

————. 1988b. "New Liberation Faith: Social Conflict Is Muted," *New York Times.* July 27, p. 2.

Sullivan, Andrew. 1990. "Gay Life, Gay Death," *New Republic.* December 17, pp. 19–25.

Teltsch, Kathleen. 1989. "Americans Donated $104 Billion in '88," *New York Times,* June 7, p. A16.

Templeman, Mark R. 1986. "Factors of Extraordinary Altruistic Behavior: The Role of Religious Belief." Paper presented at the annual meeting of the Association for the Sociology of Religion, New York, August.

Terian, Sara M. Karkkainen. 1986. "Philosophies of Helping and Respect for Persons." Paper presented at the annual meeting of the Association for the Sociology of Religion, New York, August.

Tocqueville, Alexis de. 1969. *Democracy in America.* Edited by J. P. Mayer. New York: Doubleday-Anchor Books.

Tompkins, Jean Beattie. 1955. "Reference Groups and Status Values as Determinants of Behavior: A Study of Women's Voluntary Association Behavior." Ph.D. dissertation, Iowa State University.

Torpey, John. 1989. "What's in a Number," *Nation.* October 9, pp. 393–394.

Townley, Phyllis. 1989. "Let Me Tell You About Reubens." Pp. 21–31 in *Simple Acts of Kindness.* Edited by John Griggs. New York: United Hospital Fund.

Treichler, Paula. 1987. "AIDS, Homophobia, and Biomedical Discourse: An Epidemic of Signification," *Cultural Studies.* Vol. 1:3 (October), pp. 263–305.

Valente, Michael. 1970. *Sex: The Radical View of a Catholic Theologian.* New York: Bruce Publishing.

Van Til, Jon. 1985. "Mixed Motives: Residues of Altruism in an Age of Narcissism." Pp. 243–260 in *Motivating Volunteers*. Edited by Larry Moore. Vancouver: Vancouver Volunteer Center.

———. 1982. "Volunteering and Democratic Theory." Pp. 199–221 in *Volunteerism in the Eighties*. Edited by John D. Harman. New York: University Press of America.

Voelcker, John. 1990. "The Second Epidemic," *Outweek*. July 11, pp. 48–57.

Watney, Simon. 1988. "The Spectacle of AIDS." Pp. 71–86 in *AIDS: Cultural Analysis, Cultural Activism*. Edited by Douglas Crimp. Cambridge: MIT Press.

———. 1987. *Policing Desire: Pornography, AIDS and the Media*. Minneapolis: University of Minnesota Press.

Wedin, William. 1984a. "No Cure for Anonymous Sex," *New York Native*. No. 87, pp. 21, 36.

———. 1984b. "The Sexual Compulsion Movement," *Christopher Street*. Vol. 8:3, pp. 48–54.

———. 1984c. "Sexual Healing," *New York Native*. No. 95 (July 30), pp. 26–29.

Weinberg, George. 1973. *Society and the Healthy Homosexual*. New York: Doubleday.

Weinberg, Thomas S. 1976. "Becoming Homosexual: Self-Discovery, Self-Identity, and Self-Maintenance." Ph.D. dissertation, University of Connecticut, Hartford.

Weinraub, Bernard. 1989. "Bush Calls for New Volunteer Effort," *New York Times*. June 23, p. A6.

Westmorland, Timothy. 1990. "Structural Barriers to Financing Early Intervention and Treatment for AIDS." Pp. 157–160 in *AIDS Prevention and Services Workshop*. Edited by Vivian Fransen. Princeton, N.J.: Robert Wood Johnson Foundation.

———. 1987. "AIDS and the Political Process: A Federal Perspective." Pp. 46–54 in *AIDS: Public Policy Dimensions*. Edited by John Griggs. New York: United Hospital Fund.

Whelan, Jim. 1989. "God's Love We Deliver," *New York Native*. No. 300 (January 16), p. 10.

Whitlow, Joan. 1988. "Fighting the Plague," *Newark Star Ledger*. September 11, p. 44.

Whitmore, George. 1988. "Bearing Witness," *New York Times Magazine*. January 31, pp. 14–16, 42, 50, 54.

Williams, J. Allen, N. Babchuk, and David Johnson. 1973. "Voluntary Associations and Minority Status: A Comparative Analysis of Anglo, Black and Mexican Americans," *American Sociological Review*. Vol. 38:5, pp. 73–79.

Winkle, Curtis R. 1991. "Inequity and Power in the Nonprofit Sector: A Comparative Analysis of AIDS-Related Services for Gay Men and Intravenous Drug Users in Chicago," *Nonprofit and Volunteer Sector Quarterly*. Vol. 20:3, pp. 317–328.

Wirth, Louis. 1951. "Urbanism as a Way of Life." Pp. 42–53 in *Reader in Urban Sociology*. Edited by Paul K. Hatt and Albert J. Reiss, Jr. Glencoe, Ill.: Free Press.

Wolf, Jacquelyn H. 1985. "'Professionalizing' Volunteer Work in a Black Neighborhood," *Social Service Review*. September, pp. 423–434.

Wyman, David. 1986. *The Abandonment of the Jews*. New York: Pantheon.

Yearwood, Lennox. 1976. "Black Organizations: A Study of Their Community Involvement with Reference to Decision-Making Processes." Ph.D. dissertation, State University of New York, Buffalo.

Yearwood, Lennox, and Thomas S. Weinberg. 1979. "Black Organizations, Gay Organizations: Sociological Parallels." Pp. 301–316 in *Gay Men: The Sociology of Male Homosexuality*. Edited by Martin Levine. New York: Harper.

Zwickler, Phil. 1988a. "Policing Desire: Language and the Shaping of AIDS," *New York Native*. No. 273 (July 11), pp. 16–17.

_____. 1988b. "Remembering the Little Guys," *New York Native*. Nos. 270–271 (June 20–27), p. 8.

_____. 1988c. "Service Groups Respond to City AIDS Plan and Budget," *New York Native*. No. 269 (June 13), pp. 6–7.

_____. 1987a. "Vatican Statement Still Draws Fire," *New York Native*. No. 233 (October 5), p. 8.

_____. 1987b. "Vatican Declares AIDS 'Natural Sanction' Against Homosexuals," *New York Native*. No. 232 (September 28), p. 10.

About the Book and Author

THE UNTOLD STORY in the AIDS crisis is that of the mobilization of the gay community. *Bearing Witness* is a study of how a community-based initiative—Gay Men's Health Crisis in New York—overcame the formidable obstacles of homophobia and fear of AIDS, and the resulting lack of an adequate response from political and health organizations. Philip Kayal shows how volunteers at Gay Men's Health Crisis (GMHC) confront their deepest fears about being homosexual. Rather than shun People with AIDS, they identify with them and neutralize the immobilizing power of homophobia. The volunteers have the courage to bear witness to the suffering of People with AIDS, suffering that in many ways is their own.

Kayal explores the why and how of the gay community response to AIDS from his perspective as both a sociologist and GMHC volunteer. The author's own experience allows him to illuminate the social and political meanings of volunteerism by showing how gay/AIDS volunteerism is radical political and religious work. Through collective altruism, GMHC helps to integrate the gay community and establish new concepts of what is sacred.

In *Bearing Witness,* Kayal explores the relationship between personal motives for volunteering and the broader political, social, and religious contexts in which People with AIDS have been largely abandoned. He shows how the mixing of morals, medicine, and American volunteer ideology sets both the tone of the politics of AIDS and influences the evolution of volunteer organizations such as GMHC. AIDS brings that which is deeply private into the public domain, and Kayal offers a compelling analysis of this intersection in his new study of gay/AIDS volunteerism.

Philip M. Kayal is professor of sociology at Seton Hall University. He has published extensively in the sociology of religion, ethnicity, and homophobia. His current interests are the nonprofit sector and the study of gay/AIDS volunteerism.

Index